THE CHRONICLES
OF
GEORGETOWN, D.C.

FROM 1751 TO 1878

Richard P. Jackson

**A Native of Georgetown and Member of the
Washington Bar**

*I loved her from my boyhood—she to me
"was as a fairy city of the heart."*

With a New Index by
Wesley E. Pippenger

HERITAGE BOOKS
2011

HERITAGE BOOKS

AN IMPRINT OF HERITAGE BOOKS, INC.

Books, CDs, and more—Worldwide

For our listing of thousands of titles see our website
at
www.HeritageBooks.com

A Facsimile Reprint
Published 2011 by
HERITAGE BOOKS, INC.
Publishing Division
100 Railroad Ave. #104
Westminster, Maryland 21157

Index Copyright © 2001 Wesley E. Pippenger

First Printed 1878 by R. O. Polkinhorn, Printer
Washington, D.C.

International Standard Book Numbers
Paperbound: 978-1-58549-671-6
Clothbound: 978-0-7884-8954-9

TO

MY ELDEST SON,

WILLIE JACKSON,

A PRINTER BY OCCUPATION. TO WHOM I AM
GREATLY INDEBTED FOR THE FAITHFUL
PUBLICATION OF THIS WORK;
AND TO THE
CITIZENS OF GEORGETOWN,

I RESPECTFULLY DEDICATE

THIS VOLUME.

PREFACE

To compile this book, during my leisure hours, has been more a labor of love than an expectation of gain; to snatch from oblivion what otherwise would be lost, and to refresh the memories of our citizens of the facts and events that have transpired in a lifetime, and leave to the rising generation a history of the town (though imperfect) to which reference can be made to learn how our ancestors struggled amidst adversity to build a city, with churches and institutions of learning, that should be a credit to themselves and a benefit to posterity.

What little knowledge I possess I have gleaned from the citizens of Georgetown, among whom I was born and reared; and what little property I enjoy I owe to their patronage. The older citizens of the town were well acquainted with the father of the Chronicler.—He was no general; he never commanded an army and slew thousands of men and gained a victory; neither was he the governor of a province, and starved the peasantry to feed an idle court, but a peaceable, quiet citizen, a store-keeper by occupation; and when he died, he left the Chronicler, then thirteen years of age, an heir to his good reputation.

To the Lady Superior of the Academy of the Visitation, and to General Humphreys and Major Weiss of the Engineer Department; to Colonel Theodore Samo, of the Washington Aqueduct; to Benjamin Fawcett, clerk of the Chesapeake & Ohio Canal Company; to Rev. J.S. Sumner, S.J., editor of the *College Journal*; to Josiah Dent, president of the Linthicum Institute, and Charles M. Matthews, Joseph Libbey, William Shoemaker, M.D., William W. Winship, secretary to trustees of the Presbyterian Church, and other citizens, I feel grateful for their kind assistance to me while compiling this book.

THE CHRONICLER.

TABLE OF CONTENTS

CHAPTER I.

CHAPTER II.

CHAPTER III.

CHAPTER IV.

CHAPTER V.

CHAPTER VI.

CHAPTER VII.

CHAPTER VIII.

CHAPTER IX.

MAP OF GEORGETOWN STREETS
Before Names Changed in 1880 for
the District of Columbia System

CHRONICLES OF GEORGETOWN.

CHAPTER I.

INDIAN HISTORY—HOW THE TOWN WAS LAID-OUT—COPY FROM A
LAND PATENT—TEST OATH—DIVISIONS OF THE TOWN AND
REFERENCE TO THE DEED BOOKS IN WHICH THEY ARE
RECORDED—CHARTER AS AMENDED, AND IN FORCE FROM 1789 TO
1871—SKETCH OF THE TOWN AND ITS SURROUNDINGS—WHO
FRAMED THE ORIGINAL CONSTITUTION—WILLIAM WIRT—LUDICROUS
SCENES—DUELS—DEPRESSION IN BUSINESS AND BEGINNING OF
THE CANAL—CHANNEL OF THE RIVER, AND CONTEST FOR THE
UPPER AND LOWER ROADS LEADING TO FALL'S BRIDGE—THE
HOLLAND LOAN, AND OPPOSITION TO THE ALEXANDRIA
AQUEDUCT—BASIS OF AN AGREEMENT FOR THE CONSOLIDATION OF
WASHINGTON CITY AND GEORGETOWN—SKETCH OF ITS
LEGISLATION—OFFICERS OF THE CORPORATION—NAMES OF THE
STREETS—ILLUMINATING THE TOWN—ANTS FROM THE WEST
INDIES—A BREEZE IN TOWN—LONG BRIDGE—POPULATION.

The original inhabitants of Maryland, out of which the District
of Columbia was carved, were Indians. According to a letter
written by Captain John Smith in 1626, to Queen Anne of Great
Britain, who had been sent to America to explore the
Chesapeake Bay, and the coast of Maryland, reported that more
than forty tribes of Indians inhabited the shores of Maryland and
Virginia. The principal tribes were the Manahoacs, the
Powhatans, and the Monacans. It is generally, believed that the
Powhatans occupied that space of country between the
Chesapeake Bay and the Patuxent River in Maryland; the tribes
called the Manahoacs and Monacans are supposed to have
roamed the shores of Virginia, between York and the Potomac
Rivers; the Shawanees are supposed to have inhabited that tract
of land lying between the Chesapeake Bay and the Alleghany
Mountains. Mr. Elliot, in his history of the District of Columbia,
says: "that the tribe called the Susquehanocks lived on the banks
of the Susquehanna River; the Tockwocks and others occupied
Kent, Queen Anne, and Talbot Counties; the Manahoacs and
Monacans were in alliance with each other and waged perpetual
war against the Powhatans." It is generally admitted that they

1

were the occupiers of the territory which forms the District of Columbia.

Sir Walter Raleigh and Captain Smith were the great navigators who visited the New World and made maps and charts of the same, especially of the Chesapeake Bay and Potomac River, and learned the habits of the Indians. One habit Raleigh carried with him to England was, the habit of smoking tobacco; he introduced it at court, arid it became fashionable among all of the nobility. On one occasion Raleigh made a bet with Queen Elizabeth that he could tell the weight of smoke from his pipe of tobacco. The Queen covered his bet; when Raleigh filled his pipe with tobacco. He then emptied the same into a pair of delicate scales, and after weighing it, lie returned it to his pipe, and, setting fire to the same, commenced smoking. After the tobacco was consumed, lie emptied the ashes into the scales, and subtracting the weight of ashes front the tobacco, be told the Queen the weight of the smoke. The Queen remarked that she had seen many a man convert gold into smoke, but this was the first time she had seen smoke converted into gold.

Frederick County, in Maryland, was formed by an act of the Legislature in 1748. Montgomery County in 1776, was carved out of Frederick. An act was passed by Congress, July 16, 1790, to establish the permanent seat of Government of the United States, and on the 30th day of March, 1791, President Washington, then in Georgetown, issued his proclamation concerning the permanent seat of Government of the United States as being located in the District of Columbia. This proclamation closes as follows:

"In testimony whereof, I have caused the seal of the United States to be affixed to these presents, and sign the same with my hand.

Done at Georgetown, aforesaid, the 30th day of March, in the year of our Lord, 1791, and the Independence of the United States the fifteenth.

By the President:

GEORGE WASHINGTON."

THOMAS JEFFERSON.

2

HOW THE TOWN WAS LAID OUT.

The beginning of Georgetown was, by legislative enactment, of the then province of Maryland.

The Legislature of Maryland, by act of May 15, 1751, authorized Henry Wright Crabb, John Needham, John Clagett, James Perry, and David Lynn, Commissioners, to lay out and erect a town on the Potomac River, above the mouth of Rock Creek, in Frederick County, Maryland, and empowered them to purchase sixty acres—part of the tracts of land belonging to George Gordon and George Beall, at the place aforesaid, where it shall appear to them to be most convenient—and to survey the same into eighty lots, to be erected into a town, and to be called Georgetown.

The Commissioners met September 18, 1751, and chose Alexander Beall to be Clerk and Surveyor, and Josiah Beall, Coroner.

Mr. Gordon and Mr. Beall refusing to sell to the Commissioners the tract selected by them as "most convenient;" it was appraised, and two hundred and eighty pounds, currency, were awarded to the said Gordon and Beall as damages, by the following jury, viz: William Pritchett, Ninian Magruder, Nicholas Baker, James Beall, Nathaniel Magruder, Charles Clagett, Thomas Clagett, James Holman, Charles Jones, Zachariah Magruder, James Wallace, Basil Beall, William Williams, Alexander Magruder, William Wallace, and John Magruder, son of Alexander.

The survey and plat was completed February 27, 1752, and the Commissioners named the lots, streets, and lanes; and the eighty lots were assessed at two hundred and eighty pounds, currency.

To Mr. Gordon and to Mr. Beall was allowed the privilege of first selecting two lots each. Mr. Gordon chose lots 48 and 52, but Mr. Beall, having refused to recognize in any way the proceedings of the Commissioners, was notified that "if he did not make his choice within ten days from the 28th of February, he could only blame himself for the consequences." Whereupon, after a week's reflection, Mr. Beall sent the following

3

answer:

"If I must part with my property by force, I had better save a little than be totally demolished. Rather than have none, I accept these lots,—Nos. 72 and 79—said to be Mr. Henderson's and Mr. Edmonston's. But I do hereby protest, and declare that. my acceptance of the said lots, which is by force, shall not debar me from future redress from the Commissioners or others, if I can have the rights of a British subject. God save King George! *March 7, 1752.*   GEORGE BEALL."

Many persons suppose that the name of Georgetown was given in honor of the commander of the army of the Revolution; but this cannot be so, as General Washington was born on the 22d day of February, 1732, and when the town was laid out, he was quite a young man engaged in the profession of surveying under Lord Fairfax, and had not established his great reputation as a military man. Others, again, suppose that the name came from George Beall, who was an able soldier and a great fighter of Indians in the province, but more likely it took its name from George II, King of Great Britain, towards whom all the provinces in America were at that time loyal; but let the name come from whence it may, the town has grown and prospered under that name, and if it had been named differently, its adversity and prosperity would have been the same.

COPY FROM A LAND PATENT.

The original land patent issued by Henry Darnell, keeper of the great seals of the State of Maryland, November 18, 1703, to Ninian Beall for seven hundred and five acres *Rock of Dunbarton*, which tract of land is now covered by a portion of the city of Georgetown, has recently been examined and authenticated copies made for reference. The papers recite that the patent is made in consideration of there being due to Beall five hundred acres, under a warrant of the 19th of May, 1702, and the property is described as lying in said Prince George's County, beginning at the southeast corner tree of a tract of land taken for Robert Mason, standing by Potomac River side, at the

4

mouth of Rock Creek, on a point running thence with said land N.N. West six hundred and forty perches, then east three hundred and twenty perches, thence south 6½°, easterly four hundred and eighteen perches, then west twenty perches, then S.S. West one hundred and seventy-five perches, thence with a straight line by the creek and river to the first bound containing, and there laid out for, seven hundred and ninety-five acres.

TEST OATH.

When the town began to grow in size, and various offices were created, and citizens appointed to fill them, a test oath appears to have been required from all officers. Among the records of the town, now in the Surveyor's office of the District of Columbia, is a quaint old document, which the chronicler copies for the benefit of his readers. It relates to a meeting of the Commissioners, February 24th, 1772, and appointing one Thomas Branan as flour inspector; when there was administered to him the several oaths of office, he repeated and signed the following:

"I, Thomas Branan, do declare that I do believe that there is not any transubstantiation in the sacrament of the Lord's supper, or in the elements of bread and wine, at or after the consecration thereof, by any person whatsoever.

THOMAS BRANAN."

No religious test is now required to fill the office of flour inspector, or any other office in the gift of the Government.

DIVISIONS OF THE TOWN AND REFERENCE TO DEED BOOKS IN WHICH THEY ARE RECORDED.

The town, as originally laid out, only consisted of sixty acres of land. Several additions have since been added, as follows:

Beall's first addition, known by the name of the *Rock of Dunbarton*, containing sixty-one acres, was added by act of Assembly passed at November session,1783, and recorded in liber B, page 223, at Rockville, Md. Peter Beatty, Threlkeld &

Deakin's addition at November session, 1784, containing twenty acres, and divided into sixty-five lots, and recorded in liber K, No. 10, folio 31, District of Columbia. Beall's second addition, supposed to be recorded at Rockville, Maryland. Deakin & Bailey's, and Threlkeld's addition, liber W.B., No. 14, page 55 to 73; Deakin, Lee & Cazanove's addition, A.F., No. 31, page 448 to 466; Holmead's addition, deed of partition O, liber 14, page 15; liber B, No. 2, folio 702, original plan of Georgetown; liber K, No. 10, from page 8 to 28, Beatty & Hawkins; slip recorded in liber C, from 423 to folio 426; slip recorded in liber 13, liber S, No. 18, Corporation of Georgetown, to John M. Beatty and Charles A. Beatty; liber T, No. 19, page 146, map of water lots; liber W.B., No. 59, Canal Condemnations; liber W.B., No. 99, map of lots between Bridge, Gay, High, and Congress Streets.

The town was incorporated by act of Assembly of Maryland, passed at November session, 1789, to which additional powers were given in 1797 and 1799; also by the act of Congress of 1802, chap. 52, March 3d, 1805, page 310, vol. 2d; also 1809, page 332; also 1813, vol. 3, page 1; also 1824, vol. 4, page, 75; also May 31st, 1830, vol. 4, page 420 ; also 1826, vol. 4, page 183; also March 3, 1826, page 140; also August 19, 1841, vol. 5, page 449; also July 27,1842, vol. 5, page 497; also March 3d,1843, vol. 5, page 629; also June 17, 1844, vol. 5, page 721; also August 11,1856, vol. 11, page 321; also May 21, 1862, vol. 12, page 405.

This last relates to the distribution of Potomac water in which all the citizens are deeply interested. The legal style of the Corporation was known by name of the "Mayor, Recorder, Aldermen, and Common Council of Georgetown," which charter was as follows:

CHARTER OF GEORGETOWN, AS AMENDED, AND IN FORCE FROM 1789 TO 1871.

I. ORGANIZATION—II. JURISDICTION—III. GENERAL POWERS AND DUTIES—IV. MISCELLANEOUS PROVISIONS.
[NOTE.-All clauses in brackets are from the acts of Maryland.]

I.—ORGANIZATION.

[Georgetown shall be, and hereby is, erected, constituted and made an incorporate town, consisting of a Mayor, Recorder,] and two branches; the first branch to be composed of five members and the Recorder,] and to be called the Board of Aldermen; and the second branch to be composed of eleven members, and to be called the Board of Common Councilmen; [which said Mayor, Recorder, Aldermen, and Common Councilmen shall be a body incorporate and one community forever, in right and by the name of the Mayor, Recorder, Aldermen, and Common Council of the said town; and shall be able and capable to sue and be sued at law, and to act and execute, do and perform, as a body incorporate, which shall have succession forever, and to that end to have a common seal, and the same to alter and change at their pleasure.]

THE MAYOR

On the fourth Monday in February, 1831, and on the same day biennially thereafter, the citizens of Georgetown, qualified to vote for members of the two boards of the corporation, shall, by ballot, elect sonic fit and proper person, having the qualifications now required by law, to be Mayor of the Corporation of Georgetown, to continue in office two years and until a successor is duly elected; and the person having at said election, which shall be conducted by judges of election appointed by the corporation, the greatest number of legal votes, shall be declared duly elected; and in the event of an equal number of votes being given to two or more candidates, the two boards in joint meeting, by ballot, shall elect the Mayor from the persons having such equal number of votes.

In the event of the death or resignation of the Mayor, or of his inability to discharge the duties of his office, the two boards of the corporation in, joint meeting, by ballot, shall elect some fit person to fill the office until the next regular election.

No person shall be eligible to the office of Mayor unless he be a citizen of the United States, of the age of thirty years, a resident of the town for five years last past, and unless he shall have paid a tax to the corporation.

Before he acts as such, the Mayor shall make oath before some, justice of the peace for the County of Washington, in the presence of both branches of the corporation, that lie will well and faithfully discharge the several and respective duties of his office.

POWERS AND DUTIES OF THE MAYOR.

The Mayor shall leave power, upon the application of at least five members of the corporation, in writing, to convene said corporation, giving reasonable notice of such intended meeting.

He shall have and exercise the powers of a, justice of the peace in the said town.

He shall receive for his services annually, a just and reasonable compensation, to be allowed and fixed by the corporation.

It shall be his duty to see that the laws of the corporation are duly executed; to report the negligence or misconduct of any officer to the said corporation; and to lay before the corporation, front time to time, in writing, such alterations in the laws as lie shall deem necessary and proper.

He shall sign all ordinances duly passed by both branches of the corporation, unless he objects thereto, within forty-eight hours after the time the same is presented to him for his signature; and if he does so object, he shall immediately return the ordinance, with his objections, in writing, to the corporation. If it is afterwards passed according to law, lie shall sign the same. If he shall not return the same within the time aforesaid,

8

he shall sign the same.

No ordinance shall be passed unless approved by the Mayor, or passed under the provisions made in case of his objecting thereto.

[See also "IV. Miscellaneous Provisions."]

THE RECORDER.

On the first Monday of January in every year, the corporation shall, by a joint ballot of the said two branches present, choose some fit and proper person learned in the law, to be Recorder of the said corporation, to continue in office one year.

The Recorder, before he acts as such, shall make oath before some justice of the peace for the County of Washington, in the presence of both branches of the corporation, that he will well and faithfully discharge the several and respective duties of his office.

In the event of a tie vote upon any question in the Board of Aldermen, the Recorder shall have the casting vote, and power thereby to determine the same to the same effect as if it had been determined by a majority of the aldermen present.

In case of vacancy in the office of Recorder, the corporation shall, within five days thereafter, proceed to the choice of a fit person, qualified as aforesaid, to fill his place, in the manner herein before provided.

The Recorder of the corporation is hereby declared to be a member of the Board of Aldermen, to all intents and purposes whatever.

THE TWO BRANCHES.

On the fourth Monday in February, 1806, and biennial thereafter, the free white male citizens of the United States, who shall have attained the age of twenty-one years, and shall have resided in Georgetown one year immediately preceding the day of election, and shall have been returned on the books of the corporation during the year ending on the 31st of December next preceding the day of election, as subject to a school tax for that year—except persons *non compos* mentis, vagrants, paupers, and persons who shall have been convicted of any infamous crime—and who shall leave laid the school taxes due from him, shall elect by ballot five fit and proper persons, citizens of the United States, residents of the said town one year next before the election, above twenty-one years of age, and having paid a tax to the corporation, to compose the Board of Aldermen; anal the five persons voted for as Aldermen, who shall have the greatest number of legal votes on the final casting up of the polls shall be declared duly elected for the Board of Aldermen, the said Board of Aldermen to continue two years.

On the fourth Monday in February in every year, the free white male citizens of Georgetown, having the qualifications prescribed for persons to be entitled to vote for members of the Board of Aldermen, shall elect, by ballot, eleven fit and proper persons, having the qualifications prescribed for members of the Board of Aldermen, to compose the Board of Common Council; and the eleven persons voted for as Common Council who shall have the greatest number of legal votes at the final casting up of the polls, shall be declared duly elected for the Board of Common Council, the said Board of Common Council to continue for one year.

In case of vacancy in either branch, a fit person or persons qualified as aforesaid, shall be elected by the people in the same manner, five days' notice being given of such election.

Each member of the two branches, before he acts as such, shall, in the presence of the corporation, take an oath to discharge the duties and trusts reposed in him with integrity and fidelity.

POWERS AND DUTIES OF THE TWO BRANCHES, SEPARATELY.

Four members of the Board of Aldermen and seven members of the Board of Common Council shall form a quorum to do business.

Each board shall hold two sessions in each year, one to commence on the first Monday of March, and the other on the first Monday of December.

Each board shall have power to adjourn from day to day; and five members of either branch may cause the Mayor to convene the two boards, by an application to him in writing.

Each branch shall judge of the elections, qualifications, and returns of its own members; and may compel the attendance of members by reasonable penalties.

The Common Council shall choose out of their own body a president.

Either branch shall have power to elect a president *pro tempore* in the absence of the one duly elected.

Ordinances may originate in either branch, and shall be passed only by a majority of both branches during the same session.

If the Board of Alderman shall be equally divided on any question before them, the Recorder shall have the casting vote, and determine such question to the same effect as if the same had been determined by a majority of the Aldermen present; and similar power is given to the president of the second branch, in case of an equal division therein.

POWERS AND DUTIES OF THE TWO BRANCHES, TOGETHER.

If any ordinance, duly passed by both branches, shall be returned by the Mayor with his objections, in writing, within forty-eight hours after the same is presented to him for his signature, and if, on reconsideration of the same, two-thirds of each branch shall be of opinion that the said law should be passed, it shall become a law, the objections of the Mayor notwithstanding.

The two branches may remove from office, or take such other measures thereupon as shall be just and lawful, any officer of the corporation, upon the report of the Mayor and satisfactory proof of negligence or misconduct on the part of such officer.

On the first Monday in January, annually, the two branches by joint ballot shall choose some fit and proper person, learned in the law, to be the Recorder of the corporation.

In the event of an equal number of votes being given to two or more candidates for Mayor at the regular election, the two boards in joint meeting, by ballot, shall elect the Mayor from the persons having such equal number of votes.

In the event of the death or resignation of the Mayor, or of his inability to discharge the duties of his office, the two boards of the corporation in joint meeting, by ballot, shall elect some fit person to fill the office until the next regular election.

II.—JURISDICTION.

The following are hereby declared the limits of Georgetown, any law or regulation to the contrary notwithstanding: Beginning in the middle of College Street, as laid down in Fenwick's map of the town, at or near the bank of the Potomac River; thence by a straight line northerly through the middle of said street to the middle of First Street ; thence by a line drawn through the middle of First Street to a point directly opposite to the termination of the eastern line of the lots now enclosed as the property of the college; thence northerly by the eastern line of said enclosure so far as the same extends; thence in the same northerly direction to the middle of Fourth Street; thence easterly by a line drawn along the middle of Fourth Street to a point at the distance of one hundred and twenty feet westerly from the west side of Fayette Street; thence northerly by a line drawn parallel to Fayette Street at the said distance of one hundred and twenty feet west, from the west side thereof, until it intersects a boundary line of Beatty and Hawkins' addition to Georgetown; thence westerly by said boundary line so far as it extends; thence by the courses and distances of the several other boundary lines of Beatty and Hawkins' addition aforesaid, that is to say, westerly, northerly, easterly, and southerly to a point opposite the middle of Road Street, and opposite to or nearly opposite to the middle of Eighth Street; thence east by a line drawn through the middle of Road Street as it now runs, as far as it extends; thence easterly by a line drawn parallel with Back Street (now Stoddard Street) and continued in the same direction to the middle of Rock Creek; thence by the middle of the same creek and the middle of the Potomac River to a point directly opposite to the middle of College Street aforesaid; thence to the place of beginning.

The said limits of Georgetown between Seventh and Eighth Streets, are further extended so as to extend westwardly from Fayette Street three hundred feet.

So much of the territory of Georgetown as lies west of Fayette Street, and between the north line of Third Street and a line drawn parallel therewith from a point on the west line of Fayette Street at the end of sixty feet north of the line of Sixth

Street, is excluded from the limits of the town, except the following lots in Threlkeld's addition, viz: One hundred and fifty-three, one hundred and sixty-one, one hundred and sixty-two, one hundred and sixty-three, one hundred and seventy-two, one hundred and seventy-four, one hundred and seventy-six, one hundred and seventy-eight, and the south half of lot one hundred and seventy-one.

The jurisdiction of the Corporation of Georgetown is extended so as to include the bridge across the Potomac River at the Little Falls, the site thereof, and all premises appertaining to the site.

The limits of Georgetown are extended so as to include *Pretty Prospect*, the site of the Poors' house, contained within the following bounds: Commencing at a stone marked No. 4, extending at the end of four hundred and seventy-six poles on the first line of a tract of land called the *Rock of Dunbarton*, said stone also standing on the western boundary line of lot No. 260 of Beatty and Hawkins' addition to Georgetown; running thence north 78° east, thirty-eight poles; south 80° east, three poles; south eighteen poles; south 12° east, nine poles; south 11° west, twelve poles; south 73° west, twenty-three poles, to the said first line of the *Rock of Dunbarton*; thence with said line to the beginning.

III.—POWERS AND DUTIES OF THE CORPORATION.

The corporation shall have power to impose and collect a tax of seventy cents in the hundred dollars on all property by law taxable in the town; shall have perpetual succession; shall have power to regulate the inspection of flour and tobacco in the town; to prevent the introduction of contagious diseases; to establish night watches and paroles, and to erect lamps; to regulate the stationing, anchorage, and mooring of vessels; to provide for licensing and regulating auctions, ordinaries, and retailers of liquors, hackney carriages, wagons, carts, and drays within said town; to restrain and prohibit gambling; to provide for licensing, regulating, or restraining theatrical or other public amusements; to regulate and establish markets; to pass all laws for the

13

regulation of weights and measures; to provide for the licensing and regulating the sweeping of chimneys, and fix the rates thereof; to establish and regulate fire wards and fire companies; to regulate and establish the size of bricks to be made and used in the said town; the inspection of salted provisions and the assize of bread; to sink wells and erect and repair pumps in the streets; to erect work-houses; to restrain, regulate, and direct the manner of building wharves and docks, and to direct the manner in which the improvements thereon shall be erected, so that they may not be injurious to the health of the town; to direct or order the, paved streets to be cleansed and kept clean, and appoint an officer for that purpose; to make aid keep in repair all necessary sewers and drains, and to pass regulations necessary for the preservation of the same.

To appoint constables and collectors of taxes, and all other officers who may he deemed necessary for the execution of their laws, and prescribe their duties and powers;

[To sue and be sued at law; to act and execute, do and perform, as a body incorporate; to have a common seal, and alter and change the same at pleasure;]

[To cause, from time to time as they deem necessary, a correct survey of the town to be made, and establish and fix permanent boundaries and stones at such places as they may deem necessary to ascertain and perpetuate the true lines of the town; to survey the streets, lanes, and alleys, and declare the same, and to adjudge as nuisances all encroachments thereon;]

[To make such by-laws for the graduation and levelling of the streets, lanes, or alleys of the town as they may judge necessary;]

[To erect wharves on all streets, lanes, or alleys of said town, *provided* no buildings be erected on the front of said wharves;]

[To pass, make, and ordain all laws necessary to take up, fine, imprison, or punish any and all vagrants, loose and disorderly persons, and persons having no visible means of support, that may be found within the town;]

[To make such by-laws for the regulation and good government of the town, and the inhabitants thereof, and to restrain all disorders and disturbances; and to prevent all

14

nuisances, inconveniences, and annoyances within the said town, and other matters, exigencies, and things within said town, as to a major part of them shall seem meet and consonant to reason, and not contrary to the constitution and laws of this State;]

To provide for licensing, taxing, and regulating within the town all traders, retailers, pawnbrokers; and to tax vendors of lottery tickets, money changers, hawkers, and peddlers;

To abate, break up, and abolish, by such means as they may deem expedient and proper, all places and depots of confinement of slaves brought to the District of Columbia as merchandise;

To introduce a supply of water into the town; and to cause the streets, lanes, and alleys, or any of them, to be lighted by gas or otherwise; and to provide for the expense of the same, either by a special tax or out of its corporate funds, or both, at its discretion;

To lay, impose, and collect every year, a school tax of one dollar *per annum*, upon every free white male citizen of the age of twenty-one years and upwards;

And to pass all laws not inconsistent with the laws of the United States, which may be necessary to give effect and operation to all the powers vested in said corporation.

IV.—MISCELLANEOUS PROVISIONS—FINES—PENALTIES —AND FORFEITURES.

[The by-laws made by the corporation shall be observed by the inhabitants of the town, and all persons trading therein, under such reasonable penalties, fines, and forfeitures as shall be imposed by the said by laws, not exceeding seven pounds ten shillings current money, or twenty dollars; said penalties, fines, and forfeitures to be levied by distress and sale of the goods, or execution of the person so offending.]

[The corporation may pass, &c., laws to take up, fine, and punish vagrants, &c.: *Provided,* That they shall not, in any case, pass, make, or ordain any law to fine for any one offence a sum exceeding twenty dollars, or to imprison exceeding thirty days.]

The corporation shall have power to impose and appropriate fines, penalties, and forfeitures for breaches of their ordinances.

[If any person committed to jail under this act shall not, at the expiration of the term for which he was committed, pay the amount of his fine and prison fees, or give security therefor, it shall be lawful for the sheriff, with the written consent of the Mayor, to sell such person as a servant for any term that the Mayor shall prescribe, not exceeding four months.]

The corporation may recover all fines, penalties, and forfeitures incurred under their charter, laws, and ordinances, by warrant before any justice of the peace in the District of Columbia; subject to appeal to the Circuit Court, as in other cases of small debts.

BRIDGES—ROADS, &c.

The two bridges over Rock Creek, between the cities of Washington and Georgetown, shall be kept in repair and rebuilt at the joint expense of the two cities.

The Corporation of Georgetown shall contribute and pay to the levy court of the County of Washington, one-fourth of the expenses incurred by said court on account of the orphan's court, the office or coroner, the jail of said county, and one-half the expenses incurred by said court in the opening and repairing of roads in the County of Washington, west of Rock Creek, leading to Georgetown.

The Corporation of Georgetown shall keep the road leading to the bridge across the Potomac River at the Little Falls, and the bridge, free and in repair forever.

SPECIAL TAXES.

The corporation nay lay and collect a special tax, annually, not exceeding seventy-five cents in the hundred dollars, upon all property by law taxable, and on all money vested or held in banking, exchange, insurance, or brokerage companies, upon all stocks, and money loaned, to pay their subscription to the stock of the Metropolitan Railroad Companies, and to pledge the, same so that no part thereof shall in any event be applied to any other object.

16

TAXES.

Public notice of the the and place of sale of any real property chargeable with taxes in Georgetown shall be given once in each week for twelve successive weeks in some one newspaper printed in Georgetown and Alexandria, and in the *National Intelligencer,* in which shall be stated the number of the lot or lots, or part of lots, intended to be sold, the value of the assessment, and the amount of taxes due and owing thereon.

Public notice of the time and place of sale of any real property chargeable with taxes in Georgetown, in all cases (except where the property is owned by persons not residing in the District of Columbia) shall be given once in each week for twelve successive weeks in some one newspaper in the County of Washington, in which shall be stated the number of the lot or lots, or parts thereof, intended to be sold, the value of the assessment, and the amount of taxes clue and owing thereon.

If, before the day of sale, the taxes, with all costs, shall not be paid, said lots, or so much as may be sufficient to discharge the same, shall be sold for cash to the highest bidder; a certificate from the proper officer shall be issued to the purchaser, stating that he is the purchaser, and the amount paid by him. And if, at the expiration of twelve months from the day of sale, the amount of the purchase money and costs, and taxes subsequently accruing, and ten *per centum* interest *per annum* on the purchase money, be not paid, a title in fee simple shall be made to the purchaser: Pro*vided,* That no real estate shall be sold for taxes where there is personal property belonging to the owner or tenant sufficient to pay the same.

All titles to property sold for taxes shall be conveyed by deed from the Mayor under the seal of the corporation; which conveyance shall be effectual in law to convey the title, the requisitions of this act having been complied with.

The amount of the purchase money over and above the taxes, costs, and charges upon the property, shall be paid to the owner, on his application for the same.

If taxes are collected from a tenant, he may retain possession of the property until the rent accruing shall discharge the debt so created, and twenty-five, *per centum* on the amount

17

of taxes so paid by him, except where he has previously been in arrears for his rent.

STREETS, ETC.

The corporation may tax any particular portion of the town, for paving the streets, lanes, or alleys, or for sinking wells or erecting pumps, which may appear for the benefit of such portion: *Provided,* The rate of tax so levied shall not exceed two dollars per front foot.

In addition to the above, the corporation shall have power upon petition, in writing, of the majority of the holders of the real property fronting on any street, lane, or alley, if, in their judgment, it shall be deemed necessary, to lay such additional sum on each front foot as will be sufficient to pave said street, or part of a street, lane, or alley petitioned for.

[The corporation shall have full power and authority to make such by-laws and ordinances for the graduation and levelling of the streets, lanes, and alleys of the town, as they may judge necessary for the benefit thereof.]

The corporation may lay out, open, extend, and regulate streets, lanes, and alleys under the following regulations: The Mayor shall summon twelve freeholders, inhabitants of the town, not interested in the premises, who, being first sworn to assess and value what damages would be sustained by any person, by reason of extending or opening any street, lane, or alley (taking all benefits and inconveniences into consideration), shall proceed to assess what damages would be sustained by any person, by reason of such opening or extension, and shall declare the amount, in money, each individual benefitted thereby, shall contribute and pay towards compensating the persons injured thereby; and the names of the persons benefitted, and the sums which each shall be obliged to pay, shall be returned under their hands and seals to the clerk of the corporation, to be kept in his office; and the persons benefitted as aforesaid, and assessed as aforesaid, shall pay the ruins charged and assessed to them, with *six per centum* interest thereon from the time limited for the payment, until paid; and the sums assessed and charged to each individual benefitted, shall be a lien upon and bind all the property so benefitted to the full amount thereof: *Provided,* No street, lane, or alley shall be laid out, opened, or extended until the damages assessed to individuals shall be paid, or secured to be paid: *And provided, also,* That nothing herein shall authorize the laying out or opening of any street, lane, alley, or other way, through any of the squares or lots in Thos. Beall's second addition, north of Back Street, without the consent in writing of the owner or proprietor first had and obtained; which consent shall be acknowledged in the presence of, and such acknowledgment certified by, the Mayor or some justice of the peace for the County of Washington.

GENERAL ASSESSMENT.
The corporation shall, on or about the first day of April, 1825, and every five years thereafter, cause three respectable freeholders, resident in said town, being previously sworn, to assess and value, and make a return of all and every species of property by law taxable in said corporation; and in making their said valuation, they shall determine it agreeably to what they believe it to be worth in cash at that time.

SCHOOL FUND.
The school tax, which shall be levied and collected every year, shall constitute a fund, or be added to any other fund, now or hereafter to be constituted by act of said corporation, for the establishment and support of common schools, and for no other purpose.

ELECTION PRECINCTS AND JUDGES.
The corporation shall establish not less than two election precincts, and appoint not less than three judges of election for each precinct.

NON-RESIDENT INSANE PERSONS.
Upon the application of the Corporation of Georgetown, and at their expense, any indigent insane person, who did not reside in the District when he or she became insane, may be admitted

into the Insane Hospital of this District.

BUYING AND SELLING VOTES.

If any person shall buy or sell a vote, or shall vote more than once at any corporate election, or shall give or receive any consideration therefor, or shall promise any valuable consideration, or vote in consideration of such promise, he shall be disqualified forever thereafter from voting or holding any office under said corporation.

CLERK OF THE CORPORATION.

The clerk shall record in a look, to lie kept for the purpose, all the laws and resolutions duly passed by the corporation, and deliver a copy of there to the public printer, to he printed by him for the use of the people.

The clerk shall, on the presentation of the collector's receipt showing the person has paid his school tax, enter the name of the payer on the books of the corporation, and furnish the judges of election at each precinct, before or on the morning of the day of election before the hour of opening the polls, a list of the names of all persons who shall have paid their school tax for that year.

FIRE REGULATIONS.

The corporation shall annually appoint an inspector of fire engines, whose duty it shall be to examine and report the condition of the fire apparatus belonging to each fire company once a month.

The corporation shall have full power and authority to make all necessary provisions for the prevention and extinguishment of fires; for the preservation of order and protection of property at any fire; for the removal from any fire of suspicious persons, and those who are disobedient to the regulations of the corporation; for the punishment, by fine and imprisonment, of such person as, being present at, refuses to assist and obey the commands of the proper officer in extinguishing any fire; for the removal of such property as may be necessary to be removed; to prevent and arrest the progress of any fire; and to aid, protect, and obtain obedience to the officers in command of the several fire companies, and to protect the members thereof while in the discharge of their duty at any fire.

SKETCH OF THE TOWN AND ITS SURROUNDINGS.

To have a good view of our town let the spectator ascend the heights to Holyrood Cemetery, at the intersection of High and Fayette Streets, and take a glance over the horizon, he will discover that the town is situated at the confluence of Rock Creek and the Potomac River, about three miles front the Little Falls, to which tide-water rises, and is separated by Rock Creek from Washington City, with which there is ready communication by means of four bridges crossing the creek at the intersection of Water, Aqueduct, Bridge, and West Streets. Cars run every few minutes over the M Street and West Street bridges, from the center of the town to the Navy Yard. The position of the town is salubrious; and, being elevated on hills that slope towards the creek and river, it has ample drainage, and has always escaped certain epidemics that have prevailed in other cities. In the distance we behold the heights of Arlington, late the residence of G.W.P. Custis, now made memorable by the late war, in laying it out as a cemetery for the dead. Not far from the mansion is the famous springs where the inhabitants of Georgetown and Washington would congregate to enjoy a conversation with the "old man eloquent," or step it off on the light fantastic toe; Mr. Custis having erected, at his own expense, a pavilion for the accommodation of all parties who came, with or without music, to spend a pleasant day. Above the town is the rocks called "the Three Sisters," on which it was proposed to build a wire suspension bridge for railroad and common travel, the plan of which was furnished to the town at a cost of two thousand dollars, but never erected, although a bill is now reported upon favorably by the District committee for the construction of a permanent bridge in that locality.

Near the Aqueduct stands the brick mansion where lived the author of "the Star Spangled Banner," Francis S. Key, when he was a citizen of Georgetown, and prior to being appointed

District Attorney, when he transferred his residence to Washington.

Southwest of us is the Georgetown College, known to fame as the *alma mater* of many distinguished men who have here received their education and gone forth in the world to fill various offices in church and state. A little north of the college is the Monastery and the Academy of Sisters of the Visitation, embracing a large extent of ground, some thirty-three acres, with ample buildings fronting on Fayette Street. We will leave a further description of these institutions until we come to treat on education.

Alexandria can be seen in the distance, with its church-spires and thousands of houses, over which rolled the clouds of smoke and flame on the 18th day of January, 1827, when from eighty to one hundred houses were destroyed.

The Long Bridge extends itself across the Potomac from the District to the Virginia shore, and looks as if it might be carried away lay a freshet. Away to the east is seen the dome of the Capitol, and the Washington Monument in an unfinished condition. Also the National Observatory, located on Camp Hill, where the professors record the appearance of the planets and comets. It is said that General Braddock landed his army and drilled his men here preparatory to his toilsome march with colonial troops to Fort Duquense, by a route through the city of Frederick to Cumberland. On the borders of Rock Creek stands Lyon's Mill, a great place of resort in the summer season. A little to the east is *Kalorama*, famous for having been the residence of distinguished men. Joel Barlow, the author of the "Columbiad," once resided here, also did Fulton, the inventor of the steam engine, make here his home when experimenting on the powers of steam. Here, also, were interred the remains of Commodore Decatur, who fell in a duel with Barron on the 22d day of March, 1820. Here, also, lived Col. George Bomford, when at the head of the Ordnance Bureau.

Immediately west of Georgetown is the Alexandria Aqueduct, which connects the Chesapeake and Ohio Canal with Alexandria. The architect of this magnificent work was Major Turnbull, of the United States Corps of Engineers. It cost about six hundred thousand dollars to erect the aqueduct, of which amount Congress gave four hundred thousand. As we shall write a chapter on this work, we leave its history to a future page.

Just opposite the town is Analostan Island, with its beautiful trees and verdant fields, embracing near one hundred acres, and is denominated Mason's Island, being the former residence of the late General Mason, who entertained Louis Phillipe when on a visit to the United States in 1798. James M. Mason, late Confederate Minister to Europe, was born here. The dwelling, in which so much princely hospitality was exhibited, was burnt down during the civil war. The island is now used as a pleasure resort. A stone causeway connects the Island with the Virginia shore, which was erected in 1805, at a heavy expense, for the purpose of improving the channel of the river by throwing the whole body of water on the eastern side of the island.

Just above the town, on the north bank of the river, is located the former "Columbian Foundry," belonging to the late John Mason, formerly called Foxall's Foundry, where was manufactured cannon, shot, and shell that were used in the late war with Great Britain. Since Mason's death the property has been sold, and is now used for milling purposes and a distillery.

Further up the Potomac, three miles above the town, is the "Little Falls," a great place of resort in the summer season for fishing parties, also for picnics, and for persons seeking pleasure and amusement. The water has a fall here of thirty-three feet, and a narrow, contracted channel, through which the water shoots with great impetuosity.

Twelve miles above the town is the "Great Falls," just above whose waterfall a dam has been erected to supply the reservoirs and tunnels with a full supply of water for the use of the cities of the District. A description of the water works will be found in our chapter on the Washington Aqueduct.

On the heights of the town are situated some of the finest mansions in the country, occupied by citizens whose wealth enables them to retire from business and to devote their leisure in improving and embellishing their estates. *Monterey*, the residence of the late Edward M. Linthicum, is a beautiful situation. This house was formerly occupied by John C.

Calhoun, when Secretary of War under the administration of Monroe. Then comes *Tudor Place*, the former residence of the late Thomas Peter, but more recently of Commodore Kenyon, who lost his life on board of the ill-fated steamship *Princeton,* on the 1st of March, 1844. Next is the residence of the late Brooke Williams, where the Russian minister was captivated by the beauty of an American lady in May, 1841. The residence of the late David Peter, which was formerly occupied by an English ambassador, Baron Sir John Crampton, and afterwards by the minister from France, was unfortunately destroyed by fire during the war. Henry D. Cook purchased the grounds for fifty thousand dollars, and on Stoddard Street has erected handsome buildings. The next in order is the residence of the late Captain Boyce of the United States Navy, who unfortunately lost his life by a railroad accident in 1855. Then comes the fine mansion of the late Samuel Turner, now owned by Joseph Weaver, and is fitted up in princely style. There are several other desirable residences on the heights, occupied by John Marbury, A.H. Herr, the Worthington family, William Dougal, C.T. Peck, and *Evermay*, the residence of the late Samuel Davidson, now of John McPherson.

Having now taken a circumspective view of the town from an elevation, let us descend into the city, and see what has been going on there. The town, being fortified by its charter, as already mentioned, then came into existence as a city. For many years a very active business was done by our wholesale and retail merchants and numerous buildings and improvements were erected by our mechanics, which were an ornament to the town.

Education was not neglected. Several private schools were conducted in the town at different periods of time: John Kellenberger taught in a school-house near the Bank of Columbia; James Graham in a building on the lot where the residence of Phillip T. Berry stands; Matthew McLeod in a frame building on Gay Street. The Rev. James Carnahan taught a classical school, of high repute, until 1823, when Rev. James McVean conducted his classical and mathematical academy on West Street, which was afterwards conducted by Rev. Mr.

Simpson, from 1849 to 1857. Miss Lydia English taught a ladies' seminary at the corner of Washington and Gay Streets. William R. Abbot conducted a classical academy on West Street until his death in 1852. A Lancasterian school was conducted by the late Robert Ould on Beall Street, in the building occupied by the late McKinney Osbourn. A school was also taught on High Street by John McLeod; also, at another period of time, by Rev. William Allen. A ladies' school was also conducted by Miss Searle; and a military academy by Captain Cobb, on Prospect Hill. We mention these places where the, juveniles received the first rudiments of education, leaving to a future chapter a more extended notice of the institutions of learning.

WHO FRAMED THE ORIGINAL CONSTITUTION.

As a matter of some importance to the rising generation to know who framed the original Constitution of our country, we transcribe from the tombstones at *Kalorama*, as follows: "Abraham Baldwin, a Senator in Congress from Georgia, died 4th March, 1807, aged 52 years. His devotion to his country his greatest fame, her constitution his greatest work." Abraham Baldwin was a member of the convention to draft the Constitution of the United States. After his death the original manuscript of the constitution was found among his papers.

Joel Barlow, patriot, poet, and philosopher, died December 26, 1812, aged 57 years. Henry Baldwin, Judge of the Supreme Court, died April 21, 1844. Ruth Baldwin, his wife, died May 29, 1818, aged 62 years. George Bomford, Colonel U.S.A., died May 25, 1848, aged 66 years. Clara, wife of Colonel Bomford, died 10th December, 1855, aged 74 years. The remains of Commodore Decatur were subsequently transferred to Philadelphia; his widow, Mrs. Susan Decatur, resided for many years near Georgetown College. She died June 21st, 1860, aged about 70 years, and was buried in the family lot of the Fenwick's, within the college grounds.

Any reader desiring to peruse a history of the Decatur duel, will refer to George Alfred Townsend's book, entitled "Washington Outside and Inside;" he will there learn "how hard it is to be a duelist and live, and how hard it is to be a duelist and die."

WILLIAM WIRT.

We cannot refrain from mentioning that William Wirt, the author of the "British Spy," and Attorney General of the United States, for twelve years, under the administrations of Monroe and Adams, received the rudiments of his education in Georgetown. From his life I make the following extract: "In 1779 I was sent to Georgetown, eight miles from Bladensburg, to school—a classical academy kept by Mr. Rogers. I was placed at boarding with the family of Mr. Schoofield, a member of the Society of Friends. They occupied a small house of hewn logs at the eastern end of Bridge Street. Friend Schoofield was a well-set, square-built, honest-faced, and honest-hearted man; his wife was one of the best of creation. A deep sadness fell upon me when I was left by the person who accompanied me to Georgetown—when I could no longer see a face that I knew, nor an object that was not strange. I remember the sense of total desertion and forlornness that seized upon my heart, unlike anything I felt in after years. I sobbed, as if my heart would break, for hours together, and was utterly inconsolable, notwithstanding the maternal tenderness with which good Mrs. Schoofield tried to comfort me. Almost half a century has rolled over the incident, yet full well do I recollect with what gentle affection and touching sympathy she urged every topic that was calculated to console a child of my years. After quieting me, in some measure, by her caresses, she took down her bible and read to me the story of Joseph and his brethren. It is probable I had read it before, as such things are usually read without understanding it; but she made me so comprehend it, that, in the distress of Joseph and his father, I forgot my own. His separation from his family had brought him to great honor, and possibly mine, I thought, might be equally fortunate. I claim some sense of gratitude. I never forget an act of kindness, and never received one, that my heart has not impelled me to wish for some occasion to return it. So far as my experience goes, I am persuaded, too, that doing an act of kindness, and still more repeated acts to the same individual, are as apt to attach the heart of the benefactor to the object, as that of the beneficiary to the person who does him the service. It was so in this instance. I went to see Mrs. Schoofield after I became a man, and a warmer meeting has seldom taken place between mother and son.

"I passed one winter in Georgetown, and remember seeing a long line of wagons cross the river on the ice. I conjecture that it was the winter of 1779-'80, and that these wagons were attached to the troops which were going south. I remember, also, to have seen a gentleman, Mr. Peter, I think, going out gunning for canvass-backs—then called white-backs—which I have seen in those days whitening the Potomac, and which, when they arose, as they sometimes did, for half a mile together, produced a sound like thunder."

I mention this, being struck with the different state of this game now on the Potomac.

LUDICROUS SCENES.

Some ludicrous scenes have taken place in our legislature. On the 26th of September, 1810, an ordinance was passed authorizing Richard Parrott to make a rope to survey the width of the Potomac River. The rope was made according to order, and on a day appointed, the surveyor, with the fathers of the town and a number of citizens, assembled to span the vast Potomac. The rope was made fast on one side, and all hands got hold of the end on the other, and such a pulling rope never had before; but, alas, for the onward progress of human legislation, the whole town could not draw the rope into a straight line. The attraction of gravitation prevailing here, caused the rope to describe a curve in opposition to the surface of the earth; it swagged into the water, got a ducking, and was then drawn ashore. Thus ended rope surveying.

On the 24th of January, 1825, the corporation passed an ordinance to purchase a steel triangle, which was swung in a steeple built upon the town house. This triangle was used to triangulate the town with its music every night at ten o'clock. It carried the sound of time through the town as fast as the magnetic wires carries news to Baltimore; and when the town officer commenced triangulating, the darkies would move off in parallel lines for home: but sometimes they would come in contact with a triangular watchman who would ensconce them in the watch-house until day. The triangle lasted but a short time. On account of the laws of gravitation prevailing here and elsewhere, the treacherous cord by which it was swung gave way one night while the system of triangulation was in full blast, and the triangle leaped through the steeple on the roof of the house, and, bounding from thence to the ground, broke up into fragments. Thus ended triangulation. The old system of blowing tin horns at ten o'clock was re-established, and the watchmen were ordered to cry the hour to time the citizens through the darkness of the night.

DUELS.

It was about the year 1826, as well as the chronicler can remember, that the duel between John Randolph and Henry Clay took place, one afternoon, on the banks of the Potomac, above the Fall's Bridge. Randolph was a man of talent, but nearly a madman. He vilified Clay, who was Secretary of State under John Q. Adams, by attacking him in the Senate—styling him a black-leg. On the word being given, Mr. Clay fired without effect. Mr. Randolph fired his pistol in the air. The moment Mr. Clay saw that Randolph had thrown away his fire, he instantly approached Mr. Randolph, and said; "I trust in God, my dear sir, you are untouched. After what has occurred, I would not have harmed you for a thousand worlds." This was a bloodless duel, and, probably, fortunate for our country it was so. Both were distinguished men; but the duel fought upon the same ground on the 16th of February, 1844, between Julian May, a citizen of Washington, and J.W. Cochrane, terminated fatally to one of the parties. They fought with rifles, and Cochrane fell at the first fire, shot through the head. In June, 1836, a duel was fought between two young men of the Navy—Daniel Key, son of the late Francis S. Key, and J.H. Sherburne, both being midshipmen, in which Key was killed; and in February, 1838, Jonathan Cilley, of Maine, and W.T. Graves, of Kentucky, had a duel with rifles, in which Cilley was killed. This last duel caused Congress, on the 20th day of February, 1839, to enact a law against dueling. (See volume 5, statutes at large, page 318.) The author of "the Star Spangled Banner" had another son killed on the 27th day of February, 1859, by Daniel E. Sickles. The chronicler mentions these events, as Philip Barton Key, Daniel Key, and Julian May were his school-mates.

DEPRESSION IN BUSINESS AND BEGINNING OF THE CANAL.

The business of our town began to languish; houses ceased to be built; and many of those that had been erected were without tenants. What was the cause of this was a question which presented itself to the inquiring mind. Our merchants and mechanics were industrious and willing to work; but business was slack. This was due to the rapid growth of Washington, whose citizens purchased the productions of the soil from the people of the surrounding counties, and who, in return, sold them goods on their way for home. They passed through our town without stopping to purchase. Affairs went on this way for many years, until Washington grew to be a large city; and by building towards our town her prosperity has diffused itself into our city, like a stick thrown into a pond of water, it makes a ripple until it reaches the shore. Both cities must now flourish, being in conjunction. The prosperity of one is the prosperity of the other.

To improve the trade of the town, a charter was obtained from the State of Virginia on the 24th of September, 1824, assented to and confirmed by Congress on the 3d of March, 1825, and also by the State of Pennsylvania, to make and construct a canal from Georgetown to the Ohio River. Our citizens subscribed liberally to the stock, believing it would eventually pay a dividend to the stockholders, some of them subscribing as high as five thousand dollars, and paying all their installments. It was considered that the canal, if it did not pay directly on its completion, would indirectly pay by increasing the business of the town and increasing the value of property. On the passage of the charter by Congress, the citizens of the town were in high glee; bon-fires illuminated the streets at night, and everybody thought that prosperity had come upon us.

Friday, the 4th of July, 1828, was a gala day for Georgetown. The President of the United States, accompanied by the heads of the departments, the Diplomatic Corps, the president and directors of the Chesapeake and Ohio Canal, and the corporate authorities of the three cities of the then District of Columbia, assembled early in the morning at the Union Hotel, on Bridge Street, when a procession was formed and moved on to the excellent music of the Marine Band to High Street wharf, where they embarked on board the steamboat *Surprise*, and other boats, and coursed their way up the Potomac until they reached the termination of the old Potomac Canal, where they landed and marched a few hundred yards to the canal-boats prepared to receive them. After being seated in these boats they glided along until they reached the point of destination, where the old powder magazine formerly stood. On landing from the boats the procession formed a large circle, in the centre of which was the spot for the commencement of the work. The president of the Canal Company addressed the President of the United States in a brief speech. After he concluded, he handed to John Q. Adams the spade by which the sod was to be turned. The President, on receiving the implement, stepped forward and addressed the multitude in an eloquent and able speech, from which I take the following extract:

"Friends and fellow-laborers: We are informed by the Holy Oracle of truth, that at the creation of man, male and female, the Lord of the Universe, their Maker, blessed them, and said unto them: "Be fruitful, and multiply, and replenish the earth, and subdue it." To subdue the earth was, therefore, one of the first duties assigned to man at his creation; and now, in his fallen condition, it remains among the most excellent of his occupations. To subdue the earth is pre-eminently the purposes of the undertaking, to the accomplishment of which the first stroke of the spade is now to be struck. That it is to be struck, by this hand, I invite you to witness."

Attending this action was an incident which produced a greater sensation than any other event that occurred during the day. The President, in attempting to run the spade into the ground, struck a root which prevented its penetrating the earth. He tried it a second time with no better success, when a wag in the crowd cried out that he had come across a "hickory root." Thus foiled, he threw down the spade and hastily stripped off his coat and went to work in earnest. The people around on the hills who could not hear, but could see and understand what was going on, raised a loud cheering, which continued for some time after the President had overcome the difficulty. The excavation of the canal was immediately put under contract. During the excavation of the canal through the town, some accidents occurred: In undermining a heavy bank of earth between High and Congress Streets, it suddenly fell and destroyed the lives of two men. On the section between Market and Frederick Streets a sand blast was fired by a contractor, when large rocks were hurled through the air. One rock struck the dormer window in the house of Doctor Charles A. Beatty, on Water Street, and smashed it to pieces; another rock, weighing one thousand and forty-five pounds, struck a horse at the corner of Potomac and Water Streets, producing instant death. The indignation was so great against the contractor that he fled the town. The work progressed so rapidly that, by the 4th of July, 1831, the water was let in from the first feeder to the Columbian Foundry. The number of locks on the canal are seventy-three; being one hundred feet long, fifteen feet wide, with eight feet lift; are built of cut stone and laid in cement. The distance from our town to Cumberland is one hundred and eighty-four miles, to which point the canal is finished. In subscribing to the stock of the Chesapeake & Ohio Canal, at one hundred dollars per share, the United States subscribed to ten thousand, the city of Washington to ten thousand, Alexandria to twenty-five hundred, and Georgetown to twenty-five hundred shares, which, with private subscriptions, amounted to three million five hundred thousand dollars—at that time thought to be sufficient to complete the canal to Cumberland. When the reader peruses the chapter on the Chesapeake & Ohio Canal, in this work, he will see that the estimate was far below the actual cost. The cities of the District employed Richard Rush to negotiate a loan of one million and five hundred thousand dollars on the credit of the citizens of Washington, Alexandria, and Georgetown, to meet their subscription towards the work; which money was obtained in Holland, of the house of Messrs. Crommelins at Amsterdam.

CHANNEL OF THE RIVER, AND CONTEST FOR THE UPPER AND LOWER ROADS LEADING TO FALL'S BRIDGE.

The channel of the river, below the town, began to fill up, so that a brig or large vessel, when loaded, could not pass down the river. As the town had paid large sums of money into the Treasury of the United States, when a large importing and exporting business was done, Congress passed an act on the 2d of March, 1833, appropriating one hundred and fifty thousand dollars—"to enable the town to remove obstructions to the navigation of the river, and for the further purpose of enabling the citizens to make a free turnpike road to the District line in Virginia, and to purchase the bridge at the Little Falls of the Potomac River and declare the same free, and to keep the road and bridge in repair forever."

The Corporation of Georgetown made a contract with E. and T.P. Ellicot, of Baltimore City, to deepen the channel below the town. They brought a powerful dredging machine to accomplish their contract, and by the year 1835, they had excavated a cut through the bar; below the town, that gave a sufficient depth of water to float large ships. The cut made through the bar was four thousand feet in length by one hundred and forty feet wide, with a depth of fifteen feet at low tide, and nineteen feet at high tide. Before the excavation, the depth of water over the bar was from ten to twelve feet.

The chronicler makes the following extracts from the report of the Commissioners appointed to supervise the work on the channel:

"Statement showing expenditures in excavating the channel through the bar below Georgetown—commenced in 1833, and continued to December 31,1835:

Expenses in the year 1833 : For preliminary surveys . $236.31
Estimate of excavations in 1834:
    38,570 cubic yards, @ 30 cents 11,571.00
Contingent expenses: Engineers' pay during
    the year 1834 . . . . 816.04
Estimate of excavation, per contract of
    1835: 10,068 cubic yards, @ 30 cents 3,020.40
Estimate of same work, being an angle of the bars:
    4,815 cubic yards, @ 30 cents 1,444.50
Estimate of excavation during residue of
    the year 1835: 58,294 cubic yds. @ 30 cts. 17,488.20
Contingent expenses, exclusive of pay of
    Engineers 680.50
                                      $35,256 95

Leaving a balance yet due to the contractors, the Messrs.
Ellicots, according to contract, as security for completion,
$3,000.

                                WALTER SMITH,
January 26, 1836.   JOHN KURTZ,
                              WILLIAM LAIRD,
                              Commissioners.

    Considerable discussion sprang up in our Boards of
Aldermen and Common Council, whether all the money left from
deepening the channel should not be applied to the making of
two roads to the Fall's Bridge; one by the side of the canal, and
the other from the intersection of High and Seventh Streets,
across the country to intersect the canal road. We had at this
time a property qualification in electing the Mayor and members
of the Corporation; and the consequence was, we elected able
men to the council that would have done honor to the floors of
Congress: There was Thomas Corcoran, Francis Dodge, Samuel
McKenney, and others, men of strong minds and able debaters.
The question was debated for several weeks. Colonel Corcoran,
being the advocate for the lower route, was overwhelming in his

argument; and the question was finally decided in favor of the road by the side of the canal (on being submitted to a vote of the people) by a majority of five votes. On the 11th of March, 1833, the Corporation appropriated fifty thousand dollars to purchase all claim and right to the Fall's Bridge and the road leading to the same.

The friends of the upper route were not dismayed by the decision of the people, and at the next election, held on the fourth Monday in February, 1834, they elected a majority of upper route men, and on the 21st of October, 1834, they passed a bill for making the upper road, and appropriated fifteen thousand dollars out of the Congress fund to construct the same; but the cost of the road before completion was twenty-seven thousand dollars.

THE HOLLAND LOAN, AND OPPOSITION TO THE ALEXANDRIA AQUEDUCT.

On the 20th of May, 1836, Congress passed an act to relieve the cities of the District from the Holland loan, incurred by their subscription to the stock of the Chesapeake & Ohio Canal. Washington City owed one million of dollars, Alexandria two hundred and fifty thousand dollars, and Georgetown the same amount as Alexandria, making one and a half millions assumed and paid by the United States.

In the same year (1836), while the Alexandria Aqueduct was being constructed, under a charter passed by Congress, dated 26th May, 1830, also, under a large donation of four hundred thousand dollars given by Congress to aid in the construction of the work, the corporate authorities of Georgetown undertook, by an injunction, to stop the further progress of the work. The case came on for a hearing before the Circuit Court of the District of Columbia, when the Court decided against the town on a demurrer to the bill. An appeal was taken to the Supreme Court of the United States; that court held "that the plaintiffs, in their corporate capacity, could not maintain this suit in behalf of the citizens of Georgetown. It was not like the common case of the creditor's bill, where the persons bringing the suit by names have an interest in the subject-matter which enables them to sue; and the others are treated as a kind of co-plaintiffs with those named. The appellants have no authority to vindicate, in a court of justice, the rights of citizens of their town in the enjoyment of their property." (12 Peters, p. 91.) This was an unfortunate suit for the town. It generated bad feeling between Alexandria and Georgetown, and when we went to Congress and asked for a free bridge by the side of the Aqueduct, Alexandria opposed it, and we obtained nothing.

BASIS OF AN AGREEMENT FOR THE CONSOLIDATION OF WASHINGTON CITY AND GEORGETOWN.

In the year 1856, on the 17th and 24th of September, and 15th and 17th of October, a committee from the town, appointed by the corporate authorities, met a committee of Washington City at the City Hall, for the purpose of devising some plan to consolidate the two cities; the following propositions were submitted and argued at length by the gentlemen on both sides.

"1. Georgetown, as such, is no longer to have any separate existence as a corporation. All of its powers of legislation and distinct corporate action are to be surrendered.

2. Georgetown is to form two wards of Washington City, to have a representation in the Councils of Washington, as such, and to have the rights and incur the obligation of such.

3. The people of Georgetown, in becoming citizens of Washington City, will assume their proportion of the debt of Washington, and submit to such revenue system and taxation as is or may be imposed upon the citizens of Washington City, for the purpose of paying the principal and interest of said debt.

4. The debt of Georgetown, funded and floating, is to be assumed by Washington.

5. The property, real and personal, now owned by Georgetown, the debts owing to it, the stocks held by it, and assets of any and every kind belonging to it, are to vest absolutely in Washington City.

6. The obligations incurred by Georgetown, so far as they bind it, and no further, are to be assumed by Washington.

7. The present western or Virginia Channel of the Potomac is not to be altered or in any manner affected, except by the consent of the people resident in the aforesaid two new wards, or of a majority of their representatives in each of the branches of the Corporation of Washington.

8. The people of Georgetown, in becoming citizens of Washington, will assume their just and fair proportion of all the obligations, past and future, incurred by Washington City.

9. Georgetown and Washington City will unite in an effort to have any plan of union agreed upon carried out by appropriate legislation by Congress.

10. Any plan agreed upon by the joint committee is to he submitted to the people of Washington City and Georgetown, respectively, for ratification, and shall only be effectual when ratified by both cities and confirmed by Congress."

All the propositions were agreed to except the seventh, to which the Washington committee objected; but our committee held on to the seventh proposition, when, no agreement being accomplished, the meeting adjourned *sine die.*

In the year 1838, on the 29th and 30th of January, and at other times, several meetings were held at the old Lancaster School room, on Beall Street, to consider and discuss the question of retrocession to Maryland of all that part of the District lying west of Rock Creek, including Georgetown. Samuel McKenny addressed the citizens in favor of the question in an able speech, that occupied two evenings in its delivery; he was replied to by others, when it was agreed to submit the question to a vote of the people. On an election being held in the town a majority of sixty-five votes was declared in favor of retrocession. Consequently, a committee was appointed to visit Annapolis and lay before the Legislature of Maryland a petition of the citizens of Georgetown for annexation to the State of Maryland, which was favorably received and considered; but the Congress of the United Status took no action on the petition. In 1851, several meetings ware held at Forrest Hall to discuss the question of retrocession. Able speeches were made for and against retrocession by Henry Addison, Samuel McKenney, and Robert

Ould and others, but no vote was submitted to the people, and the question rested. The chronicler at that time penned an allegory on the question of retrocession to Maryland, or annexation to Washington, published in the *Georgetown Advocate*, in 1851, which we will now insert:

> *"Is it best to marry widower Georgetown to*
> *Miss Maryland or to Lady Washington?*

MR. EDITOR: It is proposed to marry Georgetown to Maryland, a buxom lady of seventy-five years of age, with a debt resting upon her shoulders of fifteen million dollars, running on interest at 6 per cent. per annum, making the interest for the first year nine hundred thousand dollars. Now we well know, according to the rules and laws of matrimony, that widower Georgetown must take Maryland with all her advantages and disadvantages, and if Maryland has not enough to pay her debts while single, the property of her husband, Georgetown, must be taken to pay her liabilities. Now, Lady Maryland has been accustomed to high life, and high living. She has given soirees and parties frequently at her palace at Annapolis, and invited the surrounding country and legislature to feast on champagne and oysters, while old Georgetown has been accustomed to live upon Potomac herrings and corn-bread, and by his economy has laid up a little property; which he is now going to throw away upon his extravagant lady-love, Maryland. Why, Lady Maryland has been accustomed to move in a high and noble sphere. She has invoked herself in debt by making railroads, on which she could take pleasant rides with her company and enjoy a season at Harper's Ferry, in beholding the surrounding scenery, the hills and valleys of Virginia, and the meanderings of the Potomac from the unbroken plains. She has luxuriated at Martinsburg, then at Winchester, then next at Cumberland, where she settled down and built a palace to feast the inhabitants of Alleghany. We next hear of her preparing for a departure from that city, with more than a dozen cars in her train, carrying her company, baggage, and boxes, with a snorting, fiery locomotive ready for the word, and when she takes her departure, we cannot tell

37

where she will spend the next summer, whether upon the hills of Pittsburg, or slumbering upon the banks of the Ohio, at Wheeling. Now, would it be well to marry widower Georgetown to such an extravagant lady as this? The best we can do is to unite Georgetown to Washington. Lady Washington is but little in debt compared to Miss Maryland, and she has an uncle, called 'Uncle Sam,' who is very liberal towards her. He owns large possessions; he owns the Capitol and the departments, the Smithsonian Institute, large tracks of land in the West, and all California. He has a large revenue of fifty millions, out of which lie generally gives two or three hundred thousand a year to his niece, as pin money, which enables her to adorn her person in fine attire, and beautify her city by making rough places smooth, and filling up her valleys, and laying off her streets and avenues, lighting up the city with gas, and having a guard to attend her person. In fact, so kind is he towards his niece, that it is generally believed, when the old man dies, he will leave her all his property, and she will become the richest lady in the world. Now to his distant relative, Georgetown, he has occasionally given something to keep him from starvation. He once gave him one hundred and fifty thousand dollars to help to buy a bridge and make a road to the same, and on another occasion he went his security to the Dutch for one-fourth of a million, which be had to pay—both principal and interest; and he has never given him anything since. Now, as old Georgetown is rather poor, and hard pushed for money to get along, would it not be well to marry him to Lady Washington so that be can share in her prosperity and wealth? He would certainly have a life-estate in all her possessions, and would be entitled to receive the emblems and income of her vast property; and if heirs should be born alive (of which I hope there will be a great many after the union), then Georgetown would, in case of the death of Lady Washington or the removal of the seat of Government, become tenant by the courtesy during his natural life. He would then be entitled to all the Capitol, the public buildings, and the innumerable wealth of 'Uncle Sam.' Then we need not go to Washington for a walk, nor go there to laugh and talk, &c., &c."

SKETCH OF ITS LEGISLATION.

Our charter was our guild and strength. It gave us power to act and to do in all things relating to the welfare of the town. In an evil hour we were, life Sampson of old, lulled to sleep by a false Delilah, in the shape of a bill to create a form of Government for the District of Columbia, passed by Congress on the 21st of February, 1871. Section 37 was as follows:

"SEC. 37. That there shall be in the District of Columbia a Board of Public Works, to consist of the governor, who shall be president of said board; four persons to be appointed by the President of the United States, by and with the advice and consent of the Senate, one of whom shall be a civil engineer, and the other a citizen and resident of the District, having the qualifications of an elector therein; one of said board shall be a citizen and resident of Georgetown, and one of said board shall be a citizen and resident of the county outside of the cities of Washington and Georgetown. They shall hold office for the term of four years, unless sooner removed by the President of the United States. The Board of Public Works shall have entire control of and make all regulations which they shall deem necessary for keeping in repair the streets, avenues, alleys, and sewers of the city, and all other works which may be entrusted to their charge by the Legislative Assembly or Congress. They shall disburse, upon their warrant, all moneys appropriated by the United States, or the District of Columbia, or collected from property holders, in pursuance of law, for the improvement of streets, avenues, alleys, and sewers, and roads, and bridges, and shall assess in such manner as shall be prescribed by law upon the property adjoining, and to be specially benefitted by the improvements authorized by law and made by them, a reasonable proportion of the cost of the improvement, not exceeding one-third of such cost, which sum shall be collected as other taxes are collected. They shall make all necessary regulations respecting the construction of private buildings in the District of Columbia, subject to the supervision of the legislative assembly. All contracts made by the said Board of Public Works

39

shall be in writing, and shall be signed by the parties making the same, and a copy thereof shall be filed in the office of the secretary of the District; and said Board of Public Works shall have no power to make contracts to bind said District to the payment of any sums of money except in pursuance of appropriations made by law, and not until such appropriations shall have been made. All contracts made by said board in which any member of said board shall be personally interested shall be void, and no payment shall be made thereon by said District or any officers thereof. On or before the first Monday in November of each year, they shall submit to each branch of the legislative assembly a report of their transactions during the preceding year, and also furnish duplicates of the same to the governor, to be by him laid before the President of the United States for transmission to the two Houses of Congress; and shall be paid the sum of two thousand five hundred dollars each annually."

This section gave the Board of Public Works uncontrollable power to dig down, fill up, and change the grade of the streets wherever they thought best. The consequence was, the District of Columbia was, within three years, overwhelmed with a debt of twenty-two millions of dollars, of which Georgetown had to bear its share in the shape of heavy taxation, to pay the interest on said debt.

The Board of Public Works entered the town to make what they called improvements, in altering and changing the grade of the streets, to the great detriment and injury of a large class of property holders. If ever a set of sensible men were guilty of a wrong, it was in filling up Bridge Street between High and Market Streets; also Market Space on the east and west side of the market house. They filled up at the head of the market house thirteen feet with earth, and at the foot twenty feet; thus leaving the market house in a hollow, as well as the row of buildings on both sides of Market Space. The consequence was, the District of Columbia had to raise the buildings to the new grade of the street at a cost of one hundred and fifty thousand dollars; and the cost of raising the market house and underpining the same was twenty-four thousand, nine hundred and eighty four dollars. (See the acts of legislature of June 25, 1873, page 11, of the statutes relating to the District of Columbia.) By thus filling up Market Space a most serious injury was done to the property holders. The grade of the streets was destroyed, and all communication was cut off from the canal and river—the south side of the canal being twenty feet below the foot of Market Space. Your chronicler has seen thousands of hogsheads of tobacco, and barrels of flour, hauled to the river down Market Space, in days gone by, to the vessels at the wharves, to be shipped to Europe; but all this communication is now cut off, and stores and dwellings which formerly sold, before the grade of the street was destroyed, from three to four thousand dollars, would not bring at the present time more than one-third of that amount.

After the District of Columbia had been in existence as a municipality a little over three years, under the act of 21st of February, 1871, Congress repealed the law, and passed an act on the 20th of June, 1874, establishing three commissioners to manage the affairs of the said District, to abolish all useless offices, and reduce the expenses of said District.

The salaries of the officers in the employment of the said District, amounted to five hundred and forty thousand five hundred and ninety dollars per annum, as per report of the comptroller made to the legislature on the 5th of May, 1873. (See journal of the House of Delegates, volume 5, page 65.) Such heavy salaries were sufficient to sink the District of Columbia into bankruptcy, if continued for a length of time. To get clear of this great expense, the commissioners consolidated some offices and abolished others, and reduced the expenses of the District to an economical working condition. The salaries of the public school teachers being two hundred and ten thousand dollars, and the salaries of the officers employed in managing the business of the District, about ninety thousand dollars, making in the aggregate, three hundred thousand dollars.

[A bill has been introduced in Congress to form a government for the District, and if it should pass and become a law, while penning these chronicles, it will become a part of this book.]

The great evil under which the District of Columbia suffers, is its enormous debt of twenty-two million dollars, the interest on which exceeds a million dollars per annum, which is nearly equal to two-thirds of the revenues of the District. Now, what is a million of dollars? The chronicler will here give you a definition of a million: Place a million of silver dollars on the floor of a room, and the chronicler will allow an accountant to count one hundred per minute, day and night, and at the end of a week he will have counted a million.

OFFICERS OF THE CORPORATION.

Although our town was chartered in 1789 by the legislature of Maryland, from that year to the first day of June, 1871, it never had but two clerks: the late John Mountz was clerk from the passage of the charter until 1856, when he was superseded in office by the late William Laird, Esq. Mr. Mountz became disqualified for the active duties of clerk by advanced age, but was still retained by our corporate authorities as consulting clerk until the 1st of August, 1857, when he died at an advanced age—"An honest man the noblest work of God."

Mr. Laird, his successor, had no superior as an accountant in this country. Being the son of an eminent merchant of our town, and qualified by a liberal education and long service in the counting-room, he fulfilled the expectations of the people.

Now that our charter has passed away, and we have entered upon a municipal District government, the question is, Shall we be benefitted by the change? We are now, with Washington, one town, one city, and one people. If our new government is strangled in its infancy with too much "pap," we shall perish; otherwise we shall float upon the tide of prosperity, and the Genius of our commerce will again spread her white wings over every sea, until we shall become renowned throughout the habitable globe.

On the fourth Monday in February, every two years, the citizens would elect a Mayor and five members of the Board of Aldermen to serve two years; and on each and every year they would elect eleven members of the Board of Common Council, to serve one year. Prior to the amended charter of 1830, the

Mayor was elected by the joint meeting of the two boards. I will now mention those citizens who have served as Mayor and Recorder from the time the charter was granted:

MAYORS.

Robert Peter, Mayor from 1789 to 1798; Lloyd Beall, from 1798 to 1803; Daniel Rentzel, from 1803 to 1805; Thomas Corcoran, from 1805 to 1806; Daniel Rentzel, from 1806 to 1808; Thomas Corcoran, from 1808 to 1811; David Wiley, from 1811 to 1812; Thomas Corcoran, from 1812 to 1813; John Peter, from 1813 to 1818; Thomas Corcoran, from 1818 to 1819; Henry Foxall, from 1819 to 1821; John Peter, from 1821 to 1822; John Cox, from 1822 to 1845; Henry Addison, from 1845 to 1857; Richard R. Crawford, from 1857 to 1859; Henry Addison, from 1859 to 1867; Charles D. Welch, from 1867 to 1869; Henry M. Sweeny, from 1869 to 1871.

All the other officers of the corporation were elected by the joint meeting of the two boards every year, on the first Monday in January.

RECORDERS.

John Mackall Gantt, from 1789 to 1809; James S. Morsell, from 1809 to 1813; Francis Scott Key, 1813 to 1816; John Wiley, from 1816 to 1819; James Dunlop, from 1819 to 1839; Clement Cox, from 1839 to 1847; Robert Ould, from 1847 to 1851, also from 1853 to 1859; Walter Cox, from 1851 to 1853; Hugh Caperton, from 1859 to 1861; Walter Cox, from 1861 to 1866; Charles M. Matthews, from 1866 to 1868; Charles A. Peck, from 1868 to 1869; Hugh Caperton, from 1869 to 1870; Charles A. Peck, from 1870 to 1871.

NAMES OF THE STREETS.

There are in the town thirteen streets running cast and west, also thirteen streets running north and south. Some of these streets had various names for certain distances; but to have uniformity in the names of all the streets, our town authorities enacted an ordinance on the 13th April, 1818, that the following alteration be made in the names of certain streets in Georgetown, to wit: Water Street and High Street; High Street continued and Commerce Street shall be henceforth called and known by the name of *High Street.* The streets known by the name of West Landing, Keys, Causeway Street, and that part of Wapping in a line therewith, shall be henceforth called and known by the name of *Water Street.* The street known by the name of Back Street, in Beall's addition to Georgetown, running parallel with Beall Street, shall be henceforth called and known by the name of *Stoddard Street.* The streets known by the name of Duck Lane and West Lane shall be henceforth called and known by the name *of Market Street.* Cherry Street, commencing at the street at present known by the name of Keys, and running northerly, including Market Space to Potomac Street, shall be henceforth called and known by the name of *Potomac Street.* The street known by the name of Gay Street shall be henceforth called and known by the name *of Lingan Street.* The street known by the name of Bridge Street and Fall's Street shall be henceforth called and known by the name of *Bridge Street.* The street known by the name of New Street and Mill Street shall be henceforth known by the name of *Monroe Street.* That West Street, in Beatty and Hawkin's addition to Georgetown, be called *Madison Street.* The street known by the name of Fishing Lane and Congress Street be known by the name of Congress Street.

ILLUMINATING THE TOWN.

On the 6th of September 1810, the corporate authorities passed an ordinance for the erection of lamp posts and lamps at the corners of the various streets in the town, to give pedestrians an opportunity to find their way to and from church on a dark night. These lamps were trimmed with oil purchased from the yankee vessels, which traded with our town, loaded with onions, potatoes, and oil. These lamps lasted for many years, until the posts, from advanced age, began to topple over, and were never replaced until their number were reduced to four—located at the corners above the market. These stood perpendicular for a number of years, when, by an unfortunate accident their number was again reduced: A team ran off with a wagon, and its wheel striking one of the posts, shivered it into fragments; of course, the lamp shared he same fate. There was then but three lamps left, which cast a triangular light at each other, making darkness visible in the distance. Under this state of affairs, our citizens began to complain for more light, when, on the 20th day of July, 1854, Congress granted a charter, creating a gas company, by which it was enacted, that, David English, Robert P. Dodge, Richard Cruikshank, Wm. M. Fitzhugh, Richard Pettit, W.F. Seymour, Adolpheus H. Pickrell, and Wm. Bucknell, are hereby declared to be a body corporate by the name and style of "Georgetown Gas Light Company." Our corporation responded to the gas company by passing an ordinance, on the 6th of June, 1853, allowing the gas company to lay pipes through the streets of the town (and the corporation at the same time erecting gas posts), to illuminate the streets. Our citizens introduced gas into their stores and dwellings, as a substitute for candles (which were manufactured at O'Donnoghue's Soap & Candle Factory, situated in the west end of the town.) In those days, when tallow dips were used, we had candle-sticks made of brass or tin, and occasionally of a block of wood, and when a candle burnt down considerably below the wick, it required snuffing, to give a brighter light, when the thumb and finger were brought into operation to decapitate the luminary at the expense of smutting one's fingers.

ANTS FROM THE WEST INDIES.

John Laird & Son, tobacco merchants of our town, who shipped large quantities of tobacco every year to Europe, in brigs or barks, had ordered to Georgetown some vessels in ballast, to be loaded with tobacco. The vessels came and threw out their ballast on the wharves at the foot of Frederick Street. This ballast contained a large number of ants, taken on board in the West Indies, and being cast into town in the summer season, they multiplied by thousands and millions, and entered into every store and dwelling, as they multiplied and marched onward due

45

north.

Never having gone east of Potomac Street, they infested the walls of buildings, and concealed themselves in the cracks and openings. The chronicler has many times struck with a stone a brick or stone wall, when thousands would come to the surface and run in every direction. Their bite or sting was painful; and such a nuisance had they become to the property of the citizens (depreciating it in value), that our corporation offered a reward for their destruction by paying one dollar per quart for all dead ants brought to the office. After paying out several hundred dollars, the cold winter of 1840-'41 set in, which completely destroyed them.

A BREEZE IN TOWN.

One Sunday morning, in April, 1848, quite a commotion was raised in the town by a number of citizens, who had given out, on the Saturday evening previous, a supply of provisions to be cooked next morning for breakfast. One expected muffins; the second, warm rolls; and the third, buckwheat cakes and fried chicken. No breakfast being ready, the ladies of the house went to see what could the matter be, when, to and behold, there was no "Polly to put the kettle on." The fires were out, and the kitchens were dark and cold. The servants had absconded, and where had they gone, was the inquiry. It was discovered that a schooner, named the *Pearl*, had a few days before unloaded her cargo of wood, and sailed away in the night, and was supposed to have carried off all the runaway slaves. Immediately the steamer *Salem* was chartered, and many of our citizens volunteered their services, being armed and equipped according to law, and started in pursuit of the missing vessel. After steaming down the Potomac for a day and a night, they came upon the *Pearl* in Cornfield Harbor, near the mouth of the river. They immediately boarded the schooner, fastened down the hatches, and secured the captain and the few hands who sailed the vessel; they then lashed the schooner to the steamer and headed for Georgetown, where they arrived in the latter part of the week. Captain Edward Sayes and Daniel Drayton, of the schooner *Pearl*, were committed to jail, and at the June Term of the Criminal Court they were convicted and sentenced: Drayton to pay seventy-three times one hundred and forty dollars; and Captain Sayes, seventy-three times one hundred dollars, and to stand committed until paid. They were afterwards pardoned, August 12th, 1852. The number of slaves carried off were seventy-seven; consisting of thirty-eight men, twenty-six women, and thirteen children.

LONG BRIDGE.

There has been, almost from time immemorial, a great opposition, by the citizens of Georgetown, to the construction of the Long Bridge. They regarded the bridge as injurious to the channel of the river, and a great detriment to the commerce of the town. When the bridge question was agitated in Congress, as far back as 1807, our corporate authorities, by an act of the Corporation, passed January 6th,1807, employed Charles Evans, a celebrated stenographer (at ten dollars per day), to report the debates on the bridge question. Our corporate authorities did their best to prevent the passage of the bill chartering the Potomac Bridge Company, which was incorporates February 5th, 1808; the charter to last for sixty years. What the town could not do, the Potomac River did for us. The freshet of 1829 broke the bridge asunder in many places, and the company, being unable to repair the same, sold all their right and title to the United States for twenty thousand dollars, by act of Congress passed July 14, 1832; and by a subsequent act approved March 2d, 1833, the sum of two hundred thousand dollars was appropriated by Congress to erect a new bridge. Our town desired that a new bridge should be erected above the town at the Three Sisters, but Washington opposed it, on the ground that the distance from the City Post Office, through Georgetown to Alexandria, crossing the river at the Three Sisters, is ten and one-half miles; while the distance between the same points, crossing the river by the Long Bridge, is only five and three-quarter miles.

It is to be presumed, that by the acts of Congress of July

14th 1832, and March 2d, 1833, the final settlement of the question, as to the permanence or removal of the Long Bridge was settled. After the passage of the above acts, the corporate authorities of Georgetown presented a memorial to Congress, praying an appropriation for removing obstructions in the river, and making free the road to the bridge over the Little Falls. In this memorial document (No. 32, H.R., 22d Congress, 2d

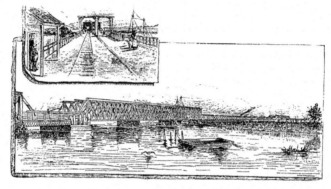

LONG BRIDGE.

Session) they say: "Without, at all, complaining that Congress has appropriated money to erect a new bridge and make it free of tolls—for since it is considered necessary that a bridge must be erected there, at the sight of the Long Bridge, no doubt, it ought to he free of tolls—your memorialists must, nevertheless, take leave, respectfully, to invite the attention of your honorable body to the fact, that a free bridge must unavoidably deprive them of the remaining trade with the neighboring counties of Virginia, unless corresponding facilities are afforded for reaching Georgetown; since none will choose to pay a toll to cross the river when it can be crossed free of toll. They ask for the sum of one hundred and fifty thousand dollars for the objects set forth in the memorial, viz : To improve the navigation of the Potomac River between Georgetown and Alexandria, and making free the bridge over the Little Falls and the road leading to it." The appropriations, relating to the Long Bridge and Falls Bridge, were

48

passed, and all controversy about the location of the bridges was considered settled.

This memorial, presented by the citizens of Georgetown, to Congress, was backed by an argument upon the facts and questions of law in the case, and signed by the late John Cox, Mayor of Georgetown. It is presumed that this able paper was written by the late Clement Cox, who was at that time, one of the most distinguished members of the Washington Bar.

The bridge, as erected by the United States, was thrown open for travel in the month of October, 1835, when the President of the United States with his Cabinet crossed it on foot, and returned in carriages. The bridge, as then constructed, had a drawer over the Virginia Channel, sixty-six feet wide, and over the Washington Channel, thirty-five feet; and was substantially the same as that which now exists—that is, the solid causeway occupies about one third of the bridge; the rest of the bridge being built of wood resting on piles. For some years the bridge escaped without any damage, but, in 1840, a portion of it was destroyed by an ice freshet. Without exact date, it is impossible to enumerate the different occasions in which it has been injured. It was injured by the freshets in 1856, 1860, 1863, and 1867; in several instances, spans of the bridge were carried away and travel suspended for several months at a time; but Congress has always been liberal in making appropriations to repair damages. The bridge is something that Georgetown has always thrown a "brick" at, and at every session of Congress a committee was generally appointed to attend to the interests of the town before Congress, and represent their grievances—the bridge always receiving due consideration; but, as we are now under one form of government, and almost one town, one city, and one people, we may harmonize better in the future, when liberal appropriations shall be made by Congress for all parts of the District.

POPULATION.

The population of Georgetown was—
in 1800, two thousand nine hundred and ninety-three;
in 1810, four thousand nine hundred and forty-eight;
in 1820, seven thousand three hundred and sixty;
in 1830, eight thousand four hundred and forty-one;
in 1840, seven thousand three hundred and twelve;
in 1850, eight thousand three hundred and sixty-six;
in 1860, eight thousand seven hundred and thirty-three;
in 1870, eleven thousand three hundred and eighty-four;
in 1878, eleven thousand five hundred and seventy-one.

This last census was taken by the officials of the District of Columbia.

CHAPTER II.

The Potomac River, which has its rise in two branches, north and south, in the Alleghany Mountains, is a noble river. In its course towards the ocean, it is joined by several minor streams, the longest of which is the Shenandoah, which rises in Augusta County, Virginia, and flows two hundred and fifty miles before it unites with the Potomac at Harper's Ferry, where the latter bursts through the Blue Ridge Mountains, affording a sublime and interesting spectacle to the admirers of nature. In its descent to the Chesapeake Bay, it forms the greater part of the boundary line between Maryland and Virginia, and waters the District of Columbia two hundred and fifty miles from the Atlantic Ocean. The termination of its tide-water is three miles above Georgetown, where the tide rises about four feet. Mr. Jefferson, in his "Notes on Virginia," gives a graphic description of the scenery at Harper's Ferry. He says:

"The passage of the Potomac River through the Blue Ridge, is, perhaps, one of the most stupendous scenes in nature. You stand on a very high point of land. On your right, comes up the Shenandoah, having ranged along the foot of the mountain a hundred miles to seek a vent. On your left, approaches the Potomac in inquest of a passage, also. In the moment of their junction, they rush together against the mountain, rend it asunder, and pass off to the sea. The first glance of this scene hurries our senses into the opinion, that this earth has been created in time; that the mountains were formed first; that the river began to flow afterwards; that in this place, particularly, they have been dammed up by the Blue Ridge Mountains, and have formed an ocean which filled the whole valley; that continuing to rise, they have at length broken over at this spot, and have torn the mountain down from its summit to its base. The piles of rocks on each hand, but, particularly on the Shenandoah—the evident marks of their disrupture and avulsion from their beds by the most powerful agents of nature—corroborates the impression; but the distant finishing

51

which nature has given to the picture is of a very different character. It is a true contrast to the foreground. It is as placid and delightful, as that is wild and tremendous. For the mountain, being cloven asunder, she presents to your eye through the cleff, a small catch of smooth blue horizon at an infinite distance in the plain country, inviting you, as it were, from the riot and tumult roaring around, to pass through the breach and participate in the calm below. Here the eye ultimately composes itself, and that way to the road happens actually to lead.

"You can cross the Potomac above the junction, pass along its side through the base of the mountain. For three miles its terrible precipices are hanging in fragments over you, and, within about twenty miles reach Frederick Town and the fine country around that. This scene is worth a voyage across the Atlantic to view it; yet, here, as in the neighborhood of the Natural Bridge, are people who have passed their lives within a half-dozen miles of it, and have never been to survey these monuments of a war between rivers and mountains, which must have shaken the earth itself to its centre."

ICE-FLOES.

The chronicler of these events occasionally spent some hours at the Arlington Springs, in conversation with G.W.P. Custis, the proprietor of *Arlington*, whose mind was replete with revolutionary history, and the events of the times that tried men's souls. On several occasions he related a description of an ice freshet that took place after the revolutionary war. Said he:

"The ice, in the memorable year of 1784, moved twice: It first descended in vast quantities from the upper Potomac, till it reached the Three Sisters, where it stopped and accumulated in great masses and froze together again; then came the deep snow, followed by a general thaw and violent rains. The second movement carried all before it. The shoving off of a strongly built stone house or stable from the bank, of where now is your town, is a well remembered story of the past. Both branches of the river around Analostan Island were open in those days; the eastern branch being used as the ship channel. The freshet of

1784 tore open the western branch, and formed in the one freshet, a channel way that would have admitted the passage of an Indianian to Georgetown, being from twenty-seven to thirty-feet depth up to the wharves of the town.

THE CAUSEWAY.

"This channel was in all its usefulness when I came to live in your vicinity in 1802, and would have been a ship channel for the largest shipping up to this time, but for the unfortunate erection of the *unfortunate causeway*, which, while doing good to none, has done infinite harm to every one. It has rendered its vicinity unhealthy, in an eminent degree, and will, until its removal, render the island (that must soon be occupied as a commercial part of Georgetown) uninhabitable. By blocking up one-half or more of the vent for the passage of the water, the whole force of the river is now thrown upon the wharves and warehouses of Georgetown. Again, it would require but one-half of such a freshet as 1784, to do as much mischief as that memorable freshet did; for while one-half of the passage way for the waters of 1784, is now filled up, the river at Georgetown is but one-half as deep, being thirty feet from shore to shore fifty years ago, is now not over fifteen feet, and a vast accumulation of mud next to the causeway. What shall we do? I answer, knock away that nuisance to every one, *the causeway,* and take the chances. What happened in 1784, may happen again in 1852, and a single freshet make a channel-way to Georgetown, that may carry an Indiaman to her wharves. Five years ago (1836), you had a pretty fair sample of a freshet without ice, in the navigation of your lower streets by boats. Had the river at that time been encumbered with icebergs, all the wharves and warehouses of Georgetown would have been an affair for history, for not a wreck would have been left behind.

"The western channel is intended by nature to be the principal channel to the town, for it is the *nearest and most direct,* and water chooses the nearest and most direct route always. In 1784 the Potomac had her choice, and she chose the western channel. It is a melancholy reflection that, from circumstances beyond the control of her citizens, Georgetown is destined, in a limited number of years, to have no harbor at all. The same causes produce the same effect all the world over. From each pier of the Aqueduct, there will extend a tongue of land, made by the alluvial deposits of the river, which will unite in the harbor and fill it up.

"The engineers have pronounced it practicable to make an artificial channel through the present bar below the island, only by a heavy expense in works of art. Perhaps old Potomac may take the engineering into her own hands, and give a channel, as she did in 1784, after a mariner speedily, efficient, and entirely her own.

"With the rapidly increasing commerce of the canal, it behooves you of Georgetown to look out for more commercial room by annexation of Analostan Island; but, if the causeway is to form part of the new annexation, rely upon it that the population of the new Territory will require a pretty smart sprinkling of doctors, apothecaries, nurses, and grave diggers, who will be in full employment from the 1st of June to the 1st of December."

FRESHETS.

We have had many freshets in the Potomac. The great freshet of June, 1836, over-flowed the wharves and cellars along the line of Water Street, and did great damage to the canal. The freshets of April and September, 1843, were equally as destructive. So was the freshet of October, 1847, when the banks of the canal were rent asunder, and navigation suspended until the spring of 1848. The freshet of April, 1852, was very destructive; navigation was suspended on the canal all summer, and it cost the company several hundred thousand dollars to repair damages. The water in the river was so high that it ran over the causeway, which joins Analostan Island with the mainland, and washed away the stone wall, and made a new channel for the river, which damage cost the town several thousand dollars to repair. We have had, since, a number of freshets in the Potomac during the years 1856, 1860, 1863, 1866, and 1867, but none of them doing much damage. The freshet of October 1st, 1870, was very destructive; carrying away more than one-half of the Chain Bridge, and washing away the causeway and south draw of the Long Bridge. The canal was greatly damaged, several lock-gates were seen floating down the river, and navigation suspended for several weeks, which cost the company between eighty and one hundred thousand dollars to repair the injury. The freshet of 24th, 25th, and 26th of November, 1877, was higher than either of the freshets of 1847, 1852, or 1870, doing serious injury to the banks of the canal, which cost the company two hundred and fifty thousand dollars to repair, and again washing away the stone causeway, which joins Analostan Island with the main-land, giving a chance to the Commissioners of the District of Columbia to repair the damage.

COLD WINTERS.

The severity of the winter of 1780, or '84, is described by Jefferson in his "Notes on Virginia." He says: "That the winter was so cold that the Chesapeake Bay was frozen from its head to the mouth of the Potomac River, and at Annapolis, where the bay is five miles wide, the ice was five inches thick."

The winter of 1827, was of remarkable severity in this latitude. Alexandria was nearly burnt down on the 18th day of January of that year, and many citizens of our town skated on the ice to Alexandria, and assisted in extinguishing the conflagration. The winter of 1829-'30, was very cold, and the ice broke up with a freshet, carrying away the schooner *Washington* from Crittenden's wharf, where she had been made fast with numerous cables, which were rent like pipe stems, and the vessel carried down the river until she grounded on Easby's Point. At the same time the Long Bridge was shattered to pieces by the ice, fourteen gaps being made by the force of the freshet. Congress then purchased the remnant of the bridge of the Potomac Bridge Company for twenty-thousand dollars, and afterwards erected the present structure. The winter of 1831-32, was very long and extremely cold. The chronicler was, at that time, a scholar at Professor Hallowell's school, located in

Alexandria, and well remembers the severe coldness of the weather. The cold weather commenced in November, 1831; the Potomac River was soon ice-bound, and the boys enjoyed fine skating. On corning home to spend the Christmas Holidays, we crossed the river at the Ferry near the Aqueduct, and saw on the ice, at the time, a wagon loaded with wood, being drawn by four horses. The mercury (in the Thermometer situated constantly in the shade on the west side of our dwelling), indicated four degrees below zero. In the first part of January, 1832, we had a thaw, and the ice passed quietly away; but in the latter part of the month the weather again turned suddenly cold, and the Potomac was frozen over. On the 28th of January, of that winter, after two nights freeze, I attempted to come home by way of the Long Bridge. On arriving at the bridge, I found no track broken for the Ferry Boat, and to cross on the ice was considered impossible, as the river is more than a mile wide. Having my skates with me, and not liking to turn back, I put them on, and taking the branch of a tree in my hands, I crossed over in safety, to the satisfaction of the crowd who stood looking on at my fool-hardy venture. As I skated on the ice, it was so thin that it would crack and bend under my light weight, and I could distinctly see the leaves and twigs floating in the water under my feet. Having arrived on the Washington shore, I felt so well satisfied, that I would not have returned for the fortune of Stephen Girard. The winter of 1835, was the coldest ever experienced in this latitude. We had some weeks a thaw, and then the weather would turn extremely cold. The mercury indicated in January, sixteen degrees below zero. We had three severe cold spells of weather during that year; one of which was in March. On the 3d of that month I skated on the Potomac, playing "Bandy" and "Prisoner's Base." The winter of 1839-'40, was long and cold. The ice broke up in the Potomac on the 10th of February, 1840; and carried away the Chain Bridge, and the draw of the Long Bridge. The winter of 1840-'41, was long and cold; though the degree of cold was not as great as some previous winters. The 12th of February, 1841, was the coldest day during the season, and it is well remembered by the inhabitants of this town as the day that General Harrison paid Georgetown a visit just before his inauguration as President of the United States. We all remember the winters of 1855,1856, and 1857; the snows were deep, and the cold was severe. During the winter of 1857, sleighing was enjoyed by our inhabitants. Fleet horses were brought on from other cities to race on Pennsylvania Avenue, and when the drivers would be arrested for driving at an improper speed, they would pay the fine, crack the whip over the head of justice and go it again. This was the winter that a locomotive was run on the ice across the river, from Maryland to Alexandria; also, sleepers and rails were laid upon the ice at Havre de Grace, across the Susquehanna River, and trains of cars crossed over for more than a month.

There is a law of nature, that one extreme is followed by another. The extreme hot summer of 1834, was followed by the cold winter of 1835; and the centennial year of 1876, was very warm; the heat set in about the 20th of June, and never broke until the 13th of July, when we had a few pleasant days, when the heat set in again and lasted until the 1st of September. The winter of 1876-'77, was severe. The extreme cold set in on Saturday, the 9th of December, and continued to the 13th of January, when we had a thaw.

SEVENTEEN-YEAR LOCUSTS.

I heard a citizen remark at one time, that every locust-year was followed by a cold winter. This remark will hold true, though no philosophical reason can be assigned for it. On examining some old registers in manuscript, I found that the locusts appeared in 1800, and was followed by an extreme cold winter; then again in 1816, and another cold winter. I well remember their appearance in the summer of 1834, which was followed by the severe winter of 1835, as above stated; they again appeared in the summer of 1851, and the winter of 1852, was one which young and old will long remember. In 1867, they again made their appearance, which was followed by the cold winter of 1868. There may be something providential in all this, which the obtuse intellect of man may not be able to fathom; that swarms of locusts should come out of the ground once every seventeen years, spreading destruction among the trees and shrubbery, deposit their eggs, then tumble into naught, and their departure followed by an extreme cold winter, which may cause the eggs to remain in a torpid state, for seventeen years, before the locust is produced again.

CHAPTER III.

POTOMAC CANAL—FALLS BRIDGE—MILITARY COMPANIES—CONTESTED ELECTIONS—BANKS IN GEORGETOWN.

These chronicles would be imperfect if they did not contain a brief description of the Potomac Canal, chartered by the Legislature of Maryland in 1784. This canal runs around the principal falls of the Potomac River. At the Great Falls, where the difference of level is seventy-six feet nine inches, it was surmounted by five locks of solid masonry of stone; each one hundred feet in length, of various widths of from ten to fourteen feet, with a lift of from ten to eighteen feet; also, guard locks, and extensive basin—a canal twelve hundred yards in length lined with stone. The two lower locks were excavated entirely from the solid rock, and exhibited an imperishable monument of perseverance and skill. At the Little Falls, the difference of level is thirty-seven feet, and was surmounted by four locks of solid masonry of stone, of the dimensions of eighty feet in length, and twelve feet wide, and by a canal two-and-a-half miles long; on the margin of which were found inexhaustible supplies of valuable stone for building purposes. The canal, at both the Great and Little Falls, was excavated of the following dimensions: Twenty-five feet wide at the surface, twenty feet wide at the bottom, and four feet deep. Gondolas and small canal boats only navigated this canal. In 1825, an assignment of all the right, title, claim, and franchise, of the Potomac Canal Company, was made to the Chesapeake & Ohio Canal Company, and being vested with all the privileges of the Potomac Canal, the Chesapeake & Ohio Canal Company made the bed of the Potomac Canal as a part of its own structure; which surrender is recorded in liber W.B., No. 33, page 58. The boats that navigated the old Potomac Canal, only carried from eighty to one hundred barrels of flour; the boats now navigating the present canal, will carry from one thousand to twelve hundred barrels of flour or one hundred and twenty tons of coal.

FALLS BRIDGE.

Falls Bridge is located at the Little Falls of the Potomac River, three miles above town. From a carefully prepared profile drawing in the office of Colonel Theodore B. Samo, the channel at this point is shown to be very deep, the bottom rocky and uneven, the current swift and running close to the Virginia Shore. The long stretch of rock flats, nearly five hundred yards in width, between this channel and the canal on the District side, is seldom covered with water, except in times of freshets. Immediately below the Little Falls the depth of water is over eighty feet, and continues very deep until the Aqueduct is reached.

In order to understand how the Falls Bridge was originally built, it will be requisite to refer to the Legislature of Maryland. The Legislature of Maryland, by an act of 1791, chapter 81, incorporated the Georgetown Bridge Company, for the purpose of erecting a toll bridge at the Little Falls of the Potomac River; and subsequently, by an act of 1795, chapter 44, on petition of that company, authorized them to construct a road from the bridge to Georgetown; which said road was declared to be "a public highway forever, and kept in repair by said company." Afterwards, upon the destruction of the bridge in February, 1811, Congress authorized the company to make a new assessment upon its stockholders to rebuild the bridge and keep the same in repair, together with the road leading thereto from Georgetown. The bridge and road were constructed by the same company, chargeable upon and to be kept in repair by the same company, for the use of the public. It was under this state of circumstances, that Congress, in pursuance of its general policy to make the road and bridges leading to and through the District of Columbia free to all, passed the act of 1833, chapter 66, appropriating a sum of money, to enable the Corporation of Georgetown, among other things, to make a free turnpike road to the District line on the Virginia side of the river, and to purchase of the present proprietors, and make forever free a bridge over the Little Falls of the Potomac River; coupling with its bounty, the condition, "that before the said sum be paid over to the said corporation, it shall pass an ordinance to make said road and bridge free, and to be kept in repair by said corporation."

This bridge, built of timber, was supported by immense cable chains stretching from pier to pier, from which the term "Chain Bridge," is derived. In 1832, during the winter of that year, the Falls Bridge, commonly called the Chain Bridge, was taken down by the bridge company, on account of the great accumulation of ice in the river and the banking of the same against the bridge. The chronicler remembers seeing the fiats, lying between the tow path of the Chesapeake & Ohio Canal and the river, being banked up with ice, mountains high, and so covered with debris and drift wood, that persons who went fishing at the Little Falls in the month of May or June, could always find a lump of ice to put into a bucket of water. This bridge was replaced by a more substantial structure, and paid for out of the one hundred and fifty thousand dollars given to the town by Congress, which remained a thoroughfare for a number of years, until carried off by an ice freshet during the winter of 1840, when the corporation built a new bridge of timber four hundred feet long, and costing thirteen thousand five hundred dollars, which lasted until destroyed by the ice freshet of April, 1852, but was afterwards rebuilt.

In 1842, Congress extended the jurisdiction of the Corporation of Georgetown, so as to include the bridge which had then ,just been constructed, by that corporation, at the Little Falls. This act provides, "that as often, and so long, as said bridge shall hereafter, from any cause, be impassible, it shall be lawful for the proprietors of land on both sides of the river through which the ferry road, to connect with the Falls Bridge turnpike, shall pass, and they are hereby authorized and empowered to establish and keep a ferry, &c."

In 1858, Congress, by an act making appropriations for sundry civil expenses of the government, placed the bridge under the protection of Georgetown, with power to regulate the speed of travel, and the passage of droves of cattle over the same, but expressly forbid that any tolls should be charged.

In 1860, an appropriation was made to reimburse the Corporation of Georgetown for money advanced towards the construction of the Little Falls Bridge.

In a report made by General Michler to the Secretary of War in 1869, upon the subject of "a railroad bridge across the Potomac River, and the channel of the river," considerable statistical information is given concerning the bridges in this District, and regrets expressed that but few of the reports, plans, and estimates of the different bridges are now to be found among the archives of the several departments, and that the most important facts concerning these works, aside from the various amounts appropriated and expended on them, are only to be obtained from the Statues at Large.

The Falls Bridge, since its partial destruction by the freshet on the first of October, 1870, various appropriations have, from time to time, been made for its repair, &c., but such expenditures proving to be unsatisfactory by reason of the floods, Congress, by an act approved June 10th,1872, appropriated one hundred thousand dollars for rebuilding the Falls Bridge, with a proviso that it "shall be rebuilt as a substantial iron structure, upon plans approved by the chief of engineers of the army, and under his supervision and direction." Proposals were advertised for, and finally the bid of a bridge building firm from Connecticut was accepted. These parties forfeited their rights by delay, and the contract was then made with Messrs. Clarke, Reeves & Co.

So disastrous hitherto have the floods been to the bridges here, that General Babcock has taken the precaution in this instance, of having all the old piers raised two feet additional, thus giving more elevation, and affording more room for the ice and drift-wood.

The plan for the new bridge selected by General Babcock as best adapted for this site, is what is known as the "Murphy Whipple Truss." It is divided into eight spans; two of one hundred and sixty feet, and six of one hundred and seventy-two feet each. The entire length is one thousand three hundred and fifty-two feet. The spans are separate and independent of each other, resting on cast-iron bridge seats, securely anchored to stone copings; one end of each span is fixed, and the other rests upon friction rollers provided for the expansion and contraction of the iron. The trusses are twenty-eight feet in depth and placed twenty-two feet apart from centre to centre. Each truss of one hundred and seventy-two feet span is divided into twelve panels, and each truss of one hundred and sixty feet into eleven panels of fourteen and one-half feet each. The upper cords, main and intermediate posts, are formed of Phoenix column iron, and the lower cords, main and intermediate ties of the forged links, without welds. The posts are fitted to cast-iron caps and seats, the bottoms of the former and the tops of the latter being truly turned for that purpose. Turned wrought-iron pins, three inches in diameter, lock in one connection the caps of the column and the diagonal ties, also the bottom cords, the seats of the columns, the diagonal ties, and the floor beam suspenders. The floor beams are fifteen-inch Phoenix rolled beams, and the floor ,joists and flooring are of the best North Carolina pine, three inches thick and not over six inches wide, with edges sawed straight, laid close, and securely spiked. There is no side walks, but an iron railing four feet high, placed on either side of the carriage way, and to prevent collision during the dark nights, it was deemed necessary to light the bridge. Four sixteen-inch railroad reflectors were purchased and placed on the bridge, two to light the approaches, and two in the middle of the structure. The width of the broadway is twenty feet, and the bridge is proportional so as to safely carry in addition to the weight of the structure, one hundred pounds for each square loot of roadway, and the maximum strain produced by this load is ten thousand pounds per square inch of section, or about one-sixth of its ultimate strength. The contract price for the entire work was ninety-four thousand dollars, which was paid by instalments as each span was completed. The work was begun about the 1st of January, 1874, and finished during the same year.

MILITARY COMPANIES.

Many of our citizens remember the military companies which existed in our town many years past, when the disposition to be a soldier was predominant in the human mind. At that time a law of Congress, passed 3d March, 1805, made it obligatory for all male citizens between the age of eighteen and forty-five to muster once a month certain months in the year, and on failure, were liable to a fine of five dollars for neglect of duty. The

63

consequence was, many military companies were formed which flourished for a while until tired of parade duty, when they dissolved, and returned their arms to the United States. The chronicler will here mention, from. memory, the names of the different companies organized in Georgetown: Morgan Rifles, Infantry, commanded by James Thomas; Green's Rifles, Infantry; commanded by Wm. Jewell; Blue's Muskets, Infantry, commanded by Thos. Corcoran; Artillery Company, commanded by Wm. W. Corcoran; Artillery Company, commanded by John Kurtz; Boys' Company, commanded by Lloyd Beall; Troop of Horse, commanded by Thos. Turner; Potomac Dragoons, commanded by John Mason; Troop of Horse, commanded by Wm. Stewart; Georgetown Guards, commanded. by Jeremiah Bronaugh; Invincibles, Infantry, commanded by Levin Jones; Independent Grays, Infantry, commanded by Clement Smith; Morgan Rifles, Infantry, commanded by R. Emmet Duvall; Independent Grays, Infantry, commanded by James Goddard; Potomac Light Infantry, commanded by J. McHenry Hollingsworth; Carrington Home Guards, commanded by James Goddard; Anderson's Rifles, commanded by Charles H. Rodier.

The form of a notice to muster was as follows:

GEORGETOWN, *May 1, 1826.*

"SIR: You are notified to attend a battalion parade on the 20th instant, on the grounds immediately north of the residence of Col. James Thompson, at ten o'clock A. 115., uniformed according to law.

W. W. CORCORAN, Captain."

Uniform: Blue coat, white pantaloons, white vest, black hat, black stock or cravat.

TO GEORGE SHOEMAKER."

Captain Corcoran thought that Shoemaker, although a member of the Society of Friends, would make, by drilling, as good a soldier as General Green of the revolution, who belonged to the same society; but Shoemaker demurred to the notice, and pleaded that he was a public functionary—holding an office as

64

flour inspector of Georgetown—and therefore was exempt from military duty.

The students of Georgetown College formed themselves into military companies prior to the war. The Senior Cadets were organized in 1851, and the Junior Cadets in 1855, and were supplied with arms by the United States. They occasionally paraded the streets of our town; and by their soldierly appearance, and the promptitude and precision of their march and maneuvers, attracted the attention of our citizens as well drilled companies. They, too, like all our military companies, have passed away, and base ball and boat clubs have been substituted in their place.

CONTESTED ELECTIONS.

We have had some close elections in our town; occasionally two candidates receiving the same number of votes for the board of common council, neither being elected. Another election would have to be held over again. This event occurred at the election held on the 4th Monday in February, 1853, for aldermen and common council, when two candidates for the council, Jenkin Thomas and Peter Berry, received an equal number of votes; neither being elected, a new election was ordered by the mayor, when Peter Berry was elected. The mayor of the town being the highest officer, more enthusiasm was manifested when two candidates were running for the mayoralty. In this year, 1853, Henry Addison and William McKenny Osbourn were the candidates before the people for the office of mayor. Addison received two hundred and sixty-four votes, and William McKenny Osbourn two hundred and sixty-one, showing a majority of three votes in favor of Addison. The friends of Mr. Osbourn were anxious to have the votes examined and counted over again, but were precluded by the return made by the, judges of elections. In 1859 another election was held for the mayoralty, Richard R. Crawford being one of the candidates, and Henry Addison the other. The following opinion of Supreme Court of United States contains a clear and condensed statement of the case, and it is, therefore, given without abridgment. By virtue of this opinion, Mr. Crawford was restored to

65

the mayoralty for the unexpired remainder of the term thereof; and recovered the amount of the salary for the time he was deprived of the office.

THE UNITED STATES, *on the relations* of R.R. CRAWFORD, Pltff. in Error, vs. HENRY ADDISON.	No. 104. December Term. 1867.

This action is brought in the name of the United States, but is prosecuted, in fact, for the benefit of R.R. Crawford, who was the relator in a proceeding in their name to oust the defendant, Addison, from the office of mayor of Georgetown. Crawford was mayor of that city on the fourth Monday of February, 1859, and had been mayor for the two preceding years. At the election for his successor, he was returned by the judges as elected for the two ensuing years, and presented himself before the joint convention of the councils of the city and offered to take the oath of office prescribed by the charter. But, upon counting the votes cast for the different candidates, the councils declared that the defendant, Addison, was elected, and he was accordingly sworn into office, and entered into the discharge of its duties. A proceeding by *quo warranto* was immediately instituted by the United States, on the relation of Crawford, in the circuit court of the District, to determine the right of the defendant to the office into which he had been installed. It is unnecessary to detail the various steps taken in the proceeding. It is sufficient that they resulted in a judgment of ouster against the defendant. To review this judgment he immediately sued out a writ of error from this court and tendered the bond in suit. This bond, the circuit court held, operated as supersedeas, and refused the prayer of counsel for process to enforce the judgment. Application was then made to this court for a *mandamus* to the circuit curt to compel the issue of process, notwithstanding the writ of error and bond. Counsel for the relator intends that the case was not one in which a writ of error would lie; that, to authorize the writ, the matter dispute must have a pecuniary value of at least one thousand dollars; that the matter in dispute was a public office of personal trust and confidence, which as not the subject of pecuniary estimation; that the salary annexed was not to be considered as the value of the office, but as an equivalent for the services to be rendered, and even that was payable in monthly instalments; and that a *mandamus* should accordingly issue, especially as the term of office would expire about the commencement of the ensuing term of the court to which the writ of error was returnable. The counsel of the defendant, on the other hand, insisted that the pecuniary value of the office was determined by the salary annexed, and, as it amounted to a thousand dollars a year, the court had jurisdiction to review the judgment on writ of error, and that the bond stayed process on the judgment. And so the court held and refused the *mandamus*.

In January, 1861, the writ of error was dismissed, and on the 21st of that month the judgment of ouster against the defendant, Addison, was enforced, and the relator was installed in office. He then brought the present suit on the bond. By the judgment of ouster against Addison, his right to the office of mayor was determined; the relator thereupon became entitled to the office, either by virtue of the declaration of the judges who had returned him elected, or by virtue of that provision of the charter, which enacts "that the mayor shall hold over until his successor is elected." By the writ of error and the suspension bond, the enforcement of the judgment was prevented, and, until the writ was dismissed, the relator was excluded from the office and deprived of the salary annexed to it. The amount of the salary received by the defendant, Addison, during the period of such deprivation, constitutes, under the decision in the *mandamus* case, the measure of damages which the plaintiff is entitled to recover upon the suspension bond.

The second instruction to the jury, which the plaintiff requested, correctly presents the law of the case, and should have been given. The rule which measures the damages upon a breach of contract for wages or for freight or for the lease of buildings, has no application. In these cases the party aggrieved must seek other employment or other articles for carriage or other tenants, and the damages recovered will be the difference between the amount stipulated and the amount actually received or paid. But no such rule can be applied to public officers or personal trust and confidence, the duties of which are not purely ministerial or clerical. An attempt is made to avoid the liability of the defendant, Addison, by showing that, on the trial of the *quo warranto*, the jury in the first instance returned a special verdict, to the effect that there was a tie in the votes cast for him and the relator respectively. This verdict is not evidence of the fact, for it was not received by the court or in any way made a matter of record. With the assent of the attorney of the defendant, the Court directed the jury to retire to their room and consider their verdict. They did retire, as directed, and returned the verdict upon which the judgment of ouster was entered.

BANKS.

The Central Bank of Georgetown and Washington was located in house No. 88 Bridge Street, now occupied by Joseph Birch, and formerly by the Potomac Insurance Company. The bank was chartered by an act of Congress, passed March 3d, 1817, but was of short duration, as, on the 2d March, 1821, Congress passed an act "that it shall be lawful for the Central Bank of Georgetown and Washington to proceed forthwith to liquidate and close all the concerns of the corporation; and after paying and satisfying all the debts, contracts, and obligations of the corporation, to divide the capital and profits which may remain among the Stockholders;" and for this purpose, all powers granted to said corporation were continued for five years longer, when the institution ceased to exist.

UNION BANK.

The Union Bank was located on the north side of Bridge Street, between Congress and High Streets, and was chartered by Congress on the 11th day of March, 1811, by the, name of the "President and Directors of the Union Bank of Georgetown." The capital stock of the bank was five hundred thousand dollars, divided into shares of fifty dollars each. Robert Beverly was president, and David English cashier. The bank did business until 1840, when it ceased to exist, and went into liquidation.

68

BANK OF COLUMBIA.

The Bank of Columbia, located on the hill, on the north side of Bridge Street, between Market Street and Bank Alley, was chartered by the Legislature of Maryland December 28th, 1793, by the name of the "President, Directors, and Company of the Bank of Columbia;" the stock to consist of ten thousand shares of one hundred dollars each, making the capital stock one million of dollars. By the 14th section of the act of incorporation, "if any person did not pay his note, bond, or obligation, negotiable and payable at said bank at the maturity of the same, within ten days after demand of payment, then the bank, on sending the note or obligation to the clerk of the court, with proof of demands of payment, might have judgment entered against the delinquent debtor and execution issued to make the money." People in our days would not like any banking institution to have such power over their property. By the act of Congress, passed March 2d, 1821, the 14th section of the act of Maryland, incorporating the Bank of Columbia, was repealed.

When the bank failed, in 1826, it created considerable excitement in the community. Those who held the notes of the bank found them worthless in their hands. Those who owned stock in the bank and lived upon their dividends found their income gone. Those who had money deposited there discovered that it was lost. It is said that the United States had on deposit with the bank four hundred and sixty-nine thousand dollars, which was swallowed up in the general wreck of the institution. The chronicler remembers seeing, in a newspaper, the picture of a white cow representing the bank, with an official holding her by the tail, another holding her by the horns, the board of directors running off with the pails of milk, while the runner of the bank was feeding her with brick-bats and crying out that she would not eat.

BANK OF COMMERCE.

The Bank of Commerce was located on Bridge Street, in the building formerly occupied by the late Union Bank. It was an unincorporated institution, being a partnership between John L. Dufief, Samuel Fowler, Timothy O'Neal, Richard M. Boyer, Richard Pettit, William T. Herron, Susan Ireland, Charles E. Rittenhouse, and Hugh B. Sweeny. The parties above named, signed an agreement to conduct and establish an exchange and banking business in Georgetown, under the name of the "Bank of Commerce." The bank was organized on the 9th day of December, 1851, and the amount of capital paid in was seventy-six thousand three hundred dollars. It subsequently had a branch in Washington City, under the name and title of Sweeny, Rittenhouse & Co. The business of the bank was not prosperous, and, on the 1st day of December, 1864, the copartnership was dissolved by mutual consent, and a process of settlement is now being had in court between the copartners, in the equity cause of Hamilton G. Fant, complainant, *vs.* John L. Dufief and others, defendants, to which the reader is referred for a more extended history.

FARMERS AND MECHANICS' NATIONAL BANK.

The Farmers and Mechanics' National Bank of Georgetown was originally a partnership concern entered into by sundry persons on the 1st Monday of February, in the year 1814, under the name and style of the "President and Directors of the Farmers and Mechanics' Bank of Georgetown." On the 3d of March, 1817; a charter was granted by Congress under the name and style of the "Farmers and Mechanics' Bank of Georgetown," with a capital stock of five hundred thousand dollars, divided into shares of twenty-five dollars each. The bank continued to do business under its charter, which was extended by act of Congress passed in 1821 to 3d March, 1836, when its charter being about to expire, the board of directors petitioned Congress for a renewal of the same. In their petition they say: "Your memorialists beg leave to mention one fact which ought, and they doubt not, will bespeak favors to this institution. The fact to which we allude is that, during the war of 1812, when our national credit was stricken beyond measure, the means and resources of this institution were tendered to and accepted by our Government; that during that dark period she never denied the call of her country, but from time to time advanced several hundred thousand dollars in response to its call; that by her funds the southwestern army which won such bright trophies at New Orleans, were mainly sustained; that, at that period, this institution was but a private association of individuals without a charter; that, consequently, for all engagements those individuals stood personally responsible; lovers of their country, they saw their country in need, and patriotism prompted them to her relief. For these facts we appeal not only to the records of the institution, but to the official documents of your Government of that day."

The charter of the bank was renewed by Congress from time to time, and the business of the bank prospered so much that the stock which was selling in 1838 for fifty cents on the dollar, rose in a short time to seventy-five, and before 1870, went above par value. When the bank was converted into one of the national banks, under the name and style of the "Farmers and Mechanics' National Bank of Georgetown," coming under the act of Congress of June 3d, 1864, the dividends declared by the bank have been four per cent. every six months, which is most gratifying to the stockholders, and shows that the bank affairs are well managed and in good hands. We now give a list of the presidents and cashiers of the bank from the chronicler's recollection: Clement Smith, president to 1844; John Kurtz, president to 1850; Robert Reed, president to 1862; George Shoemaker, president to 1865; Henry M. Sweeney, president from 1865 to the present time.

LIST OF CASHIERS.

John I. Stull, to 1844; Alexander Suter, to 1848; William Lang, to 1851; William Laird, cashier from 1851 to the present time.

This bank is the only bank in town; and, having a good set of officers, its business is prosperous. The bank suspended specie payment in 1834, when all the banks of the country suspended, also in 1837, and again in 1857, but it suspended at the request of the business community, so that the bank might continue to discount paper, and not for the want of specie.

CHAPTER IV.

POST-OFFICE AND CUSTOM-HOUSE—LIST OF POSTMASTERS—COLLECTORS OF CUSTOMS—MARKET HOUSE—FIRE COMPANIES—DESTRUCTION BY THE FLAMES—METROPOLITAN RAILROAD—LIST OF NEWSPAPERS—LITERATI.

A town without a post-office is not known in our country. It was a great invention of the Government for the transmission of news from one end of the nation to the other. In the far West, every town that has its name blazed upon a tree has a post-office, and the postmaster carries the contents of the office in his bat. Our town has been blessed with a post-office from a remote period. The chronicler remembers when the post-office was kept on Congress Street, in a small office, the size of a lawyer's office of the present day, whence it was removed to the basement of a two-story brick house on the same street, when it was transferred to Foxall's Row on Bridge Street, and afterwards to the Union Hotel, when it was again pushed back to Foxall's Row. It never had a permanent location until Congress purchased a lot of ground on Congress Street, for five thousand dollars, by deed dated October 23d,1856, and erected thereon a granite building for a post-office and custom-house at a cost of fifty-five thousand three hundred and sixty-eight dollars, under the superintendence of R.R. Sheckells, master builder. The building is two stories high and fronts sixty feet on the street, and in altitude is forty-five feet. The first story is used exclusively as a post-office, being fitted up with boxes to the number of nine hundred and fifty-six, with locks and keys; also two spacious rooms for the superintendent and clerks. The second story is used for the custom-house, consisting of two rooms for the use of the collector and clerks. The basement of the building is used for the storage of foreign goods until the duties are paid.

In 1790, there were only seventy-five post-offices in the United States, and Georgetown was one of them; but it has been ascertained that the office was in operation on the 5th January, 1776, under the management of Benjamin Franklin, who was the first Postmaster General, and who had an assistant here to manage the office. The rates of postage at that day were high compared with the present. Single letter, sixty miles or less, seven cents, one hundred miles and over sixty, eleven cents; two hundred miles and over one hundred, fifteen cents; three hundred miles and over two hundred, nineteen cents; four hundred miles and over three hundred, twenty-four cents; five hundred miles and over four hundred, twenty-eight cents; six hundred miles and over five hundred, thirty-three cents. At the present time there are over thirty-nine thousand post-offices in the whole country.

We here insert the names of the postmasters, and the date of their appointment, for the Georgetown postoffice:

William B. Magruder, appointed 16th of February, 1790; Richard Forrest, appointed 1st of April, 1797; Joseph Carlton, appointed 1st of February, 1799; Tristram Dalton, appointed 1st of January, 1803; James Armstrong, appointed 1st of September, 1817; James P.W. Kollock, appointed 20th of May, 1819; Whiteing Sanford, appointed 6th of January, 1820; William Huffington, appointed 18th of September, 1821; Thomas Corcoran, appointed 22d of October, 1823; James Corcoran, appointed 1st of February, 1830; Harriet H. Corcoran, appointed 18th of December, 1834, and 9th of July, 1836; Henry W. Tilley, appointed 3d of June, 1840; 13th of June, 1844; 17th of June, 1848; 13th of August, 1852; 9th of August, 1856, and 3d of August, 1860; Henry Addison, appointed 6th of June, 1861; George Hill, Jr., appointed 12th of July, 1865; Charles H. Cragin, appointed 17th of June, 1870; George Hill, Jr., appointed 6th of August, 1873.

The office was made a branch of the Washington post-office on the 24th of December, 1877.

COLLECTORS OF CUSTOMS.

James McCubbin Lingan, collector, appointed October 1st, 1790, and before; John Oakley, appointed October 1st, 1801; John Barnes, appointed May 6th, 1806; Thomas Turner, appointed March 7th 1826; Robert White, appointed July 20th,1840; Henry Addison, appointed July 9th, 1841; Robert White, appointed July 2d, 1845; Henry Addison, appointed July 20th, 1849; Robert White, appointed April 6th, 1853; Henry C. Matthews, appointed April 20th, 1857; Judson Mitchell, appointed June 8th, 1861; James Magruder, appointed September 15th, 1864; Charles S. English, appointed July 27th, 1871; Francis Dodge, appointed October 2d, 1877.

MARKET HOUSE.

A market house is an institution of great service and benefit to the citizens of a town, where the country people, butchers, and hucksters can assemble every morning, with the productions of the soil and meats to sell to the hungry citizens. Such an institution congregates a large number of persons, to exchange money for something to eat and express their opinions about the size of a goose or turkey, or whether a chicken offered for sale is the one which crowed when Peter denied his Master.

Our old market house was erected about the year 1806, on lots of ground conveyed by Adam King and John Mitchell to the mayor, recorder, board of aldermen, and common council of Georgetown, for the purpose of building thereon a market house, as per deeds dated October 23d, and December 27th, 1802, as recorded in liber No. 9, pages 129 and 130, one of the land records of the District of Columbia. The building was erected and used by the town up to 1864, when, becoming so dilapidated, it was torn down and a new building erected in its place in 1865, at a cost of fifty thousand dollars. During the progress of the work the town authorities rented of the owners the old tobacco warehouses, situated between Bridge Street and the canal, to be used as a market house until the completion of the new building. After the new market was ready, several butchers preferred remaining in the old tobacco warehouses, and purchased the same from the owners for thirty-six thousand five hundred dollars, and spent ten thousand dollars more for fitting up the same for conducting a market business under the name and style of the "Farmers and Butchers' Marketing Company of Georgetown." Our corporate authorities refused to grant them a license to sell. The consequence was the Farmers and Butchers' Marketing Company applied to the supreme court of the District of Columbia for an injunction against the town authorities; but the injunction was, after argument, denied. The Farmers and Butchers' Marketing Company then went to Washington and opened a bazaar on the east side of Rock Creek, near the Aqueduct Bridge, where they remained until the District government was established, under an act of Congress passed February 21, 1871, when a license being granted to them by the District of Columbia they returned to Georgetown. It is rumored, at the time of penning these events, that the Farmers and Butchers' Marketing Company have sold to the Washington and Georgetown Railroad Company all their property, to establish thereon a depot, which sale, if consummated, will be of great benefit to our town, as the railroad company will erect a magnificent depot upon lots 46, 47, and 48 that will be an ornament to the town, and increase its business by adding a large stock of horses and a number of employees. It will make a market for the farmers to sell their oats, corn, and hay to the railroad company.

The deeds of conveyance being executed, the Farmers and Butchers' Marketing Company have purchased a lot on the west side of High Street, near Gay, and erected thereon a spacious market house, eighty feet square and twenty-eight feet in altitude, containing forty-eight stalls in six rows of benches, with a basement for ice-house and cellars. This market will be a great convenience to the citizens living in the upper part of the town.

FIRE COMPANIES.

The first fire company formed in Georgetown was in the year 1803, when a fire-engine was purchased by subscription and taken charge of by the corporation; and a by-law was passed, compelling every owner of a house to have as many leather fire-buckets kept in his house as there were stories; to be numbered and the name of the owner painted on them, to be used in time of fire, and to contain not less than two and one-half gallons of water.

In the year 1817, a new fire-engine was purchased by the corporation of John Agnue, of Philadelphia, and named the *Vigilant*, when a company was formed by electing John Kurtz, president; Arnold Boone, vice-president; James Moore, secretary, and James Corcoran, treasurer; with a list of enginemen and others connected with the company. Other fire companies were formed on the 15th day of May, 1819, called the Columbian, and the Mechanical; and at a later day the Western Star and Eagle companies came into existence. These engines had long iron levers with wooden arms, to be worked by the strength of the men in throwing water from the engines—the first set of men being exhausted, a fresh set would have to take their places. This was the old method of extinguishing fires.

After the Treasury Department was burnt in May, 1833, and the Patent Office in December, 1836, Congress made liberal appropriations for the purchase of fire apparatus for Washington City. The Franklin, Union, Columbia, Perseverance, Northern Liberty, and Anacostia fire companies were furnished with new engines and apparatus. To show their strength a great parade was had on the 24th day of October, 1837. Being a very warm day, many persons were dressed in summer clothing. The Vigilant and Western Star companies united in the procession. The route of march was through Washington and Georgetown. We had no hydrant water from the Potomac at that day, and the wells were pumped dry to supply the thirsty multitude who came from the surrounding country to witness the grand pageant.

On the 26th of June, 1866, the Corporation of Georgetown purchased a steam fire-engine and new apparatus for seven thousand five hundred dollars, and appointed fire commissioners to select suitable officers for the management of the same. The engine can throw two streams, and in a horizontal direction can throw a stream two hundred and thirty-eight feet, and a perpendicular stream over the flag-staff of the Arlington Hotel. The reel has fourteen hundred feet of hose, two and one half inches in diameter. There are two horses to each piece of apparatus. The whole is managed by ten men, who sleep at the engine house, each having a separate bed and wardrobe.

DESTRUCTION BY THE FLAMES.

Our town has been more fortunate than some others in not suffering much by the devouring element. I chronicle the number of fires from my recollection:

In 1830, a row of brick houses on the south side of First

77

Street, belonging to the late Bank of the United States, were destroyed by fire; afterwards rebuilt. In 1831, December 1st, a large fire on west side of High Street, originated in the bakehouse of White & Mumby, destroying the brick dwelling and store connected with the same, also the warehouse of White & Mumby, with their stock of groceries, also dwelling occupied by Matthew McLeod, also two frame buildings. The fire was checked in its course by the fireproof warehouse of John Kurtz, now occupied by John M. May, but from that north to First Street all the buildings were destroyed. The next fire was in January, 1832; the brick warehouse on High Street occupied by William Love. The next was the fine old Union Hotel on Bridge Street, burned in August, 1832, being the property of William Crawford's heirs. The next was John Lawrence's skin dressing establishment on Fayette Street; burnt three times; the last time in 1838. Hick's cabinet store and shop burnt three times; the last time in 1843. The *Cedars*, the residence of Col. Cox, burnt on Sunday, in January, 1847. A large brick warehouse situated on Water Street east of Frederick, used as a tannery, was destroyed by fire in 1850. Brown's bakehouse, situated on Water Street, was burned in 1840, and once before in 1838. Nourse & 's large flour mill burned in September, 1844. Bradley's warehouse, occupied by Dawson as a soap and grease factory, situated on Water Street just west of Frederick, was destroyed in 1863. Two brick houses on West Street, one owned by Mrs. Abbot, the other by Miss Magruder, was destroyed by fire on the 15th day of April, 1857. One three-story brick dwelling on Jefferson Street in October, 1857. Also the fine residence of the late Commodore Cassin on Beall Street. *Carter Place*, occupied by the French Minister, Count de Sartiges, and formerly by John F. Crampton, envoy from England, was burned in 1864. A large warehouse belonging to Gilbert Vanderwerken, situated on the lots formerly belonging to the Farmers and Butchers' Market Company, and formerly used by the Corporation of Georgetown for storing tobacco, was destroyed by fire on the 15th day of August, being filled with bales of hay. William H. Hazel's livery stable was destroyed on the 3d August, 1859, and again in the year 1864. Three houses on Prospect Street was destroyed by fire in 1868.

Ramsburg & Sons' sumac mill and skin dressing establishment, situated near the Alexandria Aqueduct, was burnt in 1871, and again in 1873. Lee's buildings (feed store, and dwelling), corner Bridge and Green Streets, was destroyed by fire in April, 1871. Three houses on Bridge Street, situated west of Market Street, was burned January 1st, 1877. A merchant mill of Mark Young was destroyed by fire on 3d July, 1877.

METROPOLITAN RAILROAD.

On the 3d day of May, 1853, an act was passed by the Legislature of Maryland incorporating the Metropolitan Railroad Company, to make a railroad from a point in connection with the Baltimore & Ohio Railroad, at or near the Point of Rocks, to Georgetown, in the District of Columbia, which act was ratified by Congress. Books of subscription to the stock of said company were opened by the commissioners named in said act, and, over ten thousand shares of the stock having been subscribed, amounting to upwards of five hundred thousand dollars, the necessary steps were taken to organize the said company by the election of president and directors. By an ordinance of the boards of aldermen and common council, passed June 11, 1853, and approved by the mayor, the mayor was authorized to subscribe in their name for five thousand shares of said stock, equal to two hundred and fifty thousand dollars. That subscription was made. By a subsequent ordinance David English, Evan Lyons, Robert P. Dodge, William H. Edes, and Walter S. Cox, or a majority of them, were appointed to vote the stock of the town at any meeting of the stockholders of the said company. By an act of Congress, passed March 2d, 1855, the town was empowered to levy a tax to pay their subscription to the Metropolitan Railroad. After the election of a president and directors of said company, the first instalment of twenty-five thousand dollars upon the stock subscribed by the town was paid. On the 21st of June, 1856, the corporation passed an ordinance to pay the second instalment on their subscription to the stock of the railroad company, which was vetoed by the Mayor, Henry Addison, but the said ordinance was passed, notwithstanding the veto, by a two-thirds majority. The mayor then declared that he would not sign the bonds of the corporation to meet this second instalment.

By the 20th section of the charter, the road was to be commenced within two years and to be completed within, five years, or the charter to be forfeited. The amount of stock subscribed was six thousand three hundred and thirty-four shares at fifty dollars per share, amounting to three hundred and sixteen thousand seven hundred dollars. The second instalment due by the town to the railroad company was not paid, because the mayor refused to sign the bonds. Neither was the second instalment paid by the individual stockholders. The consequence was, the road, although apparently begun within two years, but not being completed within five years, the charter became forfeited.

Now, let us see what benefits would have accrued to the town if an obstinate, perverse mayor had not refused to sign the bonds to pay the second instalment and all other instalments due the railroad company, and all subscribers had paid promptly their subscription. We should have a railroad to-day, reaching from Georgetown to the Point of Rocks, which, if it paid no dividends to the stockholders, would have multiplied the business of the town and increased the value of real estate, and, in all probability, during the civil war the road would have paid for itself in transporting troops, munitions of war, freight, and other property of the United States, besides the thousands of passengers traveling over the road. The estimated cost of the road was one million eight hundred thousand dollars. The road would have shortened the distance between Georgetown and the Point of Rocks forty-seven miles.

LIST OF NEWSPAPERS.

Weekly Ledger, published in 1790; *Sentinel of Liberty*, by Green, English & Co., 1796; *Federal Republican*, 1812; *National Messenger*, 1817; *Georgetown Columbian and District Advertiser*, by Samuel J. Rind, 1826; *Columbian Gazette*, by Benjamin Homans, 1829; *Metropolitan*, by Langtree & O'Sullivan, from 1836 to 1837; *Potomac Advocate*, by Thomas

Turner, 1840; *National Whig Review*, 1838; *Georgetown Advocate*, from 1841 to 1845; *Georgetown Reporter*, by Joseph Williamson, 1852; *Georgetown Advocate*, by Ezekiel Hughes, from 1845 to 1860; *Georgetown Courier*, by J.D. McGill, from 1865 to 1874; *College Journal*, by Rev. J.S. Sumner, from 1872 to the present time.

LITERATI.

As this book is intended to chronicle the events of the town, and not to contain a biography of the citizens, the chronicler cannot refrain from mentioning several of the literati who have resided among us.

John J. Piatt, the editor of *The Capital*, whose productions are identified with the scenery of the Potomac River, formerly resided here. Mrs. Emma D.E.N. Southworth, the author of the "Lost Heiress," "Deserted Wife," "Missing Bride," "Wife's Victory," and other works of fiction, has her residence on Prospect Hill. Professor Samuel Tyler, the author of a discourse on "Baconian Philosophy," "Progress of Philosophy," "Memoir of R.B. Taney," "Treatise on Pleading in Maryland Courts of Law," and other works, departed this life on the 15th of December, 1877, at his residence on Washington Street. Charles Lanman, the author of "Essays for Summer Hours," "A Summer in the Wilderness," "Life of Daniel Webster," "Dictionary of Congress," and other productions, resides at his cosy dwelling on West Street. Wm. L. Shoemaker, M.D., whose lyrics and sonnets have been read with pleasure for many years by his fellow citizens, and whose muse deserves a much wider recognition than they have hitherto enjoyed, is a native and resident of the town.

CHAPTER V.

Poor-House, Will of John Barnes, and Donation of W.W. Corcoran—Commerce—Alexandria Aqueduct—Washington Aqueduct.

A town without a poor-house is no town at all. As the misfortunes in this life are numerous, no man knows how suddenly he may fall into them. We have had an alms-house for nearly half a century, and to it have gone many citizens who had baffled the waves and billows of this life, until, overcome by adversity, they were compelled to seek the shelter and charity of the town. The chronicler has seen men, who, when he was a child, were living in comfortable mansions, but, before he grew to manhood, they had fallen into adversity, and were living at the expense of the people. Old age and poverty are two hard things, therefore it becomes men, when young and strong, to lay up something for the future period of life, so that, if they should live to become old, they will not have to depend upon others for a support.

The incipiency of a poor-house was first conceived by the mind of John Barnes, who was collector of the port of Georgetown. He died on the 12th of February, 1826, leaving a will, in which he says:

"It has often occurred to me that the time was not far distant (indeed it has already become urgently necessary), when a poor-house or bettering house for this county or town (it matters not by what name denominated) should be established, and if proposed through the honorable and respectable Corporation of Georgetown, I doubt not that it would be ultimately successful, and, thereby, a good foundation would be laid towards perfecting a useful and meritorious work worthy the enlightened, benevolent, and opulent inhabitants of the District and its vicinity, and the humane at large, of contributing to the comfort and improvement of the suffering objects of such institutions. Whenever any progressive proceedings towards such an end becomes certain and conclusive, a sum not exceeding one thousand dollars, as occasionally wanted and demanded, I freely bequeath towards its establishment, and I do direct my

82

executors, having a regard to the bequeaths heretofore contained, to pay the same to the authorities having power and right to receive the same for such a purpose. And as the establishment of a poor-house, hospital, or bettering house for this county or town, is an object very near my heart, I do direct that if my executors or trustees, for the time being, shall, in the exercise of the discretion hereby vested in them, suffer the surplus, the annual proceeds, to accumulate, then I give another one thousand dollars out of such accumulation, in addition to what I have herein before directed to be applied to that purpose, as aforesaid, in further aid of the establishment and maintenance of such poor-house, hospital, or bettering house, but neither of such bequests is to be applied until my executors or trustees for the time being, shall perceive that such proceedings have been begun, as will render the final accomplishment and completion of said poor-house or hospital reasonably certain."

These devises of Barnes' will was contested by his heirs, but the matter was afterwards compromised, and on the 27th of October, 1827, the corporation purchased a piece of land, being lot No. 276, in Beatty & Hawkins' addition to Georgetown, paying one hundred dollars per acre for the same; and on the 6th of November, 1830, the town, authorities appropriated five thousand dollars to build and erect a suitable building for a poor-house upon said lot.

Although our town was chartered in 1789, and amendments to the same were made in 1797, also by Congress in 1805, 1809, and in 1824, it was not discovered, until John Barnes died, that such impecunious individuals as "poor people," were to be found in our jurisdiction; when, all of a sudden, it was discovered that the town had no charter-power to build and erect a poor-house. An application was made to Congress, when authority was given by the act of 20th of May, 1826, when, by an ordinance of the corporation, approved on the 30th day of December, 1826, James S. Morsell, John Little, John Baker, William G. Ridgely, Daniel Bussard, John McDaniel, Charles A. Burnett, and Gideon Davis, with the Mayor of the town as their president, shall constitute a board of trustees for the poor of Georgetown until the first Monday in January, 1828, and until successors be

83

appointed.

The corner-stone of the poor-house was laid by the Masons in 1831, in the midst of a large concourse of citizens, and in the presence of the mayor, recorder, aldermen, and common council of the town. The Rev. Mr. Wallace, the then pastor of the Methodist Protestant Church, preached a most eloquent discourse on the occasion. The building was soon erected, and has an imposing appearance as seen from the road. It is two stories high with a wing at each end; one wing being used by the family of the superintendent. The lower rooms in the main building were used for the kitchen; Nos. 1 and 2, dining room for boys; No. 3, dining room for girls. The rooms in the second story and dormitories were used for sleeping apartments. The rooms extend in depth to the width of the building. The first superintendent was Charles Shoemaker; the second, Jos. Brooks; the third, J.M. Barnecloe; the fourth, Reazin Stevens; the fifth, W.B. Pomeroy.

In those days the grounds were cultivated. Fruit and vegetables were raised in abundance to supply the inmates of the poor-house as well as for sale in the market, and the house and grounds showed a flourishing condition, that was captivating to the visitor.

They had a custom of washing off every person who was committed to the poor-house by the police magistrate of the town, by stripping them of their clothing; whether the weather was cold or warm, and standing them in a tall chimney, two stories high (the top of which was covered with a sieve), when a man would carry up a large bucket of water and pour the contents upon the head and body of the prisoner. The consequence was, if the weather was cold, it was a chilly reception, and in two cases, to the chronicler's knowledge, when the shower bath had been used upon individuals who were committed for intemperance, in cold weather, were attacked with *mania a potu* and died from its effects.

Whether the building will be continued to be occupied as a poor-house, is a question to be determined. The chronicler is informed that it may be converted into a Home Industrial School, and the inmates of the alms-house sent to the poor-house located on the Eastern Branch. This, we think, would be a violation of the original design of the founder of the institution, and if converted to any other purpose than a poor-house, the property might revert to the heirs of the late John Barnes. Although, a Home Industrial School is a good institution where the boys can learn habits of industry, that will carry them forward into any pursuit of life, nevertheless, this building has been dedicated for a poor-house, and should be used for that purpose in all time to come, and our District Commissioners should see that the grounds are cultivated in a successful manner according to the rules of husbandry, by the inmates of the institution, so they can raise their supply of fruit and vegetables, and not depend upon the neighboring markets for everything to eat, by taxing the citizens with appropriations.

The chronicler is informed that, at the time of penning these events, there are twenty-five boys attending the Home Industrial School in town, who are lodged and fed at the poor-house, while the number of poor persons, who have been sent there for support, does not exceed thirteen.

DONATION OF W.W. CORCORAN.

On the 29th day of May, 1848, William W. Corcoran, being desirous to signify his attachment to Georgetown, the place of his birth, and to the inhabitants thereof, did, by his endorsement made on fourteen bonds of the Chesapeake & Ohio Canal Company (each bearing date the 3d day of May, 1848, and numbered as follows: six bonds of one thousand dollars each, numbered 130, 131, 132, 133, 134, and 148, and eight bonds of five hundred dollars each, numbered 135, 143, 144, 145, 146,147,151, and 152, making an aggregate of ten thousand dollars,) transfer and assign the said bonds to the mayor, recorder, aldermen, and common council of Georgetown, to be held by them and their successors forever; the interest accruing from said bonds to be applied to the support and maintenance of the impecunious citizens of the town. This generous donation has now been in existence for thirty years, and has carried gladness to the hearts of many families who, otherwise, would have suffered for want of the necessaries of life. The chronicler is informed that the interest is paid over to the ladies of the Benevolent Society of our town, who purchase fuel and provisions and distribute them among the most needy citizens. This donation of Colonel Corcoran's is sufficient to entitle him to the grateful thanks of all the citizens of our town; but what shall be said when the chronicler writes a chapter upon Oak Hill Cemetery, showing that his donations amount to upwards of a hundred thousand dollars, given towards this beautiful city of the dead.

COMMERCE.

To attempt to write an account of the commerce of a city, is to give a history of its export and import trade. But what the chronicler understands by commerce, is not only transportation by water, but whatever conduces to the traffic of a town or city, either by land or water, in multiplying business.

The commerce of our town bad its origin in the first settlement of our country, by the farmers of the surrounding country bringing to market the various productions of the soil to be bartered or exchanged for domestic goods. Among the numerous articles of commerce brought to town for sale was tobacco, which was hauled from a long distance in wagons, and, after undergoing inspection, was sold to our merchants to be shipped abroad. The tobacco warehouse was then located on a large lot lying south of Bridge Street and west of Market Street; or rather between Market and Frederick Streets, was a frame building called Loundes' warehouse, where all the tobacco was inspected and sold. The shipping at that time was confined to the west end of the town, near the Alexandria Aqueduct, where there were spacious wharves and warehouses; and our ships that carried the tobacco to foreign countries sailed down the western channel, between Analostan Island and the Virginia shore, before the stone causeway was erected in 1805. After the erection of the causeway the vessels sailed through the eastern channel, and our merchants commenced building warehouses along the south side of Water Street and nearer to the river center of the town.

In course of time the tobacco trade had increased to such an extent that there was a demand for room. In the year 1822, the corporation passed an ordinance for building two new tobacco warehouses, three stories high, and fire-proof, on lots 46, 47, and 48, situated west of High and south of Bridge Street. The roofs were covered with slate and the doors and shutters with sheet-iron. The buildings were large enough to hold several thousand hogsheads of tobacco, but were found insufficient to receive the quantity of tobacco brought to the town for sale. Consequently, the corporation erected wooden sheds in addition to the brick warehouses. The inspection of tobacco multiplied, and the business so increased, that as high as five thousand hogsheads of tobacco were shipped to Europe in one year. The removal of the inspection of, tobacco from Loundes' warehouse to the new buildings, was ordered by the town authorities on the 26th of July, 1824.

The tobacco business of the town continued prosperous until the death of John Laird, on the 11th of July, 1833, when the firm of Laird & Son was dissolved, and the trade died with them, as there appeared to be no other tobacco merchants in the market.
On the 18th day of March, 1836, George B. Magruder, the tobacco inspector of the town, addressed a letter to the corporation, regretting that he would have to give up the cooperage on tobacco, finding by experience in the last two years that, after paying for labor and nails on twenty-one hundred hogsheads of tobacco, coopered at seventy-five cents per hogshead, it had left him about two hundred and fifty dollars a year for himself and pay of a clerk, requesting a salary for his services, and to have a cooper appointed. If this proposition should not be agreed to, he would try the inspection one year more, provided the corporation would give him the outage on all tobacco inspected by him.

In the month of September, 1844, the large merchant mill erected by Colonel George Bomford, at the foot of the market

house, was destroyed by fire; and in the spring of 1845, Colonel Bomford erected a cotton factory on the ruins of the old mill, which went into operation in 1847. Colonel Bomford considered that a cotton factory would be of more benefit to the town than a flour mill, in giving employment to a large class of its population. The factory was run under his ownership until 1850, when it was sold to Thomas Wilson, of Baltimore, who run the factory until the breaking out of the late war, when the supply of cotton was cut off. In 1866 the building was purchased by our enterprising fellow-citizen, A.H. Herr, who converted it again into a merchant flour mill.

We here exhibit the trade, foreign and coastwise, of the port of Georgetown. Amount of duties on goods accrued; expenses attending its collection in payment to officers; also, the value of American goods and produce exported to foreign markets; also, the value of American produce and manufactures shipped coastwise; and the aggregate tonnage engaged in carrying on the trade in its different branches for a number of years:

No. 1. Amount of duties secured, beginning with the year 1815, and ending in 1835 ...		$457,396
Payment of salaries	$40,000	
Bonds unpaid	4,479	44,479
Paid over to the United States		$412,917
No. 2. Value of produce exported to foreign markets from 1815 to 1835		$4,077,708
Being an annual average of	$203,885.40	
No. 3. Value of American produce shipped coastwise from 1826 to 1835		$5,190,540
Items as follows:		
Flour: 919,940 bbls. valued at	$4,710,540	
Tobacco: 5,400 hhd's " "	300,000	
Other articles exceeding $20,000 per year ...	180,000	
	$5,190,540	
Average per year... $576,726.66⅔		
No. 4. American and foreign goods brought into Georgetown		$3,505,000
Items as follows:		
Dry Goods	$1,500,000	
Groceries and Hardware	1,500,000	
Lumber	200,000	
Wood	125,000	
Anthracite Coal	75,000	

Bituminous Coal	5,000
Domestic Produce	100,000
	$3,505,000

No. 5. Tonnage engaged in trade per annum:

Average tonnage arriving from foreign ports . .	1,290 tons.
Departing to foreign ports	2,868 "
Arriving coastwise with merchandise, ...	60,000 "
Lumber and trade	30,000 "
Coal and Wood	60,000 "
Other Items	16,000 "
	170,158 tons.

By returns during the year 1835, of the officer supervising the coasting trade to Georgetown, it appears there were near three thousand arrivals, whose tonnage was a fraction less than two hundred thousand tons.

Many of our citizens remember the ships, *Eagle* and *Shenandoah*, which sailed regularly to Europe loaded with tobacco, and brought in return cargoes of salt. In course of time our ships went the way of all ships—by being stranded at sea, and our noble town felt the great loss of the vessels that were wont to unload at our wharves, amid the shouts of the boatmen and songs of the sailors.

A number of enterprising citizens afterwards purchased four ships named the *Francis Depau, Southerner, Caledonia,* and *Catherine Jackson.* They made their appearance in our harbor, in the summer and autumn of 1836, and after making several voyages to Europe, were finally sold as being too large for our commerce. Our merchants, then engaged in the coasting trade, having a number of vessels sailing to Boston, Newburyport, New York, and other cities, carrying away large quantities of flour and produce, brought down the Chesapeake & Ohio Canal, which extends into the interior of Maryland. Others extended their commerce to the West Indies, and had large quantities of sugar and productions of the West Indies' brought in every few months, and sold upon the wharves at public sale. In course of time the sailing packets passed away, and we have, in their place, steamers plying between our town, Baltimore, New York, Philadelphia, and Norfolk, which always arrive heavily loaded with freight, and carry away in return, cargoes of flour.

The heaviest trade carried on, at this time, is in the article of coal. Thousands of boat-loads of coal arrive at our town by way of the canal from Cumberland, which is shipped in vessels to distant ports, and is largely used by the ocean steamers and manufacturing establishments. The river is frequently covered with vessels with their forests of masts reaching towards the sky, awaiting their turn to be loaded with coal, before sailing to a distant clime.

The town is so located, that the Potomac River has a fall of thirty-three feet, within four miles, from the Little Falls to the canal basin; and the canal flowing through the town (having the same fall) to the river, renders its banks desirable for milling purposes. The consequence is, we have a number of merchant mills in our town, located on the canal, propelled by water power. The first is the mill of David L. Shoemaker; second, F.L. Moore; third, Beall & Shoemaker; fourth, William H. Tenney & Son; fifth, James S. Welch ; sixth, George Shoemaker; seventh, Ross Ray & Bro.; eighth, A.H. Herr, at the foot of the market, and George Hill, Jr.'s Paper Mill. The flour mills will shell out from one hundred and fifty to three hundred barrels of flour per day. Besides these, we have other mills in the neighborhood of the town, as the Lock Mill on the canal, and about two miles above town is Lyons' Mill, and the Columbian Mill, located on Rock Creek, all of which are supplied with grain brought down the canal or by vessels from a distance.

The flour and produce trade has become one of great importance in our town, and the most of our merchants are engaged in that line of business. There was a time, many years past, when the wholesale grocery business occupied nearly all the warehouses on Water Street. Our merchants attended the cargo sales of groceries in New York, where they purchased supplies for the District market. These groceries were brought to Georgetown in the sailing packets, that plied regularly between New York and our town, and were sold to the retail dealers in the District—embracing Washington and Georgetown. A large and extensive business was done in this way, until the railroad was constructed between Washington and Baltimore, in the year

1835, when our retail dealers began going to Baltimore and New York to purchase their supplies, instead of looking to our Water Street merchants; in this way the wholesale grocery business of Georgetown declined, while the flour and produce trade has taken its place.

The quantity of flour inspected in our town bas reached three hundred thousand barrels per year, all of which was transported down the canal, or manufactured at our merchant mills.

Our principal flour inspector was George Shoemaker, who was elected annually on the first Monday in January, in each and every year. He served the town faithfully in that office for forty-nine years, until his death in July, 1865. By his sound judgment in the grades of flour, he raised the Georgetown brands to such a degree, that the flour, with his inspection, was demanded in all the markets of the country.

In May, 1868, James A. Magruder, being then the collector of the port of Georgetown, addressed a letter to the then commissioner of public buildings, in reference to the channel of the river and custom-house business. He says:

"The tonnage of vessels belonging to this District is twenty-two thousand four hundred and fifty-five and eighty-eight one hundredths tons. The number of vessels entered for the past year, is three hundred and seventy-three; number of vessels cleared, for the same time, is two hundred and five." He further says: "You cannot judge of the amount of business done in this District from the number of vessels entered and cleared; for vessels in the coasting trade are not required to enter or clear at the custom-house, unless they have foreign goods, or distilled spirits on board. I suppose there are at least twenty vessels arriving here, which do not enter or clear, for each one that has to do so."

ALEXANDRIA AQUEDUCT.

A charter for the construction of the Alexandria Aqueduct and canal was passed by Congress on the 26th day of May, 1830, giving the company power to construct an aqueduct across the Potomac River, and excavate a canal to Alexandria. The work was begun in 1833 and completed by the 4th of July, 1843, when the water was turned into the aqueduct. The construction of two abutments and eight piers of stone, built upon the rock of the river at a great depth below the surface, was a triumph of engineering skill, not surpassed by any similar work in the country.

It was decided by the engineers in charge of the work, that the aqueduct should consist of eight piers one hundred and five feet apart at high water mark; two of the piers to be twenty-one feet thick, and the others twelve feet thick at high water mark; the southern abutment to be twenty-one feet thick, with circular wing walls thirteen feet average thickness at the base, sixty-six feet in length, to connect with the slope walls of the causeway. Each of the piers have an ice breaker upon the up-stream end in form of an oblique cone, sloping forty-five degrees, extending five feet below and ten feet above high water mark, made of cut granite; the down-stream ends to be circular, and to have a slope the same as the sides, one inch to the foot. Upon this plan each pier was erected.

The first coffer-dam constructed was built in a depth of eighteen feet of water and seventeen feet four inches of mud, being the second from the Virginia shore. The figure, of the dam was a parallelogram, eighty-two feet long by twenty-seven feet wide. The inner row of piles were of white oak, forty feet long and sixteen inches in diameter at the larger end, shod with iron pointed with steel, weighing twenty-five pounds. They were placed four feet apart from center to center, and driven to the rock with a ram weighing seventeen hundred pounds. The outer row of piles, fifteen feet from and parallel with the inner row, was also of oak, thirty-six feet long and sixteen inches in diameter. After the dam was constructed puddling clay was thrown in between the two rows of piles and well rammed to make the dam tight; then the steam engine was used for pumping the water and excavating the mud. Seventeen feet of water was discharged by two pumps in four hours and thirty-two minutes. After a large portion of the mud was removed, a break would frequently occur; and a dam has been known to fill more than a dozen times before succeeding in reaching the rock of the river. It was a spectacle so unusual to see men busily at work so far below the surface of the river, that it was an exceedingly interesting sight to the public; but to the engineer, whatever might be his confidence in the ability of the dam to resist the immense weight which he knew to be constantly pressing upon it, the sight was one calculated to fill his mind with anxiety. The ice breaker at the head of each pier is of cut granite, the two lower courses, being five feet below high water mark, were twenty-two inches thick, and no stone being less in size than twenty cubic feet. The piers were erected to the height of twenty-nine feet above high water mark. After the piers were erected, then came the work of removing the dams, which was easily done by the steam-engine in drawing fifty piles a day.

To describe the construction of each dam and pier separately, would fill a volume. It is sufficient to say that the *modus operandi* of construction was the same in all, until the piers and abutments were erected to the required altitude above the surface of the river.

If it had not been for the United States, probably this work never would have been completed. Congress, by an act passed June 25th, 1832, gave one hundred thousand dollars towards this work, and, by a subsequent act passed March 3d, 1837, gave three hundred thousand dollars more. The whole cost of the aqueduct was six hundred thousand dollars, the canal five hundred thousand dollars, and the locks at Alexandria fifty thousand dollars.

The original plan of the aqueduct was to be all of stone, consisting of twelve arches supported by eleven piers and two abutments, the arches to be one hundred feet span and twenty-five feet rise; but, the immense cost being beyond the means of the company, it was abandoned, and a wooden superstructure for the trunk of the aqueduct substituted.

Several ingenious plans used in the country were duly considered. Benjamin F. Miller, the master carpenter and superintendent of the work, invented a model, which, having been tested in the presence of the directors and board of engineers, was adopted; and all the timber used in the construction was subjected to "Kyan's Process" for preserving timber.

The length of the wooden trunk is eleven hundred feet; its width, from timber to timber, twenty-eight feet; width of trough, seventeen feet; width of towpath, five feet, and depth of trough, seven feet.

Major Turnbull, who was the principal engineer in charge of the work, says:

"When I reflect upon the numerous difficulties which we have overcome in the progress of the work, and recall the disheartening predictions of that numerous portion of the community who looked upon the attempt to establish foundations at so great a depth and in a situation so very exposed and dangerous, and who did not fail to treat it as an absurdity, I cannot but congratulate myself upon having so happily succeeded; and, while so doing, I recollect, with a very grateful sense of what I owe them for it, the very generous confidence which the president and directors of the company always reposed in me; and I recall with pleasure and admiration the unhesitating promptness with which they always seconded me bringing to my aid their own spirit of zealous perseverance, backed by all the disposable means of the company."

The aqueduct being completed, and thought to be durable, was in use as a public highway from July 4, 1843, to May 23, 1861, when the United States took possession of the same, drew off the water, and converted the aqueduct into a bridge for the transportation of troops and munitions of war. It was used also as a road for common travel by the public (without paying any toll) until after the close of the war, when it was surrendered by the United States to the aqueduct company, but in such a dilapidated condition that it would hold neither wind nor water. The consequence was, the company was not able to repair the structure, and made a lease of the same to Henry H. Wells, Philip Quigly, and William W. Duncan for ninety-nine years, on condition that the said lessees should rebuild the aqueduct and erect over the same a bridge, suitable for railway or common travel, and collect tolls for crossing the sane. A new aqueduct was immediately rebuilt after July 27, 1868, out of North Carolina timber. It has now been ten years since it was reconstructed, and, from present appearances, it will have to be rebuilt again to hold water and sustain the weight of travel.

This was an unfortunate investment for Alexandria—the sinking of one million one hundred and fifty thousand dollars—when, if she had constructed a set of locks, four in number, at Georgetown, to lock boats into the river, then tow them to Alexandria by steam tugs and back again to Georgetown, the expense would have been a bagatelle compared to the cost of the canal and aqueduct.

WASHINGTON AQUEDUCT.

Before beginning to write a sketch of the Washington Aqueduct, it will be well to examine into the history of water-works and see what other cities have done in days gone by. We extract from the cyclopædia that, "the Pools of Solomon, near Bethlehem, were three large reservoirs connected with each other, from which water was conveyed to Jerusalem, six miles distant. One of these pools was five hundred and eighty-two feet long, and a hundred and eighty feet wide. Jerusalem is still supplied with water from them. In Egypt and Babylonia, similar works were constructed in very early ages. Enough remains of the ancient aqueduct of Carthage to show that it was one of the most remarkable of these great works. Upon it, the waters from the mountains were conveyed through an arched conduit six feet wide, and four feet deep. The whole length was seventy miles. The Romans exceeded all other nations, ancient or modern, in the construction of these works. There were nine different aqueducts which brought into the city daily, twenty-eight million cubic feet of pure water. Strabo says: 'I that whole rivers flowed through the streets of Rome.' It is estimated that fifty million cubic feet of water must have been supplied daily to a population of one million, or three hundred and twelve imperial gallons to each individual." The Croton Aqueduct of New York surpasses all modern constructions of this kind in extent and magnificence. It was completed in 1842; having been five years in building, under the superintendence of Mr. John B. Jervis, chief engineer. The whole expense was twelve million five hundred thousand dollars. The entire length is, from its source to Fifth Avenue, forty and one-half miles. On this line are sixteen tunnels, having a length of six thousand eight hundred and forty-one feet, cut through rock. A dam constructed across the Croton River, raised the water forty feet, and formed the Croton Lake which covers about four hundred acres; and with a depth of six feet of water, contains five hundred million gallons.

Having given a sketch of other water-works, we will now turn our attention to the one in which we are more directly interested:

The Washington Aqueduct was begun November 8, 1853, under the administration of Franklin Pierce, President of the United States. The names of the engineers who designed and built the works, are Montgomery C. Meigs, captain of engineer; Alfred L. Rives, William H. Bryan, C. Crozet, C.G. Talcott, William H. Hatton, E.T.D. Myers, Silas Seymour, J. James R. Croes, and Theodore B. Samo, civil engineers; Nathaniel Michler, and George H. Ellicott, majors of engineers; Orville E. Babcock, colonel of engineers, now chief engineer of the Washington Aqueduct. The source of supply is the Potomac River above the Great Falls. In 1853, the estimated cost of the work was two million three hundred thousand dollars, and is yet unfinished; but the actual expenditures for all purposes from 1853 to 1876 is three million seven hundred and twenty-eight thousand two hundred and sixty-seven dollars. The cost of maintenance of works, including engineering, superintendence and repairs, is fifteen thousand dollars. The population of Washington and Georgetown being one hundred and forty-six thousand, the quantity of water used by the citizens and departments of the Government, is twenty-three million gallons in twenty-four hours. The Steam pump supplies the reservoir on Georgetown heights with one million gallons daily. The conduit of the Washington Aqueduct is circular in section—nine feet in the interior diameter. It is twelve miles long, with a fall of nine and one-half inches to one mile. The engine for propelling water to the reservoir on the heights of Georgetown, is a Knowles & Libbey Engine, which is under the control of the Water Registrar of the District of Columbia. There are two reservoirs, the receiving and distributing. The receiving reservoir, covering fifty-one acres, is a natural basin formed by building an earthen dam across the valley of Powder Mill Branch, and is seldom used. The distributing reservoir covers forty-four acres, and is nearly a rectangle in form, built by excavating clay from its bottom and forming embankments thereof; the inner faces of which are protected by a slope wall of dry rubble masonry, generally one foot thick, laid on a bed of small broken stone six inches in depth. The pipes laid through Georgetown and Washington are cast-iron, from 2, 4, 6, 8, 10, 12, 20, 30, 36, and 48 inches in diameter. Pipes laid in 1858, and taken up in 1875, were found to be in a good condition. There are six hundred and seventy-four hydrants for fires; the McClelland pattern, made in Washington, is generally used, and has taken the place of nearly all others. Stop-cocks of various kinds have been used. The stop-cocks manufactured in Troy, New York, have the preference. Those used on the thirty-six-inch main were manufactured by the Norris Iron Company, of Pennsylvania. The workmanship is considered first-class. About thirty meters of various patterns have been used for experimenting on the flow of water in the aqueduct for the purpose of ascertaining the amount consumed (but not for ascertaining the discharge of the conduit), nearly all of which have been abandoned as failures. Of late years, the quantity of water consumed has been ascertained by shutting the conduit off from the distributing reservoir, and recording the height of the surface of water every hour, for forty-eight hours. The amount of water consumed is about twenty-three million gallons in twenty-four hours.

There have been no difficulties in the construction of the water-works from the beginning. The last three miles of the conduit have been, and are now run under a head. Where built on an embankment, leaks have occurred, which have been repaired with hydraulic cement, and the embankments strengthened by widening and raising them. Since this was done, there have been no leaks, although the lower end of the conduit is run under a head between three and four feet.

There are twelve tunnels on the line of the Washington Aqueduct. Tunnel No. 1, is one thousand four hundred and thirty-eight feet in length; No. 2, three thousand eight hundred and sixty-five feet; No. 3, eighty-six feet; No. 4, seven hundred and sixty-six feet; No. 5, ninety feet; No. 6, eighty-eight feet; No.

7, six hundred and seventy-five feet five inches; No. 8, four hundred and twenty-one feet nine inches; No. 9, seven hundred and twenty-five feet; No. 10, eighty six feet; No. 11, six hundred and twenty-six feet; No. 12, dalecarlia, eight hundred feet. The number of bridges are six. The span of No. 1, is fourteen feet; No. 2, ten feet; No. 3, seventy-five feet; No. 4, two hundred and twenty feet; No. 5, one hundred and twenty feet; No. 6, two hundred feet. The first four bridges are constructed of cut stone; the two last of iron pipes. The cost of bridge No. 1, was four thousand and six dollars; No. 2, seven thousand seven hundred and seventy-nine dollars; No. 3, seventy-six thousand and sixty-eight dollars; No. 4, two hundred and thirty-seven thousand dollars. Bridges No. 4, over Cabin John's Run, and No. 6, over Rock Creek, have been much admired. Their elevation and plans have been published in the scientific journals of Europe. Both bridges are new among engineering structures. The Cabin John Bridge being the widest stone arch in existence; and the Rock Creek Bridge being the only one in which the arched-ribs are utilized to convey the water supply for a city, and at the same time, to support a roadway. The length of the line of the Washington Aqueduct is eighteen miles, and the number of culverts twenty-six. Over the conduit is one of the best roads in the country, being macadamized, over which there is a large amount of travel by farmers living in the surrounding neighborhood, who use this road in hauling their produce to market. It is, also, a pleasant drive in the summer season, when a large number of our citizens avail themselves of the opportunity of visiting the Great Falls of the Potomac, to fish in the rolling tide, or view the swelling hills and sunken valleys of Virginia, and the course of the rivulets from the unbroken plain.

The Aqueduct Bridge over Rock Creek, was constructed upon two iron mains forty-eight inches in diameter, springing from two abutments on either side of the stream, and are used for the purpose of conveying water from the aqueduct into the city of Washington.

By an act of Congress, passed May 17th, 1862, the Washington & Georgetown Railroad Company was created, and authorized to construct and lay a double track in the cities of

Washington and Georgetown, along the following avenues and streets: "Commencing on Bridge Street at the intersection of High Street, thence along the said Bridge Street to its intersection with the street running to the Tubular Bridge over Rock Creek to Pennsylvania Avenue in the city of Washington, along said avenue to Fifteenth Street west, &c." The bridge was completed in 1862, and was immediately used as a general thoroughfare for street cars and wagons of all descriptions. The railroad company claimed to have authority for the use of this bridge, from the portion of the law above quoted (but it was used as a bridge of common travel during the war by the public, on account of the demand for passage way and the K Street Bridge not being in a good condition for travel), until an act of Congress, passed on the 3d of March, 1875, "gave authority to the chief engineer of the Washington Aqueduct, to notify the railroad company to remove their rails from the Tubular Bridge over Rock Creek, within one year from the date of said notice; and the engineer may establish and publish regulations prohibiting the passage of heavy loaded wagons and carriages over said bridge." The street cars and heavy carriages now pass over the M Street Bridge, but it is evident that the travel over the Tubular Bridge is as great as before the act of Congress passed, judging from the number of vehicles sometimes crowded upon the bridge. It should be restricted to foot passengers and light carriages.

Great complaint has been made, particularly in the summer, when the weather was warm and the dry season had set in, that the water flowing from the Great Falls through the conduit, was affected by impurities which gave it the oder and taste of fish, and it was the prevailing opinion that the offensiveness proceeded from fish in a state of decomposition in the reservoirs and pipes. To cure this difficulty, the mains and pipes were frequently flushed, but this did not remove the peculiar oder and taste, and it was the opinion of the chief engineer, that the impurities of the water were not due to the fish, either in the reservoirs or pipes. It has been generally supposed that the fishy taste of the water in time of a drought, was owing to a green moss generating inside of the reservoirs, which imparted a peculiar taste and oder to the water. When rain was plentiful, the fishy oder and taste suddenly disappeared.

As we have given the acts of Assembly of Maryland, also the acts of Congress relating to the town, we will now give the acts of Congress in reference to the construction of the Washington Aqueduct, which will be of use to the general reader and especially to the members of the Washington Bar:

The first enactment of Congress in relation to this work, is found in volume 10, Statues at Large, p. 92; approved April 30th, 1852. The second, in vol. 10, p. 206; approved March 3d, 1853, giving one hundred thousand dollars. The third, in vol. 10, p. 664; approved March 3d, 1855, giving two hundred and fifty thousand dollars. The fourth, in vol. 11, p. 86; approved August 18th, 1856, giving two hundred and fifty thousand dollars. The fifth, in vol. 11, p. 225; approved March 3d,1857, giving one million dollars. The sixth, in vol. 11, p. 256; approved March 3d, 1857. This act surrenders to the United States certain machinery, bricks, and materials. The seventh, in vol. 11, pp. 263, 264, and 265, for the purpose of acquiring land for the aqueduct. The eighth, in vol. 11, p. 323; approved June 12th, 1858, giving eight hundred thousand dollars to complete the works. The ninth, in vol: 11, p. 435; approved March 3d, 1859, transfers the control of the Washington Aqueduct to the Department of the Interior. The tenth, in vol. 12, p. 106; approved June 25th, 1860, giving four million dollars. The eleventh, in vol. 12, pp. 405, 406, and 407; which refers to the Corporation of Georgetown especially, in which all the citizens are interested. The twelfth, in vol. 12, p. 620 ; the thirteenth, in vol. 12, pp. 804 and 805 ; the fourteenth, in vol. 13, p. 384; the fifteenth, in vol. 13, pp. 133 and 134; the sixteenth, in vol. 14, p. 316; the seventeenth, in vol. 14, p. 374; the eighteenth, in vol. 14, p. 464; the nineteenth, in vol. 14, p. 466; the twentieth, in vol. 14, p. 464; the twenty-first, in vol. 15, p. 118; the twenty-second, in vol. 15, p. 174; the twenty-third, in vol. 15, p. 309; the twenty-fourth in vol. 16, p. 276; the twenty-fifth, in vol. 16, pp. 301 and 302; the twenty-sixth, in vol. 16, p. 505. See also an act of the Legislature of the District of Columbia, approved July 20, 1871, appropriating four hundred and fifty thousand dollars.

CHAPTER VI.

CATHOLIC TRINITY CHURCH—PRESBYTERIAN CHURCH—ST. JOHNS EPISCOPAL CHURCH—CHRIST EPISCOPAL CHURCH—METHODIST EPISCOPAL CHURCH—METHODIST PROTESTANT CHURCH—GERMAN LUTHERAN CHURCH—BAPTIST CHURCH—COLORED CHURCHES.

It is difficult to write a sketch of a church when no record has been kept of the events surrounding it, by which a brief history might be written. The information imparted to the chronicler concerning the old church edifice, was given to him by Rev. J.S. Sumner, editor of the *College Journal.* It appears that the first entry on the records of Trinity Church is of a marriage April 6, 1795; the first baptism recorded is of May 14th, of the same year. These are signed by Rev. Francis Neale, S.J., the first pastor of Trinity Church, and indicate the period at which the church was used for worship. The lot was purchased by Bishop Carroll, some years previously, and the church erected by contributions from people of the adjoining counties. Alexander Doyle seems to have erected the building, putting in his own means in addition to the contributions from others. The college virtually owned the church, and still continues to hold it. Mr. Doyle made an arrangement with the college by which the debt of the church to him was extinguished, namely, by contracting for the education of his sons at the college; the whole embracing a term of years. When the last one left there was still an unexpired term due his estate, and the college paid his executor the balance. The old church was frequently used by the college to hold the annual commencements, until 1832, when the college had erected a new building for that purpose. The old church has lately been remodeled to make room for Trinity Church Sabbath School. The school room is a fine hall on the first floor of the building extending its entire length and breadth, with seats for six hundred pupils. On the upper floor are class rooms for the parish school. The parish school connected with the church is in a most flourishing condition, and should be encouraged, so that its influence may extend in doing good, by educating the children of the poor and making them useful members of society, that they may become an honor to their parents and a blessing to the community.

The new Trinity Church fronts west, like Solomon's Temple. The corner-stone was laid in 1849, when Rev. James Ryder preached a most eloquent sermon. The church was dedicated on Sunday, 15th day of June, 1851 (the chronicler was present), when Doctor Ryder again preached a very impressive discourse from the II Chronicles; his text was: "The appearance of the Lord in a dream unto Solomon at the completion of the temple;" and then came a faithful description of what a true worshiper of the Saviour ought to be, and which, to our mind, was never more faithfully portrayed. There was present, on the occasion, a large company collected from far and near, consisting of all classes and denominations, among them many Protestants desirous of seeing the imposing ceremonies and solemn services. The clergy, all attired in their proper vestments and bearing the holy cross, marched up one of the aisles of the church sprinkling the holy water with hyssop, and, upon arriving at the altar, Hayden's Mass was sung and chanted by the choir. The procession then passed through the aisles again sprinkling the holy water; the music was superior to anything of the kind ever heard in our town at church dedications.

The pastors who have filled the pulpit of Trinity Church are as follows: the Rev. Francis Neale took charges of the church in 1792, and was followed by his assistant, Rev. Charles L. Thoux, in 1818; then came the Rev. Stephen Dubuisson, James F.M. Lucas, Philip A. Sacchi, Peter P. Kroes, Peter O'Flanagan, up to the year 1852. In that year Rev. Joseph Aschwanden became rector, taking control of the new church erected in 1849-'50. In 1856, he was succeeded by Rev. Anthony Ciampi, who, after a year's incumbency, gave place to Rev. Thomas Mulledy. In 1858, Rev. Joseph Aschwander returned and remained pastor until his death in 1868. The Rev. Hippolyte Gache entered upon his duties as rector in 1868. He built a pastoral residence near the church, and was followed, two years later, by Rev. Charles H. Stonestreet, who governed the parish until 1874. Next came Rev. John B. DeWolf, who, in 1876 and 1877, made an addition to the church to accommodate the male parochial school, which, for several years, had occupied premises opposite. The Rev. John J. Murphy, S.J., succeeded DeWolf in 1877. The pastors

103

of Trinity Church lived at Georgetown College until the Rev. Mr. Gache built the pastoral residence. They have all been men of distinction. Lately the Rev. John J. Murphy resigned his charge of the church, and the Rev. Anthony Ciampi has again returned to preside over the congregation.

PRESBYTERIAN CHURCH.

[History prepared from the records of the church, by Rev. R.T. Berry, pastor, September 8, 1848.]

"According to the inscription on the tablet, on the right as you enter the north door of this edifice, the gospel was first planted in this town, and this church was founded, by the Rev. Stephen Bloomer Balch, D.D., who was for fifty-two years its revered pastor, and whose remains lie beneath the tablet alluded to. As the history of this congregation is identified with that of this venerable and venerated name, it is natural that I should present a succinct biographical sketch of the leading events of his life.

"Doctor Balch was born in Harford County, Maryland, April 7, 1746. In the fall of 1772, he became a student of Princeton College, then under the superintendence of the distinguished John Witherspoon, D.D., one of the signers of the Declaration of Independence. Dr. Balch graduated in 1774, and went to Lower Marlborough, Calvert County, Maryland, to take charge of an academy. There he remained till 1778, when he visited the State of Georgia, where he studied divinity. In 1780 he was licensed to preach (and probably ordained at the same time as an evangelist, for he was commissioned by the presbytery to travel as a missionary as far north as Georgetown, then in the State of Maryland.) Here he commenced his ministerial labors; and soon after his location here he opened a classical school, which he taught, with eminent success, a considerable portion of his life. And here I think it worth while to remark, to the credit of your Presbyterian fathers, that they were not only the pioneers of religion, but of education. This community is under great obligation to the Presbyterian church for having provided, from its earliest settlement, the means of a liberal education for its sons.

"I am under the impression that, from the time of the

104

establishment of this first academy, under Dr. Balch, down to the period of the lamented death of the late Rev. James McVean, there has always existed here a school or academy of a high order under the care of a Presbyterian minister: first under Dr. Balch, then under the Rev. David Wiley, who was succeeded by Rev. Dr. James Carnahan, president of Nassau Hall, who was followed by Rev. James McVean.

"According to tradition, Dr. Balch preached his first sermon in a little log building on High Street, which stood on the site of the Lutheran burying ground. The burying ground still remains, but the building has long since disappeared. If this tradition be correct, it would seem that this Lutheran church had been in existence when Dr. Balch first came to this place. When it was established, or by whom, I have no means of knowing; if before Dr. Balch came, it seems to lave had no existence as an organized church at that time nor since.

"Subsequently, he is said to have preached for awhile in a small wooden building, which was used as a schoolhouse in the week and as a church on Sundays. It stood at the corner of Bridge and Market Streets, nearly opposite the market place. It is presumed that the number of his hearers must leave continued to increase, and it is probable the congregation began to assume something of a settled form soon after this, for we find, according to the tablet in front of this building, that as early as 1782 a church edifice was erected on the site of the present one, which was a small room about thirty feet square. As the congregation increased it became necessary to enlarge the building, which was done by extending the north front. This occurred in 1793. Soon after the removal of the seat of Government to Washington, or about the years 1801-'2, considerable accessions were made to the congregation, and it was necessary still further to enlarge the church edifice, which was done under the immediate superintendence of Dr. Balch. This second enlargement was made by extending it on the west side. This appears from an old plat of the pews still in existence. To this improvement, among others, Mr. Jefferson, then President of the United States, and Albert Gallatin, the Secretary of the Treasury, subscribed. Mr. Jefferson's subscription was seventy-five dollars. I believe at that time it was customary for the officers of the Government, when they went to church, to attend at this place. General Washington is said to have come from *Mount Vernon* on one occasion to attend divine service in this church. For some time it was the church of the District this side of the Potomac; all denominations attended here. Methodists, Episcopalians, and others, as well as the Presbyterians, received the word of God at the mouth of the Presbyterian pastor, and communed together at the same altar. Such was the liberality that prevailed in those days. About the years 1819-'20, the building being still found insufficient to accommodate all who desired to rent pews, and owing to the additions which had been already made, it not being deemed safe, it was determined to pull it down and erect another. This determination was carried into effect in 1821, in the erection of the present spacious, elegant, and substantial structure, which has recently been put into a state of repair without incurring any debt therefor. The repairs of the interior of the church were made by the contributions and zealous efforts of the ladies of the congregation.

"Up to the period of the second addition to the church, or about the year 1805, Dr. Balch was the only Protestant minister in this place. All denominations of Christians attended upon his ministry, for he was universally respected, and enjoyed the confidence of the whole community. This he did without sacrificing what he believed to be truth and duty, or compromising his principles as a Presbyterian minister. He felt, as all true ministers of Jesus Christ should feel, that he was the minister of God to all men for good, and not merely to his own flock. For many years he baptized, married, instructed, attended the dying, and performed the sad rites of sepulture to the whole community.

"After 'serving his generation by the will of God,' be calmly fell asleep, in the eighty-seventh year of his life, September 22, 1833, gathered 'as a shock of corn cometh in its season.'

"I shall now proceed to notice such other incidents in the history of the church and congregation as are of general interest.

"It has been already intimated that the congregation in its

beginning was small, consisting, it is said, of not more than ten members; but it was composed of the most respectable, intelligent, and worthy citizens of the community, who were not only the fathers of this church, but also the fathers of this town. They were, for the most part, of Scotch, German, and New England extraction.

"The corporation was not incorporated till 1806. Up to that time, it appears its temporal affairs were managed by a standing committee of the members appointed for that purpose; at least, this appears to have been the case as early as 1802.

"By certain deeds of that date, the property of the grave-yard and adjoining lots was conveyed to 'Rev. S.B. Balch, pastor, and Thomas Corcoran, George Thompson, William Whann, Jas. Melvin, John Cruikshank, James Calder, Christian Kurtz, John Peter, David English, and Henry Knowles, members of the Presbyterian congregation of Georgetown, for the exclusive use of the Presbyterian Church in Georgetown, adhering to the confession of faith of the Presbyterian Church in the United States of America, and to her Presbyteries, synods, and general assemblies.'

"I have not seen the deed for the lot on which this church stands, but it is probable that it contained a similar condition; so that it would seem that the title of this congregation to the property held by it depends upon their I adhering to the confession of faith of the Presbyterian Church in the United States of America, and to her Presbyteries, synods, and general assemblies.'

"In 1806, the trustees of the congregation were incorporated by act of Congress; they were Stephen B. Balch, William Whann, James Melvin, John Maffit, John Peter, Joshua Dawson, James Calder, Geo. Thompson, Richard Elliott, David Wiley, and Andrew Ross.

"To show the changes which the congregation has undergone, I find that of those who are recorded as having been pew holders from 1805 to 1808, all are dead or removed, as far as I can learn, but three. Of those recorded as pew holders in 1822, one year after the present edifice was erected, all are dead or removed but fifteen.[1] From this period on to 1827, the congregation seems to have been greatly weakened by deaths, and removals from town caused by the continued decline in the business of the place, and other causes; so that, in October, 1823, according to a statement of that date found among the papers, there were thirty-four pews and five half pews reported as vacant; and in 1827, as appears by a report male to the board of trustees, by Daniel Bussard, the collector, that from 'removals by death, and otherwise,' the funds of the trustees from pew rents were lessened by the amount of four hundred and forty dollars per annum. The prosperity of the congregation subsequently revived; but these changes in the materiel of the congregation have continued to take place up to this time. Since my connection with it as a pastor, at least one-third if not one-half of the congregation have changed—that is, at least one-third have been removed by death or emigration, and that in the space of about nine years. But, while many have thus been removed, others have come in to take their places, so that the congregation has been enabled to hold its own. And, as far as I can gather from its past history, the congregation is about as numerous and prosperous now as it has been, upon an average, at any period since the present edifice was erected, for I find there never has been a period since its erection when it was filled. Ever since it was built, the house has been too large for the congregation, and this has been a great disadvantage every way. All are now agreed that a great mistake was committed in erecting so large a building in so small a community, divided as it is into so many different denominations, all provided with places of public worship. I believe this house would accommodate pretty comfortably all the church-going people in this place. It is true, that when the plan of this edifice was projected, this congregation was at the height of its prosperity, and the town was prosperous and promised to increase. Moreover, the old church was not sufficient to accommodate all who at that time wished to rent pews in it, and these

---

1. After that date ninety-five were recorded as pew holders.

considerations no doubt led your fathers to plan this building on so extensive a scale. But it was to be regretted on another account: the estimated cost of the building was twenty thousand dollars, a burden which, as the result showed, was greater than the congregation was able to bear, for the walls were scarcely up before the building committee had to borrow money to carry on the building. This and subsequent loans laid the foundation of a debt, under the weight of which the church long staggered, and from which it has been entirely relieved, owing, in great part, to the liberality of its creditors, and the exertion of the Rev. John C. Smith, the late pastor, only within a few years past. Such debt rested as an incubus on the congregation, and was the occasion of the most disastrous consequences to its prosperity, and, indeed, jeoparded at one time its very existence, for, in 1823, a deed of trust, I find, was actually given on all its property to secure the payment of its debts; a most painful and humiliating sacrifice indeed, but an act of justice for which it deserved all honor, for churches, like individuals, should 'owe no man anything'. I allude particularly to this part of the history of the congregation first, as explaining much of the adversity and difficulties with which it has had to contend with; and, second, as a warning against church debts, which have been well termed church curses.

"Another cause which, doubtless, tended to weaken this congregation, and retard its growth in times past, is found in the fact that the several denominations of Christians who, in the early history of the church were identified with it, and united in its support, at different periods, erected houses of worship for themselves, and, of course, retired from this congregation; thus, in 1805, the first Episcopal Church, St. John's, was erected; and it may be mentioned, as a pleasing evidence of the liberality and good feeling that prevailed at that day, that Dr. Balch not only encouraged the enterprise, but contributed, along with other Presbyterians, to its funds; and this was but right, as the Episcopalians had contributed heretofore to the Presbyterian Church. In 1818, the second Episcopal Church, Christ Church, was erected. And here it ought to be mentioned, as an additional evidence of the liberality and good feeling of those times, that

109

these two congregations courteously tendered the use of their respective churches to each other while their's were being erected; and I find that the pastor of that church united with Dr. Balch in the dedication services of this. I will also add that at one time all the pastors and their people were in the habit of holding a union prayer meeting in their respective churches, where they mingled, in christian fellowship and catholic communion; their prayers and praises at the altar of the author of their "common salvation." In 1828, the Methodist Protestant Church was organized, and their organization took place in this church. The use of this church was also tendered to the Methodist Episcopal Church while the present edifice was in process of erection. Indeed, the Presbyterian Church here may be considered in some sort the "mother church" of this community, for it preceded all others in point of time; and while the others were without houses of their own, they found a welcome asylum here, and enjoyed here the ordinances and ministrations of God's house. It appears, from this history, that the Presbyterian Church here has ever pursued none other than a liberal course of conduct towards her younger sisters of other denominations, and in this it has but acted in the liberal spirit of its Catholic principles towards other bodies of christians.

"Of the church proper—that is, the communicants—I have but little to say, for the records of the church session were consumed when the house of Dr. Balch was burnt; the present records go no further back than 1831. Tradition has it that the church was organized about the latter part of 1780; and at the first communion that was celebrated, there were but seven members with the pastor. It seems that for a longtime there was but one ruling elder, viz., James Orme, who was the son of the Rev. John Orme, formerly the pastor of the Presbyterian Church of Upper Marlborough, Maryland, which is now extinct. Those who were ruling elders in this church, besides, at different periods, but who are now deceased, were John Peter, James Melvin, John Craven, John McDaniel, Robert Munro, John S. Nevins, William Williamson, Samuel Hawley, and James McVean.

"The present number of communicants is one hundred and

110

seven, and about seventy families. To show the changes that have taken place in the last nine years, there leave been added during that period upwards of sixty to the communion of the church, while rather more than that number have died or removed; none have apostatized. Well may we ask, in view of these changes—

'Your fathers, where are they ?
The prophets, do they live forever?'

"Having finished our inquiries about your fathers, we return upon our path, and ask a little further of the prophets who have spoken unto you here the word of God. This church has existed sixty-six years; and during that period it has had but three installed pastors: Dr. Balch, who presided fifty-two years; Reverend J.C. Smith, who presided about seven years;[1] and the present incumbent, about nine years.[2] Reverend T.B. Balch assisted his father as minister for awhile. In 1822, Reverend R.R. Gurley was invited as an assistant minister, and, in 1828, Reverend John N. Campbell, now of Albany. Reverend Dr. Cox was invited, in 1829, to become assistant pastor, but did not accept the call. I ought, also, to mention that, about the time, or soon after the building of this edifice, an unhappy schism occurred in the church—the only one, I believe, that ever afflicted it. A few—but those some of the most respectable members—withdrew, under the lead of a Rev. Mr. Baldwin. They worshiped for a time in the Lancasterian schoolroom, but failing in their effort to organize another church, after awhile they melted away.

"It ought also to be mentioned, as a part of the history of the church, that during the years 1837-'38 it was agitated and distracted not a little by the doctrinal and ecclesiastical questions which occasioned the schism which occurred in the Presbyterian body at that period, and which resulted in the secession from the Presbyterian church in the United States of America of a considerable number of its ministers and members. But this

---

1. From 1831 to 1838.
2. From 1838 to 1848.

congregation wisely and happily determined, to use the language of the deed which I have recited, to adhere, as there forefathers did, to the confession of faith of the Presbyterian church in the United States of America, and to her presbyteries, synods and general assemblies, with which it had been in communion for half a century; concluding very justly that it was best 'not to meddle with them that are given to change,' and that, 'no man having drunk old wine straightway desireth new; for, saith he, the old is far better.'"

APPENDIX.

"A.—Extract from journal of board of trustees:

"June 11, 1806.—A report being made of .the expenses incurred in the improvement of the church, and a deficiency appearing, *Ordered*, That the members individually take the subscription, and get any further moneys; and that Messrs. Maffit and Elliott be a committee to superintend the repairing the roof and the removal of the pulpit; Messrs. Ross and Elliott a committee to have the plastering measured, and Mr. Peter to contract for the washing and cleaning the church.

"August, 1806.—William Whann, collector of the grave-yard, offered to advance the money for the painting of the church, to be reimbursed from the funds of the grave-yard, to be retained by him as collector. Agreed to by the board. Messrs. Ross and Melvin, appointed the committee to superintend the painting. Mr. Melvin proposed, in conjunction with Mr. Balch and Mr. Ross, to erect a new pulpit, not to cost more than fifty dollars, provided the Sunday collections were pledged for that purpose. Agreed to.

"April 11, 1807.—Messrs. Elliott and Wiley appointed a committee to get the roof of the church made tight and have tables and benches made for the communion. Funds of the grave-yard pledged to Mr. Whann for the money advanced. Mr. McDaniel appointed to collect the pew rents. He and Mr. Elliott a committee to get doors put on the pews, and draw on Mr. Whann for the money.

"James Calder, David English, Jonathan Finley, Eleanor Curlan, William Knowles, Benjamin Betterton, Clephan & Makie, Joseph Wheaton, Mrs. Templeman, Alexander Carmichael, William King, John Baltzer, William Thompson, Jasper M. Jackson, Christian Kurtz, John Banks, Sarah Cruikshanks, Nathan Loughboro', Francis Clarke, Robert Ober, Nicholas Hedges, Richard Elliott, Jeremiah Mosher, John Craven, Daniel Reitzel, Daniel Bussard, Joseph Bromley, John Heugh, Francis Dodge, — Whetzel, Ezekiel King, John Maffit, Andrew Ross, William Crawford, John Laird, Sarah Suter, Edgar Patterson, James A. Morsel, C.P. Polk, Joshua Dawson, George Thompson, Mrs. George French, Thomas Beall (of George), David Peter, John Peter, William Whann, James Melvin, Jane White, Charles Love, James Dunlop, Sr., David Wiley.

"B.—The first movement towards building a new church was made as early as April 21st, 1815, as appears from the following resolution of the board, adopted at that time:

"*Resolved*, That Messrs. Peter, Ross, and McDaniel be a committee to make inquiry respecting an eligible site for a new church, and, also, of the means of obtaining money for the purchase of the same, and report at next meeting.

"This committee reported accordingly at the next meeting, and the report was filed.

"April 3, 1817.—*Resolved*, That Messrs. Peter, English and McDaniel be a committee to ascertain what can be obtained by subscription towards building a new church.

"*Resolved*, That Messrs. Laird, Ross, Whann, and Peter be a committee to consider and report a plan for a new church. This committee reported April 20, 1817, a plan of a building—probable cost twenty thousand dollars.

"The committee, to obtain subscriptions, reported that little progress had been made, and asked further time. On 24th April, 1817, the same committee reported that a sufficient sum could not be obtained, and asked to be discharged. Report adopted. Messrs. English, Peter, and Ross were appointed a committee to keep the subject in view. Messrs. Bussard, McDaniel, and English were appointed a committee to provide pews for the

113

accommodation of applicants.

"April 14, 1819.—A committee appointed to examine the church reported that it was becoming unsafe, and that steps ought to be immediately taken to build a new one.

"June 19, 1819.—Messrs. Thomas B. Beall, Robert Ober, John Kurtz, L.G. Davidson, and John Peter were appointed a committee to obtain subscriptions for a new church.

"July 6, 1819.—Messrs. John Laird, Andrew Ross, Lewis G. Davidson, and J. Kurtz were appointed a building committee, and authorized to contract for the same. They accordingly contracted with William Archer to build a church for twenty thousand dollars.

"Lewis G. Davidson was appointed treasurer of the funds for the erection of the new church in 1821. The subscription having, in a great measure, failed, the building committee were authorized to borrow three thousand dollars to carry on the building. This amount was advanced by John Laird, deceased.

MEMBERS OF THE BOARD OF TRUSTEES IN 1821.

"John Laird, John Peter, William Whann, Daniel Bussard, Andrew Ross, Richard Elliott, David English, James Calder, John McDaniel.

"C.—The Rev. John C. Smith, at that time the pastor, offered to collect funds to extinguish the debt on the church, provided the creditors would relinquish one-half of their claims, to which most of them agreed; and the thanks of the congregation were tendered to Mr. Smith for 'his diligent and successful exertions' in accomplishing the object. The principal creditors were the heirs of John Laird.[1]

MISCELLANEOUS ITEMS.

"Pastor's salary, from 1812 to 1825, was one thousand dollars. In 1825, it was fixed at eight hundred dollars.[2] In 1827, owing to the great falling off of the revenue from pew rents (alluded to in the sermon) at that time, it was reduced to six

---

1. See Journal of the Board, p. 112.
2. See Journal, pages 37 and 90.

hundred dollars.[1] It was subsequently fixed at eight hundred dollars, and has so continued to this time; though, in 1834, the amount available for the payment of the pastor's salary, after paying other expenses, was only six hundred and thirty-two dollars and fifty cents, and the balance had to be made up by voluntary subscription.[2]

TRUSTEES AT THIS TIME (1848).

"David English, Hon. James Dunlop, John Kurtz, Robert Dick, Robert Barnard, William H. Tenney, George Bohrer, Marinus Willet, R.S.T. Cissel.

OFFICERS OF THE CHURCH AT THIS TIME (1848).

"Ruling Elders: David English, Sr., O.Z. Muncaster. Deacons: Jacob Ramsburg, Edward Myers. Until within a few years past this church was without this class of officers, provided for in the constitution of the Presbyterian Church; and it appears that, in the early history of this congregation, the duties of this class of officers were performed by a committee of the trustees.[3]

"There has been, since 1822, and perhaps earlier, a Sunday School connected with the church, which was held, in 1822, in the Lancasterian school-room, as appears from a letter addressed to the trustees, by Miss Russell, in behalf of the teachers, requesting that more comfortable accommodations might be provided for them. Over this school, the late Rev. James McVean presided, with eminent ability and success, for more than twenty-five years. Its present officers are R.S.T. Cissel, superintendent; Samuel H. Howell, secretary; Jacob Ramsburg, treasurer, and William E. Myers, librarian."

If the destruction of any building in our town was to be deplored, it was the tearing down of the old Presbyterian Church, situated at the corner of Washington and Bridge Streets. It was

---

1. See Journal, p. 96.
2. See Journal, p. 110.
3. See Journal, page 13, where, in 1809, Rev. Stephen B. Balch, John McDaniel, and Richard Elliott, were appointed a committee to distribute what funds may be obtained for the relief of the poor, and render their accounts quarterly. There are other entries of subsequent dates to the same effect.

most substantially built; and all the brick and wood-work was in as good state of preservation as when erected in the year 1821. It was a large and noble church, and every way suitable for the worship of any religious congregation. It was one among the principal landmarks, and attracted the attention of all strangers who visited our town, as a noble building. Its destruction is to be regretted, because it was the only church in that section of the town; and since the Methodist Episcopal Congregation had sold their church on Montgomery Street, in 1850, to the town for a public school, a church was more needed in that section of the town than formerly, and the reason of its being originally built there, was to accommodate the citizens of Washington and Georgetown. If the chronicler had been a wealthy citizen, he would have purchased the building and dedicated it for religious worship to any congregation, and to the meeting of the Sabbath School children of our town, where all the schools formerly assembled to celebrate the birthday of American liberty; but as the noble edifice is now gone, the chronicler will here give an account of various articles found in the corner-stone and transferred to the new church on West Street.

The following are the articles found in the cornerstone of Bridge Street Church, and afterwards deposited in the corner-stone of the new church on West Street, laid in 1873:

"Medallion of Washington. Silver quarter of 1820. Two silver ten cent pieces of 1820. Five one dollar silver pieces of 1818; and one of 1820.

"Statement of the number of inhabitants of Georgetown and Washington: Georgetown, in 1800, two thousand nine hundred and ninety-three; in 1810, four thousand nine hundred and forty-eight; in 1820, seven thousand five hundred and nineteen. Washington, in 1800, three thousand two hundred and ten; in 1810, eight thousand two hundred and eight; in 1820, thirteen thousand four hundred and seventy-four. Total number of inhabitants of the District in 1820, thirty-three thousand five hundred and eighty-nine.

"Forty years have passed and gone, and but few tongues now remain to tell, that on this lot of ground a small building was erected for the worship of the true and living God, being the first

116

raised in this town.

"The Rev. Stephen Bloomer Balch setting out to labor in the vineyard of the Master, was directed to this people, then not more than fifteen in number, who called for his services, and the congregation was organized in connection with the General Assembly of the Presbyterian Church in the United States. At the first celebration of the Lord's Supper in this house, seven persons only made a public profession of the Lord Jesus Christ. By this ambassador of Christ, the message of reconciliation was preached, and thence forward proclaimed with silent success, and the visible members of the church militant have greatly increased in number.

"The congregation at the present time (1821) numbers eighty families, and one hundred and nine communicants. They continued under the pastoral care of the Reverend Stephen B. Balch, D.D., assisted by David English, John McDaniel, and Robert Ober, ruling elders.

"On the 28th day of March, A.D. 1806, the Congress of the United States passed an act incorporating nine persons, under the style and title of the 'Trustees of the Presbyterian Congregation in Georgetown, D.C.,' to whom John Laird, Andrew Ross, John Peter, William Whann, Richard Elliott, James Calder, David English, Daniel Bussard, and John McDaniel, are now successors.

"To the original building small additions were made, which, being found insufficient for the convenient accommodation of those who attended as worshipers, and, withal, fast falling to ruin and decay, it was determined in general meeting of the congregation that a suitable house should be erected in its place by means of voluntary subscriptions. The erection of the contemplated new building was committed by the trustees solely to John Laird, Andrew Ross, Lewis Grant Davidson, John Kurtz, and Francis Dodge, commissioners, who chose William Archer as their architect."

A silver plate, with the following inscription carved upon it, was deposited in the corner-stone of the Presbyterian Church, laid April 6, 1821:

"This corner-stone of the Presbyterian Church was laid on

117

the 6th day of April, 1821, Anno Mundi 5821, and in the forty-fifth year of the Independence of the United States of America, by William Hewitt, M.W.G.M. of Freemasons in the District of Columbia; James Monroe, President of the United States; John Peter, Mayor of Georgetown, District of Columbia; Rev. Stephen B. Balch, pastor; David English, John McDaniel, Robert Ober, ruling elders; John Laird, Andrew Ross, John Kurtz, Lewis G. Davidson, Francis Dodge, commissioners for erecting the building."

A silver plate, with the following, was deposited in the cornerstone of West Street Church with contents of the old stone:

"Building moved from corner of Bridge and Washington Streets to this place June, 1873. U.S. Grant, President of the United States; Henry D. Cooke, Governor of the District of Columbia; S.H. Howe, pastor; George W. Beall, B.R. Mayfield, C.F. Peck, A. Young, W.H. Dougal, J. Ramsburg, S.H. Howell, elders; J.S. Blackford, Joseph Williamson, C.S. Ramsburg, deacons; W.H. Dougal, F.L. Moore, W.W. Winship, M.V. Buckey, W.W. Curtis, R. Brace, Thomas Harrison, C.M. McGowan, James Goddard, trustees."

ST. JOHN'S EPISCOPAL CHURCH.

[A historical account of the church, by Rev. C.M. Butler, rector, October 17, 1843.]

"The Lord hath done great things for us, whereof we are glad."—

PSALM cxxvi, 3.

"This grateful exclamation of the Psalmist, my brethren, becomes us on this occasion. After more than four months intermission of our services, we are permitted, by the good providence of God, to meet again as a congregation in our enlarged, improved, and beautified edifice.

"Gratitude to God that he has enabled us to bring this good work to completion, should fill our hearts. To the zeal of the vestry, who, feeling the. necessity of larger accommodations for the stability and support of the church and for the spiritual wants of the community, suggested the enlargement of the building to the congregation; to the ready response of the congregation to the appeal of the vestry, with a large, Christian, self-denying liberality worthy of all commendation, manifested by a subscription for the object which, taking into consideration the number and means of the contributors, is seldom equaled in amount—to the skill of the gentleman[1] who furnished the plan for the enlargement of the building; to the liberality and labor of the ladies of the congregation, who procured and prepared the furniture of the pulpit, desk and chancel; to the unwearied and faithful diligence of the building committee,[2] and, I may add, to the successful efforts of the builder[3] to render the edifice complete and commodious—to these, under God, do we owe it, that we are permitted to meet this morning, none of our number lost by death, in our pleasant and beautified sanctuary, hallowed by many sacred associations, and to realize 'how amiable are thy tabernacles, thou Lord of Hosts!' Brethren, if our love be as large as our mercies, and our lives express in any good degree the gratitude which we owe, we shall be a devoted people.

"A sketch of the history of this church will show that the Lord hath indeed done great things for us, whereof it becomes us to be glad!

"The records in possession of the church of its past history are very few and imperfect. Such as remain have been collected with great care, and re-written with much labor by a member of the vestry,[4] to whose zeal and industry I am indebted for fair copies of every remaining paper having reference to the history of the church which is in its possession. Instead of the connected and minute detail which would he interesting if it were in my power to furnish it, I can give but scattered and unconnected notices of the past history of the church, gathered

---

1. Captain George F. De la Roche, engineer and draughtsman in the Navy Department.
2. Messrs. L. Thomas, A.H. Marbury, and John Waters.
3. Matthias Duffey, contractor.
4. Mr. John H. Offley. Besides the papers here referred to, others, it is believed, are in existence; and it is much to be regretted that the efforts made to procure them have failed, as they are supposed to be most interesting.

from those incomplete records which remain, and from conversation with the Reverend Mr. Addison, for many years the respected rector of the parish, and with some of the older citizens of the place.

"It is a pleasing circumstance with which to commence our reminiscences, that the first movement towards establishing an Episcopal Church in this place was made by the Reverend Mr. Addison, with the concurrence and assistance of the Reverend Dr. Balch, a Presbyterian clergyman, whose memory is still warmly cherished in this community. The Reverend Mr. Addison was at that time settled in the parish of Broad Creek, Prince George's County, opposite Alexandria. Hearing that there were some Episcopal families in this place, he paid it a visit; was invited by Dr. Balch to hold an Episcopal service in his church, and encouraged by him to endeavor to organize an Episcopal congregation. This incident is in perfect accordance with the character which this venerated man left behind him for Christian kindness and liberality. Mr. Addison continued to visit the place and to hold services occasionally during the years 1794 and 1795. In the summer of 1796, the first effort, of which any record remains, was made to organize a congregation and build a church. Whether a board of trustees or a vestry was organized or not, does not appear. The only record we possess of this effort is a list of subscribers, whose contributions were to be applied 'to building the walls and covering in a Protestant Episcopal Church in Georgetown.' This paper is dated August, 1796, and contains one hundred and twelve names, whose contributions, varying from one dollar to one hundred dollars, amount, collectively, to fifteen hundred dollars. A lot for the church (the one now occupied) was given by Colonel William Deakins. The subscription list is preceded by the promise to pay the amount subscribed, for the purpose of building a Protestant Episcopal Church in the lot in Beatty and Hawkins' addition to Georgetown.' From this expression it appears that this location was at that time beyond the limits of the town proper. The memory of one of our oldest citizens refers the chief agency in this movement to Mr. William Dorsey and Mr. Plater. From causes which do not appear, but which may be conjectured to have been the difficulty of raising a sufficient amount of money, the building which was commenced at that time was carried up only to the first range of windows, and remained in this situation until the year 1803. During this period the Reverend Mr. Addison held occasional services in this place, though with little encouragement to his hopes of completing the building.

"The next record of which we are in possession is of a meeting of the citizens of Georgetown, in January, 1803, to take measures for renewing the effort to build an Episcopal Church. The minutes of this meeting commence as follows: 'At a meeting of a number of the inhabitants of Georgetown, at Mr. Semmes' , on Friday evening, 28th January, pursuant to a notice in the *Washington Federalist*, for the purpose of adopting regulations for building a Protestant Episcopal Church, Walter S. Chandler, Charles Worthington, and Walter Smith, were appointed a committee to inquire into the situation of the building commenced for that purpose, and to examine into the state of the accounts relative thereto, and to judge of the propriety of completing the same, or to purchase ground in any other part of the town, in their opinion most appropriate; to solicit subscriptions therefor, and to make all such contracts and agreements as may be requisite for carrying into effect the object proposed.' The committee were instructed by resolution to appoint a treasurer, and to proceed to build a church as soon as sufficient funds for the object could be obtained. There are recorded the names of one hundred and fifty-four subscribers, whose subscriptions amount to twenty-five hundred dollars. Among the subscribers is found the name of Thomas Jefferson. The name of the Reverend Dr. Balch also appears as a subscriber. Another record states the whole amount of the subscriptions to have been four thousand two hundred and forty-five dollars. Consequently, aid from other sources and contributors than those which appear on the remaining list must have been received. That difficulties occurred in obtaining the amount required is manifest from a letter addressed by the Rev. Mr. Rattoone, associate rector of St. Paul's Church, Baltimore, on behalf of the trustees of this church, to the vestry of Trinity Church, New York. The letter gives us an idea of the

121

difficulties they had to encounter, and the importance of the enterprise, not only in reference to the spiritual interests of Georgetown, but of Washington also.

"At that period there was no other church at Washington than Christ Church at the Navy Yard. A part of the letter is here given:

"'To the rector and vestry of Trinity Church, N.Y.

"'GENTLEMEN: Having perused a memorial from the trustees of the church at Georgetown, at their request I am induced to certify that the statement they have given is perfectly correct. The exertions they have made, the difficulties they have encountered, and the great importance of the Episcopal Church taking a primary and superior lead, where at the seat of Government they are so divided, are considerations which I have no doubt will have their due weight when you shall take into view the facts they have stated. I should regret that from the very small number of Episcopalians residing in this place, and from the great sacrifices they have made to accommodate the poorer classes of the same society, they should not be able to complete the church, and form the most respectable establishment.

"'As Trinity parish gave so liberally to the church established at Albany, under the idea of that place being made the seat of the State government, I am induced to hope, as no evil can result from the precedent, that they will extend their liberality likewise to the permanent seat of the General Government. It may tend greatly to restore order, to diffuse the principles of equal and just liberty, and to establish, with honor and distinction, a house of public worship, where the doctrines, discipline, and worship of the Protestant Episcopal Church may be taught in purity, and from this center of the Union be widely diffused throughout the United States.'

"Whether this appeal to Trinity Church was successful, does not appear. The building was commenced, covered in, and sufficiently finished for the celebration of public worship.

"Early in 1804, the trustees[1] advertised their want of a rector. In March they were visited by the Rev. Mr. Sayrs, of Port Tobacco parish. A meeting of the pew holders was held in April, at which be was elected rector, and the trustees directed to inform him of his election. He appears at once to have entered upon his labors. In May, 1806, there was a call upon the pew holders for one year's rent, or a sum equal thereto, to *finish* the church. It is this call which leads me to infer, that at the first occupancy of the church, it was not completed, but only made sufficiently comfortable to be occupied in 1804 and 1805. The church appears to have been in a prosperous state until the death of the rector in 1809. Few are now living here who have distinct recollections of this excellent man, but those few unite in paying a sincere tribute to his memory. A scholar, a pleasing speaker, a pious and humble minister, he was well qualified for usefulness in the then important position which he occupied. The character given of him in conversation by that lamented and distinguished man, Francis S. Key, Esq., by whose Mr. Sayrs' epitaph was written, impressed my mind with a deep respect for his memory.

"The marble which commemorates his fidelity, restored by the pious care of the vestry of the church to a position which enables him being dead yet to speak, serves to remind its alike of the good example of him whose ashes sleep beneath, and of him, his parishioner and friend, whose affectionate and devoted spirit yet lives in the epitaph, whose words fall on the ear and on the heart with so sweet and solemn cadence! That marble also serves to preach to the preacher, as he stands in this place, an earnest exhortation, which seems to issue from the tomb, 'Whatsoever thy hand findeth to do, do it with thy might, for there is no work, nor device, nor knowledge, nor wisdom in the grave whither thou goest!' Oh! may all who speak in this place, reminded by that silent monitor, speak as in view of the hour of death, and of the day of judgment. 'Storied urn and animated

---

1. It appears from one of the papers, that the following gentlemen composed a board of trustees, viz: William H. Dorsey, Charles Worthington, Thomas Corcoran, Walter S. Chandler, and Walter Smith. Thomas Corcoran and Walter Smith acted as treasurers.

bust' may bear flattering memorials of the worth, and fame, and honor of the children of the world; but when truth guides the hand that writes the epitaph, no higher eulogy can be traced over the resting-place of man than this, that

> `He lived and died an humble minister
> Of God's benignant purposes to man.'

"In January, 1809,[1] the Rev. Walter Addison was called to and accepted the rectorship of this church. At that time the church was as largely attended from Washington as from Georgetown, there being still no other church at Washington but Christ Church at the Navy Yard.

"The memories of some of our older citizens recall the crowded attendance upon the services of this church at that period. No other records are possessed than those of the names of the vestry, and of the ordinary business transactions of that body, until the year 1811. That the church was in a most prosperous condition at that period, at least in reference to its external affairs, appears from a resolution of the vestry dated January 11, 1811.[2]

"On motion, *Resolved*, 'That it is expedient to enlarge the church, and that a committee be appointed to solicit subscriptions; and that Mr. Gozler be requested to furnish a plan for the said addition to be built, together with his estimate of the probable cost thereof.' The plan failed, as we have been informed, from the double difficulty of raising the means, and of making the pew holders satisfied with holding the same pews, relatively more distant from the pulpit than before, at the same valuation. The incident shows how, even in a Christian congregation, little and selfish considerations sometimes oppose themselves to, and prevent great and permanent measures of improvement. We cannot but contrast that unsuccessful effort

---

1. Vestry in 1807—Charles Worthington, W. Bowie, T. Corcoran, J. Mason, T. Plater, B. Mackall, P.B. Key and William Stewart.
2. Vestry alluded to were T. Corcoran, treasurer; J. Abbot, secretary; T. Peter, J. Goszler, L.H. Johns, R. Beverly, T. Hyde, F.S. Key, C. Smith and J. Kennedy, wardens.

for enlargement with the one in whose success we rejoice to-day, using the language of David, to express our joyful gratitude,
`The Lord hath done great things for us, whereof we are glad.'
At that time the church was thronged to an overflow with all who were most elevated in station and in wealth from the capital; the pews in the gallery were rented at high rates, and to persons of great respectability; the street before the door of the church was filled with glittering vehicles, and liveried servants; and yet, because means could not be raised for the enlargement, and a miserable selfishness could not be made to relinquish anything for the sake of extending the privileges of God's house, the enterprise was abandoned. Now, with a much smaller and humbler congregation, on whom heavy burdens have rested ever since the re-opening of the church, not largely blessed, or shall we say cursed, with this world's wealth, but, as their deeds have shown, rich in faith, with but little aid from without the congregation, the means for the enlargement of the church have been raised, and the work has not been prevented by the obtrusion of selfish and secondary considerations, and to-day we rejoice in its completion. The contrast strikingly teaches us to whom we *are*, and are *not*, to look for the extension of Christ's kingdom, and the honor of his name. I should do violence to my feelings if h did not here express my sense of the noble and Christian liberality of the little flock among whom it is my happiness to minister. Looking above the human instruments to Him who put it in their hearts to do honor to his name, to Him alone would I give the glory, and say, in the grateful language of the Psalmist—
'The Lord hath done great things for us, whereof we are glad.'

"From this period until the year 1817[1], the church continued in operation with but a moderate measure of temporal or spiritual prosperity. It appears, from a resolution of the vestry, that the Rev. Mr. Addison tendered his resignation of the parish, and that

---

1. Vestry in 1817—F.S. Key, T. Hyde, L.H. Johns, W. Bowie, C. Worthington, C. Smith, T. Corcoran and J. Abbot; J. Howe and T.G. Waters, wardens. At a meeting of the vestry, Messrs. Bowie, Corcoran and Abbot were appointed a committee 'to adopt such measures as they may deem proper to enlarge the church.'

this resignation was accepted and acted upon by the vestry.

"The resolution was in these words: *Resolved*, 'That a rector of St. John's Church be appointed on Wednesday, 30th of April, 1817, to supply the vacancy occasioned by the resignation of the Rev. Walter Addison.' Mr. Addison's resignation, however, did not take effect, and the vestry furnished him with an assistant. At a meeting of the vestry May, 13th, 1817, we find this resolution: *Resolved*, 'That the Reverend Ruel Keith be appointed the assistant minister of this church for one year.' On the 26th of April, 1818, there is again a record, 'That the Rev. Mr. Addison was unanimously appointed rector of this church.' At this time, the congregation of Christ Church was organized, and the Rev. Mr. Keith chosen rector of the church. From this period St. John's Church continued in a feeble and declining condition. In 1821, the Rev. Mr. Addison resigned the rectorship of the church, under the conviction that his usefulness had been much diminished, and that the parish might prosper better in other hands. He then took charge of Rock Creek Church and Addison Chapel, near Bladensburg, and was succeeded in the rectorship of St. John's by the Rev. Stephen S. Tyng. Mr. Tyng remained in the parish from April, 1821, to April, 1823. There were but eleven families connected with the church when he assumed the charge of it, and when he left, the number had increased to thirty-three. Mr. Tyng resigned the parish in 1823, and removed to Queen's Parish, Anne Arundel County, Maryland. Mr. Addison was recalled in 1823 and continued the settled minister of the parish till 1827. During this period he was much afflicted with weakness of the eyes, which in the end became perfect blindness. Unable under this affliction, to continue his services effectively, he resigned the charge again in 1827. He was succeeded by the Rev. Sutherland Douglass, who had charge of the parish about the same length of time. After the church had ceased to have a settled rector, the Rev. Mr. Addison, though perfectly blind, continued to hold an occasional service in the church till 1831, when it was finally abandoned.[1] *Abandoned*, did I say? If *this* had been all, it would have been comparatively well. Had it remained only open and deserted, so as not inappropriately to have borne the title of 'The Swallow Barn,'[2] by which name I hear it was often called, even in such a deserted and neglected state, it would not have been altogether divested of sacred associations. As the pious member of the church passed by the desolated house of God, where himself or his fathers worshiped, he might then have applied to it, with something of mournfulness, the plaintive language of the Psalmist: 'The sparrow hath found her an house, and the swallow a nest, where she may lay her young, even thy altars and thy tabernacles, O Lord of hosts, my King and my God!' But, a feeling of holy indignation, or of conscious shame, must, I think, have filled his heart, when he saw it given up as a workshop of a sculpture! Yes, in this Christian community, a Christian temple was allowed to undergo the most shameful desecration, and they who had worshiped under its roof, and gathered about its sacred board, or in it been dedicated to God by baptism, passed it by, and saw the statues of heathen gods and goddesses as a sign at its portico, and heard the chiselings of the workmen, where the voice of prayer and praise was wont for years to rise[3] and they suffered it to be so! I know not on whose heads the censure falls, but I should be unfaithful to my duty as an annalist, and a minister of Christ, if I did not designate such gross indifference to God's house as inexcusable and disgraceful. If, which God in his mercy avert, these walls should ever again be deserted and left without worshipers, may there be, at least, such a decree of godly jealousy for the honor of God's house left among you, brethren who may linger last about its forsaken altar, as will lead

---

1. Vestry at this time: Dr. Charles Worthington, Gen. John Mason, Messrs. G.B. Magruder, Thomas Peter, John Goszler, Clement Cox, Charles G. Wilcox, William Stewart, William Good, and Richard Davis, wardens; F. Lowndes, register.
2. The church occupied at present long remained in an unfinished condition. Birds used to build their nests in it, and the Reverend Thomas B. Balch, then a boy, and his companions used to clamber up its walls. This was about the year 1800.
3. The building was, at this time, occupied as a studio by Mr. Petrich, the sculptor.

you to level the edifice to the dust, rather than that it should again be subjected to such wanton desecration!

"In the r apid sketch of the history of this church, up to the period of its abandonment in 1831, names have been mentioned as identified with its fortunes which, no doubt, have called up many associations in the minds of some of those who hear me. Of the laity who were active in its organization, few remain among us. Of the clergymen who have been connected with this church, some remain to this present, but others are fallen asleep. We have already spoken of him whose ashes sleep beneath this edifice. The name of the lamented Dr. Keith will call up fresher recollections. The impression stamped by that earnest and gifted man oil this community will not soon be effaced. Alas! that the light which was so bright in its dawning and meridian, should have been so clouded at its setting. But let us remember that the sun, whose parting rays are so obstructed that they do not meet the eye, is, in itself, no less radiant, and departs in darkness from one horizon, to shine with more than its morning and meridian brightness in other climes. The Rev. Mr. Tyng is occupying a position of great responsibility, and exercising a ministry of eminent usefulness, in the city of Philadelphia. The Rev. Mr. James was successively an assistant of Bishop White, in Christ Church, and his successor in the rectorship. He died soon after Bishop White, deeply regretted, not only by his congregation, but by the church at large. The Reverend Sutherland Douglass breathed forth his ardent and zealous spirit in a foreign land, where he had gone with the hope of restoration to health, 'by strangers honored, and by strangers mourned.' The venerable Mr. Addison is still living. Afflicted for many years with blindness, this truly humble and pious man has exhibited a meek and patient spirit, which gives evidence that the eye of his soul is open, and is fixed on Christ. 'Patient waiting for Christ,' are words which well describe his condition. Looking upon the venerable man, with his hoary head and placid countenance, which bears the marks of chastening, but not of tumult or discontent, his presence seemed to breathe forth the eloquent but unrepining complaint of the blind bard of Paradise:

128

'Not to me returns
Day, nor the sweet reproach of even or morn,
Or sight of vernal bloom or summer rose,
Or flocks, or herds, or human face divine;—
But clouds instead, and ever during dark
Surround me, from the cheerful rays of men
Cut off, and for the book of knowledge fair,
Presented with an universal blank
Of nature's works, to me expunged and razed,
And wisdom at one entrance quite shut out.'

"Ah! brethren, these churches, thus bearing on their silent walls the associations of the past, preaching to us the changes and chances of this mortal life, admonish us, with an eloquence more than human, to prepare for that eternal world towards which change and chance inevitably impel us all!

"Time allows me to give but a rapid sketch of the restoration of the church to the holy purposes for which it was established. It is less needful to be done, because, having been of recent occurrence, the circumstances of that history are familiar to those who hear me. With whatever indifference the desecration of the church may have been generally regarded, there was one o whom, as he passed it in his daily walk, it was a pain and grief.[1] It became a subject of conversation among his family and friends. The idea of restoring it was suggested. The Rev. Mr. Peterkin, to whose early zeal and activity in its behalf this church is much indebted, gave of his means, as well as his services, to the object. A zealous lady, to whose activity and zeal the church is also under deep obligations, established a sewing circle of young misses, by whose industry fifty dollars[2]—the sum which

---

1. Allusion is here made to Mr. William G. Ridgely, the present register. The first action by the vestry towards re-opening the church for regular services was had on the 31st October, 1837, which resulted in the appointment of Messrs. C.G. Wilcox, William Steuart, and W.G. Ridgely (the last not then a member of the vestry), to investigate the fiscal and all other affairs of the church, and to solicit donations to repair and refit it for public worship, &c.
2. Miss H.L. Steuart, directress; and Misses Harriet B. Williams, Eliza Williams, Catharine Davidson, Eliza Davidson, Louisa J. Ridgely, Emily Ridgely, Anna Key Ridgely, Sophia M. Ridgely, Virginia Williams, Mary A. Harry, Harriet B. Harry, Elizabeth Harry, Mary E. Berry, Soloma Pickrell, Lavinia Lyne, Arianna French, Anna

had been paid for the church by the gentleman who had bid in the building when it was sold for taxes—was raised for the purpose of repurchasing the dilapidated edifice. The gentleman[1] who had hidden in the building generously returned the money, and with it a title deed to the property. A fair was held in the latter part of 1838, the vestry reorganized, the church rendered fit for public worship, and the Rev. Dr. Marbury's services obtained as rector of the church.[2] Gradually, by untiring devotedness of the little flock, and by the Christian aid and sympathy of the members of Christ Church, several of whom took pews in the church to assist in its support, the building was furnished with all the conveniences which it possessed before its enlargement, and an income obtained for the support of its pastor. Since then you know its history. Dr. Marbury resigned the charge of the church in September of 1841, and its present pastor immediately succeeded him. It then numbered about thirty families and thirty-five communicants; at this time, it has about sixty families and one hundred and ten communicants. Since that period, as well as before, the church has had reason to use the language of the Psalmist, 'The Lord has done great things for us, whereof we are glad.'

"The brief history which I have given, and the circumstances under which we meet to-day, afford important lessons which we can but suggest to your consideration:

"1st. The ruin of the church in time past, speaks to us as a congregation, 'Be not high-minded, but fear.' It is not for man to say, without divine warrant of such an event, that it was God's

---

Morton, Mary Magruder, Nancy Beard, Ellen Pearson, Josephine Pearson, Sally Hanson, members. This association, the number of members being increased, subsequently paid over to the vestry of the church, a further sum of three hundred and seventy-five dollars, to be applied towards its repairs, and for the procurement of a bell.
1. W.W. Corcoran, Esq.
2. Vestry—Messrs. J. Gozler, Dr. N.W. Worthington, R.H. Villard, F. Lowndes, W.G. Ridgely, William Steuart, C.G. Wilcox, G.B. Magruder; F. Lowndes, register. In order to secure the services of a rector of the church, and provide six hundred dollars for his salary for the first year, four members of the vestry entered into a written obligation, binding themselves for fifty dollars each, one of the four agreeing to make good all the deficiency.

judgment on the church for its worldliness, lukewarmness, and faithlessness to the cause of Christ. This, however, we may say that God's judgments are denounced against the lukewarm and worldly churches. He who walketh in the midst of the churches, and holdeth the stars in his right hand, declares of those who have become lukewarm, who have lost their first love, who have fallen into the impurities of licentious practice, or the delusions of licentious doctrine, that their candlestick shall be removed, and their star extinguished. "He that hath an ear, let him hear what the spirit saith unto the churches.'

"2d. The success which has attended this enterprise, teaches us another lesson. We are not to take the world's opinion as to what is practicable when we would do something for the cause of Christ. When the effort was made to restore this church, and when the plan for enlarging it was suggested, in both cases the enterprise was judged visionary by men of the world. The church is often made fainthearted, and frightened out of her duty, by the ridicule of such men, and their oracular decision that her plans are visionary, fanatical, and unnecessary. Now, my Christian brethren, I hope that you have learned to take counsel elsewhere than front them, as to what can be done when you would extend the privileges of the gospel. If we had listened to such wisdom, we should not this day have worshiped with grateful hearts in this our enlarged and beautified sanctuary. Let worldly wisdom busy herself about worldly things, and let us take counsel of heavenly wisdom when we are engaged in the work of heaven. Henceforth, when we find anything needful to be done for the honor of God, the good of this church, and the conversion of men, believe that it can be done, and resolve that it shall be done. You have every reason so to believe and so to do.

"3d. The success of this effort teaches us another lesson. It is this: we should show forth our gratitude to God for such a blessing; by doing and giving more than ever for his service and honor. Are any disposed to say, 'Now we have done so much, let us have a pause, let us have no more calls on us for subscriptions and contributions, let us rest?' To such I answer, 'Nay.' On the other hand, as God has done so much for us, let us do what we can for those who have not the same heavenly blessings; let us give more largely than before to missions, schools, and to every object of Christian benevolence. You have given this year much more largely than usual (as I am happy and proud to say for you as your pastor), and with great liberality. And now do you wish to be released from it? Why, brethren, I had hoped that the luxury of giving largely had just begun to be realized by you, and that you would not forego it. Let me ask you a few plain questions. Have you been, or do you expect to be, any less comfortable this year than usual? Have you been in want this year? Have you been less happy this year than usual because of giving more largely to the cause of Christ and of his Church? Nay, have you been any poorer? I do not believe that any one of you can say you have. Then I will believe that one of the greatest blessings connected with the enlargement of the church is, that it has shown you the luxury of saving and giving to a holy cause, and that it has taught you that you can give much, and be neither the poorer nor the less happy. My duty, then, is plainly to call upon you to continue to save and give, and, so long as I shall be with you, I shall not cease to do so. You are but stewards of God's bounty; and never are you so happily occupied as when dispensing it in his service. Let, then, your mite go on its way to the destitute of this and other lands, bearing with it the message of salvation; let the poor about you rise up and call you blessed; let the church of your love continue to receive your liberal contributions for all she needs; let not your dying hour be darkened by the consideration that you have withheld, from selfishness, or expended upon self; that which Christ claimed, and his spouse, the Church, needed for her welfare. And let not this duty be regarded by any one as, because a more external duty, little connected with our spiritual interests as individuals or as a church. It is, on the contrary, one of the highest importance; it is a test of our profession; it shows whether or not we have given up all for Christ; it brings down God's blessing. To what was it that the great promise was made—prove me now herewith, saith the Lord, if I will riot open the windows of heaven and pour you out a blessing, that there shall not be room to receive it? It was in reference to this duty, too often regarded by Christians who profess to be eminently spiritual, as Pharisaical and legal, and therefore held almost in contempt, that the direction was given: 'Bring ye all the tithes into the storehouse, that there may be meat, and prove me herewith, saith the Lord.' Brethren, by prayer, and by the consecration of yourselves and substances, another blessing like that which came down upon this place once before, shall visit us again. This house of prayer shall become the gate of heaven to many immortal souls. May He to whose service it is dedicated ever be present here with his people! Thus, and thus only, will it be verified, 'That the glory of this latter house shall be greater than that of the former.'"[1]

CHRIST EPISCOPAL CHURCH.

[History prepared from the records of the church, by Rev. W.W. Williams, rector, December 27, 1868.]

"Fifty eventful years have now passed away since our organization as a church, and it may lend impressiveness to the solemn lessons of this day, if we retrace all the way by which the Lord our God hath led us these many years, and recall his loving kindness in the midst of His temple.

"The records of the first establishment of an Episcopal Church in Georgetown are very few and imperfect.[2] It is a pleasing circumstance connected with the first movement which was made by the Rev. Mr. Addison, that he received the concurrence and assistance of the Rev. Dr. Balch, then the esteemed minister of the Presbyterian Church of this place, whose memory is still warmly venerated by the whole of this community.

"The kindly and fraternal feeling thus manifested by our Presbyterian friends and brethren, I rejoice to say, has still been

1. Vestry at this time—Messrs. John Waters, J.H. Offley, John Hopkins, P.G. Washington, C.E. Rittenhouse, A.H. Marbury, L. Thomas (treasurer), W.G. Ridgely (register); Messrs. Waters and Hopkins, wardens.
2. For the facts connected with the first establishment of an Episcopal Church in Georgetown, I am indebted to a sermon of Rev. C.M. Butler, D.D., preached on the re-opening of St. John's Church.

kept up, and has quite lately laid us under great obligations, by generously placing their commodious chapel at the disposal of our congregation when the work of enlarging the church had derived us of a place of worship. May coming years cement and deepen the fraternal feeling which now exists, and the great Head of the church so guide and govern us by his good Spirit that all who profess and call themselves Christians may hold the faith in unity of spirit, in the bond of peace, and in righteousness of life. At the time Dr. Balch thus extended a helping hand to the movement of establishing an Episcopal church in this place there were but few Episcopal families in the town. The Rev. Mr. Addison, at this time settled in Broad Creek Parish, Prince George's County, opposite Alexandria, was induced to visit them, and invited by Dr. Balch to hold an Episcopal service in his church. Occasional services were thus held during the years 1794 and 1795. In the summer of 1796 the first effort was made to organize a congregation and build a church. Whether a vestry was organized does not appear. The only record of this effort is a list of subscribers, whose contributions were to be applied 'to building the walls and covering in a Protestant Episcopal Church in Georgetown.' The amount collected was fifteen hundred dollars, and a lot given upon which St. John's Church now stands. What causes prevented the completion of the building does not appear; but it was carried up only to the first range of windows, and remained in that unfinished state until the year 1803. During this period of seven years the Rev. Mr. Addison continued to hold occasional services, but the prospect of establishing the church seemed far from encouraging.

"In January, 1803, however, another effort was made, and a meeting of the citizens of Georgetown called for that purpose. The minutes of this meeting commence as follows: 'At a meeting of a number of the inhabitants of Georgetown, at Mr. Semmes' tavern, on Tuesday evening, 28th of January, 1808, pursuant to a notice in the *Washington Federalist*, for the purpose of adopting regulations for building a Protestant Episcopal Church, Walter S. Chandler, Charles Worthington, and Walter Smith were appointed a committee to inquire into the situation of the building commenced for that purpose, and to examine into the state of the accounts relative thereto, and to judge of the propriety of completing the same, or to purchase ground in any other part of the town, in their opinion most appropriate, to solicit subscriptions therefor, and to make all such contracts and agreements as may be requisite for carrying into effect the same.'

"Among the list of subscribers is found the name of Thomas Jefferson, and also Dr. Balch, and the amount raised on this occasion was about four thousand dollars, not enough, it would appear from the records, to complete the unfinished structure, for we find a letter was addressed about this time, by the Rev. Mr. Ratoone, associate rector of St. Paul's, Baltimore, to the vestry of Trinity Church, New York, asking their assistance, and urging the 'great importance of having an Episcopal Church firmly established at the seat of the General Government; so that from it, as a center, the doctrine, discipline, and worship of the Episcopal Church might be widely diffused throughout the United States.' There was but one Episcopal Church to minister to the spiritual wants of both our cities-that of Christ Church, Navy Yard, and its location would necessarily preclude the attendance of the Episcopalians of this place. Whether this appeal to Trinity Church was successful does not appear, but in this year (1803) the building, which had remained so long unfinished, was covered in and sufficiently completed for the celebration of public worship. In 1804 the first rector of St. John's, Rev. Mr. Sayrs, of Port Tobacco, Maryland, entered upon his labors, and, under his faithful ministry the first Episcopal Church gained a permanent foothold in the place. In 1809 the Rev. Mr. Sayrs died, and was succeeded by the Rev. Walter Addison, who, with the interval of two years, continued the beloved and efficient pastor of St. John's until the year 1827, when the increasing infirmities of age and a malady of the eyes, which ended in total blindness, disqualified him for labor and terminated his connection with the church.

"The earlier years of his ministry here were eminently blessed; the church grew in numbers and spirituality; many high in station and authority attended upon its services, and the church was so thronged that the seats in the gallery were in great demand and rented at high rates. In 1811, an effort was made to enlarge the church, the capacity of the building being far below the wants of its increased numbers. But it failed, and this led to a movement, six years after, which resulted in the organization of a new congregation. It is, at this point, our own history as a church commences. On the 10th of November, 1817, a meeting was held at the residence of Mr. Thomas Corcoran, 'for the purpose (as stated in the minutes) of organizing a new congregation, and devising a plan for building an additional Protestant Episcopal Church.' Mr. Corcoran was appointed chairman, and Mr. Wm. Morton, secretary of the meeting, arid steps were at once taken to accomplish their object. A committee was appointed to procure a suitable building for holding public worship, until a church could be erected, and also secure the services of the Rev. Ruel Keith, then assisting Mr. Addison at St. John's. The names of those who inaugurated this movement, and by whose energy and zeal it was brought to a successful issue, deserves a lasting place in our remembrance; they were, under God, the founders of Christ Church. As given in the records of that first meeting, they were the following: Thomas Corcoran, Clement Smith, Francis S. Key, John S. Haw, John Myers, Ulyses Ward, James A. Magruder, William Morton, Thomas Henderson, and John Pickrell. Twenty-six names of pew holders and subscribers are appended to the original articles of agreement, and as they are, in some measure, part of the history of the community, as well as of the church, we give them in the order in which they were signed by themselves: C. Smith, J.S. Haw, Joseph Brewer, S. Henderson, John S. Compton, William Morton, John Abbott, Thomas Corcoran, Jeremiah Williams, Darius Clagett, Wm. W. Clagett, George Clarke, C.A. Burnett, H. Horel, Ninian Magruder, Thomas Hyde, James Getty, William Hayman, Jr., Ulysses Ward, Richard Burgess, Thomas Plater, Ann Key, J.J. Stull, Robert Read, Otho M. Linthicum, Francis S. Key, James S. Morsell. The promise of Him who declares 'them that honor me will I honor,' seems to have been graciously fulfilled in their case. Their descendants, to the third and fourth generation, are still represented among us, and their attachment and love to the house their fathers built,

136

has been conspicuous in their liberality and zealous efforts in the enlargement and completion of our present beautiful church edifice. On the 18th of November, 1817, a week after the first meeting, the committee made their report, recommending the Lancasterian school-house (a few doors below the present church building), as a suitable and commodious place for holding service, and also the willingness of the vestry of St. John's Church to dispense with the services of the Rev. Mr. Keith for two Sundays in the month.

"This meeting proceeded to ballot for a vestry, and the following gentlemen were elected as the first vestry of the church: Thomas Corcoran, Thomas Henderson, Clement Smith, John S. Haw, James S. Morsell, John Abbott, William Morton, and Ulysses Ward. A letter, dated November 19th, 1817, still on record, was addressed by the vestry to the Rev. Mr. Keith, asking his acceptance of the rectorship of the new congregation. After stating the causes which led to its organization, they go on to say:

"The most prominent, important, and interesting duty devolving on us in the selection of a minister, in whose devotion to the religion of Christ, and the doctrines and forms of the Episcopal Church, the utmost confidence can be reposed, we are happy in assuring you we have every reason to expect from you a conscientious discharge of the duties attached to the ministerial office, and, therefore, take unfeigned pleasure in asking you to take charge of the congregation.'

"How largely blessed they were in this choice and expectation, we need not say. Dr. Keith here made full proof of his ministry, and has left the impress of his earnest spirit and rich gifts, not only upon this community, but the church at large. His praise is in all the churches, and there are still some living who remember his apostolic fervor and eloquence, and, at times, the awful earnestness with which he pressed home upon the heart and conscience the great truths of redeeming love. As a professor of theology at Williamsburg, then in a most flourishing condition, its venerable halls filled with the youth and rising talent of Virginia and other States, his field of usefulness was a most important one, and his great intellectual gifts and ripe scholarship were doubtless largely instrumental in moulding the religious beliefs and principles of its students. After occupying this position at William and Mary College for two years, he removed to Alexandria, in 1823, and, together with Dr. Wilmer, established the Theological Seminary of Virginia, which has done so much for the resuscitation of the church, not only in that State, but for the spread of the evangelical truth throughout our whole land supplying earnest and faithful ministers to almost every diocese, and honored by God as the source from which our missionary bishop and laborers have been almost entirely recruited.

"To Dr Keith's logical, discriminating, systematic teaching of theology, and, above all, to the atmosphere of true spiritual religion, which his life illustrated, and his influence generated, is that institution, under God, largely indebted for its early success; and the honored names, who now fill its chairs and watch over its interests, are striving to keep it faithful to the great doctrines be taught and the high spiritual standard he set up. The pleasing association which connects Dr. Keith the first rector of Christ Church, and the first professor of the seminary, is a bond of union which has been increased by many subsequent ties of interest; many faithful pastors has the seminary furnished to this church, and many times, when without a minister, have its professors broken to this people the bread of life.

"To return now to our more immediate history: The invitation extended by the vestry to Dr. Keith was accepted, and the congregation assembled together, for the first time, in the Lancaster schoolhouse, on Sunday, December 21, 1817. There are, perhaps, but few representatives of that first service now living; one of them, Judge James S. Morsell, whose absence from our midst to-day we deeply regret, is now bowed with the weight of years, and waiting, like the aged Simeon, for joyful dismissal. He has been associated for more than half a century with the church, and, by his consistent Christian life and earnest devotion to its interest, adorning the gospel of Christ. Under Mr. Keith's labors the congregation greatly increased in prosperity.

"At a meeting held in April, 1818, at the Lancaster school, and opened with prayer by Mr. F.S. Key, a committee, consisting

138

of Thomas Corcoran, Charles A. Burnett, Thomas Hyde, William Clagett, Ulysses Ward, and John Myers, were appointed 'to secure subscriptions, purchase a lot, and contract for a church edifice.' The present site was then purchased, and on the 6th of May, 1818, the building was begun. On the 21st of December, it seems to have been completed; and at sunrise Christmas day,[1] 1818, the congregation assembled for the first time within its walls for prayer. On the 30th of December the church was consecrated by the Right Rev. James Kemp, Bishop of Maryland. At ten o'clock the morning service was performed, and a sermon preached by the Rev. Mr. Keith. It must have been a joyous Christmas morning, not only from its own blessed associations, but because it witnessed the successful completion of what was then the largest Episcopal Church in the District. Would it were in my power to give some extracts from the first sermon preached within these walls. What changes have half a century wrought? Your fathers, where are they? How many who here bent the knee in prayer are now in the vast regions of the dead? How many who joined in the sublime ascription, 'Thou art the King of Glory, O Christ!' do now behold Him face to face? How many who here proclaimed the blessed gospel, do now rest from their labors and are at home with the Lord? And we who now occupy their places and join in the same solemn prayers, will, in a few brief years, be gathered to our fathers and receive the great recompense of reward according to the works done in the body. Oh, that the gospel here preached may be to us 'the Saviour of life unto life,' so that when Christ shall appear, we may be found an acceptable people, well pleasing in His sight. Brief as are the early notices of the occupation of the church, we cannot fail to be impressed with the promptness, energy, zeal,

---

1. It may, perhaps, be well to mention that at sunrise on last Christmas, just fifty years after, the congregation assembled to commemorate this first service held in these walls. The memories and changes of fifty years made it a deeply solemn and touching occasion to all present. Tears came unbidden to many eyes, and all felt it was a sad, though hallowed, service.

The rector has since learned from an estimable lady who was present on this occasion, that she well remembers that first service held by Dr. Keith fifty years before.

and liberality manifested by that first vestry, in prosecuting the work in which they engaged to a speedy completion. Within the short space of a year, we behold a congregation organized, a minister called and liberally supported, and a church begun, finished, and occupied.

"Fifty years ago things moved much more slowly, and wealth was far less generally distributed than at present, so that the enterprise they exhibited is worthy of all commendation, and their labors well entitled to our grateful remembrance. There must have been among them all a sincere love for the church, and a spirit to devise liberal things, in order to carry them through the difficulties and demands of such a work. But among those early founders, entitled to our special remembrance, we must record the names of Mr. Thomas Corcoran and Mr. Clement Smith; from the first inception of the movement, through the earlier years of our history as a church, their efforts in its behalf were untiring, and when the work of building the church was embarrassed for want of means, they came forward and liberally advanced what was needed for its completion. The entire cost of the church, including the lot, was fifteen thousand nine hundred and fifty-two dollars.

"In January, 1820, the Rev. Mr. Keith resigned the charge of the congregation. Though only of two years' duration, his ministry had been signally blessed, and he had the satisfaction of leaving the church thoroughly organized, and with every promise of a prosperous career. On the 12th of April, 1819, the second election of a vestry was held, and among other names which have been mentioned, are found those of Jeremiah Williams and Thomas Plater. One item in the minutes of the vestry, at this early period, deserves a passing notice, as showing the interest then felt in a subject which, I trust, has still a place in the prayers and charities of this people. Shortly after the resignation of Mr. Keith, and prompted, perhaps, by the difficulty of finding a successor, a resolution was offered looking to the organization of a society for the education of pious young men for the ministry, to be auxiliary to that existing in the diocese of Maryland and Virginia. A committee was appointed to draft a constitution for an Educational Society, which was afterwards presented to the congregation for their adoption. That the movement was not a fruitless one, appears from the testimony of Bishop Meade, in an address delivered at the seminary, in 1859. In enumerating the benefactors of the seminary, without the bounds of Virginia, he specially mentions the congregation of Christ Church, Georgetown, as having, under the promptings of its several pastors, furnished no little aid to its support.

"On the 8th of March, 1820, the Rev. Charles P. McIlvaine was elected to succeed Mr. Keith, as rector. Not being ordained at the time of his election, he did not take charge until the following July. Of his ministry of five years' duration, it is unnecessary for me to say much; the zeal, devotedness, and success with which he here labored are well known by many still among us who were the fruits of that ministry, and for nearly fifty years he has been so prominent an actor in all the great movements of the church, as to make his name and work a familiar one to us all. During this period, we find the following names appearing among the vestry, and active supporters of the church: Jeremiah Williams, James S. Morsell, Charles A. Burnett, Richard Burgess, James Corcoran, John Marbury, John Myers, Robert Read, H.C. Matthews, William G. Ridgely, William Sewell, Thomas Hyde, Joseph Brewer, Jeremiah Bronaugh.

"During the interval between the resignation of Mr. McIlvaine and the call of the Rev. H.W. Gray, on the 19th of May, 1825, Dr. Keith officiated. Mr. Gray continued the rector until the 20th of December, 1828, when he was compelled by ill health to resign his charge. The Rev. Mr. Cobbs, of Virginia, was called, but declined. The Rev. John Thompson Brooke, then in charge of the parish at Martinsburg, was elected, and entered upon his duties on the 15th of March, 1829. His connection with the church lasted for six years, and seems to have been signally blessed. His preaching was 'in the demonstration of the spirit and with the power,' and his private life one of singular beauty and consistency. Few ministers were ever more warmly loved and respected, and so deep and lasting was the attachment of the congregation to him, that eight years after he had resigned, we find the vestry again electing him as their pastor, and, in the letter urging his acceptance, saying, 'that as soon as it became manifested that the continued ill health of their rector would sever his connection and leave their church without a pastor, all eyes were turned towards the west, in hope that you might be induced to turn *homewards*, where your old congregation are waiting to receive you with open arms.' The Tractarian movement was then beginning to scatter its deadly errors through the church, and awaken alarm, and this presented as an additional plea in urging his coming; the letter then goes on to say, 'we need not only the most skillful, but the strongest arms to stay the mighty torrent, and we call upon you to come to the help of the Lord against the mighty.' Dr. Brooke felt compelled to decline the call, but the repetition and earnestness with which it was urged, shows how deeply he had left the impress of his character upon the hearts of the congregation.

"Nothing of special interest requires our notice during this period; we find about this time, 1829, a movement on foot to withdraw the District of Columbia from the diocese of Maryland and Virginia, and erect the said District into a separate diocese; but the movement met with no more favor then than it has lately done, and the vestry declined to send delegates to attend the proposed meeting. It may be mentioned, in this connection, that the church seems to have been regularly represented in the diocesan convention, and that the choice of the vestry often fell upon Mr. F.S. Key to fill the place as delegate. After Mr. Brooke's resignation; there seems to have been some difficulty experienced in finding a successor to fill his place; the Rev. William Jackson, of New York, and the Rev. Mr. Jones, of Orange Court House, Virginia, were called, but declined. For some reason, which does not appear in the record, the vestry at this time departed from their usual custom of calling a minister, and referred the matter to the pew holders for their action; the step seems to have been an injudicious one, for after various ballotings, and ineffectual efforts by, the friends of the different candidates, no decision was reached, and the whole matter had to be referred back to the vestry, and they authorized to proceed to an election. The Rev. P. Slaughter was then chosen, and entered upon his duties in December, 1835. About this time the steeple of the church was finished; the committee having in charge its erection, and procuring subscriptions for the same, being Messrs. Morton, Richard Burgess, and H.C. Matthews. We also find in the minutes of the vestry, at this time, the resignation of Mr. John Marbury, who had filled the laborious office of treasurer for so many years, and to whose energetic efforts the debt which was contracted in building the church, and which had hung as an incubus on its prosperity, was finally discharged by the transfer of certain pews owned by the church, and funds due it to its creditors. It is but just to state that these creditors were very generous in their dealings, and one of the largest ultimately relinquished his claim and donated it to the church. In July, 1837, Mr. Slaughter's health compelled his temporary relinquishment of his charge, and the Rev. Mr. Goodrich occupied the pulpit and ministered very acceptably to the congregation. Mr. Slaughter finally resigned in October, and Mr. Goodrich was elected his successor, but declined. Several unsuccessful efforts were made to secure a rector, but it was not until September, 1838, nearly a year after Mr. Slaughter's resignation, that the vestry succeeded in securing the services of the Rev. J.F. Hoff. On Easter morning, 1841, the following gentlemen composed the vestry: James S. Morsell, John Harry, J. Davidson, C.A. Burnett, Hezekiah Miller, J. Marbury; H. McPherson, Mr. Mix, wardens; P.T. Berry, register. In March, 1843, Rev. Mr. Hoff was compelled by ill-health to resign, much to the sorrow and regret of the whole congregation. The Rev. Stephen G. Gassaway, of Ohio, was then called, and entered upon his duties as rector, on the 21st of April, 1843. We have now reached a period, so fully within the memory of the greater part of the congregation, that only the briefest notice of the remaining changes and events in our history is necessary. In 1844, a parsonage on Beall Street was purchased by subscription, and the aid of the ladies of the congregation. In 1847, we find extensive repairs and changes were made in the church building under the supervision of Messrs. Lyons, W.R. Abbott, H.C. Matthews, J. Marbury, and that the ladies of the congregation showed their accustomed zeal by raising the

143

means for beautifying the church. Two handsome chancel-chairs were the gift of Mr. W.W. Corcoran. Easter Monday, 1845, the vestry was as follows: Messrs. Evan Lyons, John Marbury, H.C. Matthews, Levin Jones, William B. Boggs, Dr. G. Tyler; William R. Abbott, register; Mr. Lyons, treasurer; Col. Stull, and R.J. Bowen, wardens. In November, 1850, Mr. Gassaway resigned his charge, and removed to Missouri. An interval of more than a year elapsed before the Rev. David Caldwell entered upon his duties in April, 1851, during which Dr. Sparrow filled the pulpit. In May of that year, a movement was made to secure a parsonage, the one before purchased having been relinquished on account of a defective title; and through the energy of the committee to whom the matter was referred, the present commodious rectory was bought and furnished. The year after (in 1852), and principally through the efforts of Mr. H.C. Matthews, for many years an active vestryman, and the efficient leader of the choir, a new and very superior organ was purchased. In March, 1854, the Rev. Mr. Caldwell was compelled to resign his position because of increasing ill-health, and four years after he was called to rest from his labors. The Rev. Dr. Norwood succeeded him on the 20th of April, 1854, and continued for seven years rector of the church. The Rev. Mr. Harris then took temporary charge of the parish until April 1st, 1864, when the Rev. J.H.C. Bonte entered upon his duties as rector, and was succeeded by the present incumbent on the 27th of May, 1866. Vestry in 1860: Messrs. Marbury, Matthews, Berry, Dr. Snyder, Lyons, Cox, Davidson, Dr. Tyler. Wardens: Messrs. Abbott and Knowles.

"From this brief outline of events, during the first fifty years, it will be seen that of the eleven rectors, who have ministered in this church, but six are now living; and of the original list of subscribers and pew holders, but a single one survives. An entirely new generation now occupy their places, and the many changes which these passing years have witnessed, admonish us that we too are 'pilgrims and strangers,' and call us to prepare for that eternal world to which we are so fast hastening.

"Time allows me to give but the briefest sketch of the rebuilding of our present church edifice. The lapse of fifty years had left its marks upon the house our fathers built; and it was felt that something was needed to adapt it to the enlarged wants of the congregation. Our homes showed a large increase in elegance, and comfort, and expense, and it was but right that God's house should keep pace with our increased prosperity, and be the exponent of our gratitude for the privilege and blessing so long enjoyed here. With great unanimity it was determined by the vestry, at a meeting held on January 28,1867, to solicit plans and estimates for the improvement of the church. On the 20th of March, the plan of the present building was selected, and a committee appointed to wait on the congregation and solicit subscriptions. They were met by a liberal response on the part of the congregation, over thirteen thousand dollars being at once subscribed. Feeling fully justified in beginning operations, having thirty additional pews to fall back upon for any expenses outside of the estimates, contracts were entered into. The last service held in the old church was on Sunday night, May 26, 1867. The following week the work was begun. On the 15th of July, the corner-stone of the old church was removed to its present position at the northeast corner of the tower, and there was deposited in it the journal of the diocesan convention for the year 1867; the minutes of the vestry authorizing the construction of the church; the names of the rector, vestrymen, wardens, building committee, architects, and contractor; some United States fractional currency, and city papers.

"The rector, soon after the work was begun, was laid aside by protracted illness from participating in the arduous duties of the building committee, of which be was the chairman, and did not assume his charge until the lecture-room was completed and occupied, on the 16th of February, 1868. I may, therefore, the more fully bear my testimony to the zeal, and unwearied diligence of the committee, who, at no little sacrifice of their time, gave their personal aid and attention during the progress of the work. The committee consisted of Messrs. Matthews, Boggs, Kurtz, and Davidson. Upon the treasurer of the committee, Mr. C.M. Matthews, the largest part of the burden of the undertaking fell; and I feel that I record but the sense of the committee and the vestry, when I say that to his unwearied

145

energy, and personal efforts, and financial skill, we are largely indebted for the successful completion of our enlarged, improved, and beautiful church edifice. Upon the well-known. taste and judgment of Capt. W.B. Boggs the building committee largely depended, especially in the ornamentation of the church. Unlooked for delays and difficulties were experienced, but I rejoice to bear witness to the united spirit on the part of the whole congregation, which has enabled us to surmount them; they have not only served to call forth greater liberality and self-sacrifice in behalf of the church, and revealed much undeveloped strength, but, I trust under God's blessing, have qualified us for a higher place of usefulness and a greater consecration to His service. To the ladies, as is the case in every good work, we are also largely indebted. Many years ago some of them raised, by their efforts, a fund which was kept for the purpose of building a lecture-room, and which, amounting to thirteen hundred dollars, was handed over to the building committee for that object. The ladies of the Christ Church Sewing Society (organized in October after I took charge); by their needle and other efforts, raised also nine hundred dollars, which was devoted to the use of the church building, and in addition to this, they carpeted the aisles and chancel, furnished the desk and pulpit, and, together with liberal donations from two of the members, procured a costly stained-glass window for the church, showing, as the result of their work for two years, the sum of two thousand dollars. On the 14th of June last, the present church edifice was first occupied, and the voice of supplication and praise resounded in its walls. Such are the items and events of our history as a church. What wondrous changes have these fifty years witnessed? When we first begun our existence, the Episcopal Church was small in numbers and influence almost entirely confined to the seaboard and few older States, it has now expanded into a communion numbering over forty bishops, two thousand clergy, and one hundred and forty thousand communicants, and spread its agencies from the Atlantic to the Pacific. Whatever changes the future may bring, God grant to us, as a congregation, that we may cling to, and love the old gospel of the grace of God, which the saintly Keith first proclaimed in these walls, and worship Him in the same simple, solemn way as our fathers, when they first knelt together here around the throne of grace. The old bible, the old liturgy, the old doctrines bequeathed to us by the Reformers, in the sixteenth century, are our heir-loom and our precious heritage. Let us strive to transmit these, unimpaired and uncorrupted. We need nothing new to adapt the Church to her work of converting souls and edifying God's people. What we do need is the outpouring of the Holy Ghost upon the gospel preached, that it may be with power and His presence in our hearts, that we may adorn that gospel by holiness and righteousness of life.

"May He to whose service this house is dedicated, be ever present with his people here, so that it shall, indeed, be the house of God, and the gate of heaven to many immortal souls. Thus, and thus only, can the declaration be verified—

"'The glory of this latter house shall be greater than that of the former.'"

I herewith give a list of the different rectors who have had charge of the church, and the respective periods of their ministry here:

Rev. Ruel Keith, November 19th, 1817, to January 29th, 1820; Rev. Charles P. McIlvaine, March 8th, 1820, to March lst, 1825; Rev. H.H. Grey, May, 19th, 1825, to December 20th, 1828; Rev. J. Thompson Brooke, March 15th 1829, to March 17th, 1835 ; Rev. Philip Slaughter, December -, 1835, to October 3, 1837; Rev. J.F. Hoff, September 17th, 1838, to March 1st, 1843; Rev. S.G. Gassaway, April 21st, 1843, to November 18th, 1850; Rev. David Caldwell, April 13th, 1851, to March 4th, 1854; Rev. William R. Norwood, D.D., April 20th, 1854, to October 4th, 1861;[1] Rev. J.H.C. Bonte, April 1st,1864, to March 26th, 1866; Rev. W.W. Williams, May 27th, 1866, to May 28th, 1876; Rev. Albert R. Stuart, May 28th, 1876, to the present time.

---

1. From this date, to October 4th, 1861, until Rev. Mr. Bonte entered upon the duties of rector, Rev. William A. Harris filled the pulpit and was in temporary charge.

METHODIST EPISCOPAL CHURCH.

This church was formerly located on Montgomery Street. The original deed for the church is recorded in liber E, No. 5, page 238, from Anthony Holmead to Lloyd Beall, Richard Parrott and others, trustees. The deed is dated March 22, 1800, about which time a church was erected on said lot, thirty feet by forty feet deep, being one and one-half stories high. In course of time the congregation increased, when the original building was taken down, and the present building (now a public school) erected in its place. This was about the year 1820. The brick building was two stories high, substantial and strong, and answered the purpose of worship for many years, when the congregation sold the church to the Corporation of Georgetown for the sum of twelve hundred dollars, (as per deed, recorded in liber J.A.S., No. 11, page 279, February 17, 1850.) Some defect was in the original deed, and the corporation had a new deed from the heirs of Holmead to the trustees of the church before they would purchase the same. A new building was then contemplated for a church, and the ground selected was lot No. 39, in Beall's addition to Georgetown, conveyed by David English to John Pickrell and others, trustees (as per deed recorded in Liber J.A.S., No. 4, page 226; deed dated May 16, 1849). The building erected on this lot is a spacious church, two stories high, the basement being used for the Sabbath school, which now numbers two hundred and ten scholars, while the main room of the church is used for public worship.

METHODIST PROTESTANT CHURCH.

The founders of this church worshiped formerly in St. John's and the Presbyterian Church, and in the Lancaster school-room, for one or two years, before they erected the present church on Congress Street. The lot was purchased by one Butler Cook, trustee of one Samuel Robertson, in April, 1829, for the sum of ten hundred and thirty-five dollars. The original trustees were Leonard Mackall, John Eliason, William King, Joseph Libbey, Jeremiah Orme, Gideon Davis, and William C. Lipscomb.

This lot was once in jeopardy, or in danger of being lost to

148

the church, by the original owner not paying in full the parties he purchased from. A note for the deferred payment fell into the hands of the United States branch bank, at Norfolk, Virginia; suit was instituted to recover the property, but the trustee, Cook, effected a compromise, and it was released and the title made perfect. In the meantime, while this difficulty was pending, it was sold for taxes by the collector for the Corporation of Georgetown. Mr. W.W. Corcoran purchased it for twenty-two dollars, and very generously relinquished his title to the church. The lot, as originally purchased, was sold for sixty feet front, but when measured it only ran out fifty-five feet front, and this is all the church holds a title to. The trustees endeavored to effect an act of incorporation, so that they might sue and be sued; sell and purchase real estate; but it never was successfully carried out.

When the trustees began to build the original church the membership was small and comparatively poor, and hence were often in straightened circumstances. Their indebtedness to the builders was a source of great disquietude; and in order to close up the matter the trustees agreed to give the builders a deed of trust for fifteen hundred dollars to secure their debt; but this debt was settled by the individual members giving their notes and paying them at maturity. But there was one debt that gave the church some trouble, which was due to the late Gideon Davis.

After his death his executor discovered there was a debt due the said Davis by the church for the sum of five or six hundred dollars. The church refused to pay unless a credit of two hundred dollars was allowed. In the meantime the widow of Davis married, and the matter was amicably, settled without a suit.

The lot on which the parsonage stands was purchased of Ninian Beall for the sum of six hundred and fifteen dollars, on May 1st, 1839. The trustees who made the purchase were William King, Joseph Libbey, Jeremiah Orme, Thomas Jewell, Fritz J. Bartlett, Thomas A. Newman, and John E. Cox. One fact in the purchase of this lot was quite commendable. The ladies of the church paid nearly the whole purchase-money. They also organized themselves into a sewing society, while the male members organized a sinking-fund, which worked well and

149

gradually released the church from debt. Upon this lot connected with the church the lecture-room was built in 1857, at a cost of seventeen hundred dollars, which was enlarged in 1867, at nearly the same cost. The present house of worship was enlarged and beautified in 1867, and dedicated in February, 1868; the cost of which exceeded the cost of the original church, the parsonage, and lecture room combined, and, after a hard struggle, this church is nearly free from debt.

The church was dedicated in 1830, when Rev. W.W. Wallace was in charge of this station. The opening sermon was preached to a large audience. The choir was quite a feature in the dedication. It was led by W.C. Lipscomb, with a corps of practical singers.

The Rev. Mr. Snether preached the opening sermon. The second dedication was during the Rev. Mr. Shermer's administration. In February, 1868, the Rev. Augustus Webster preached the dedicatory sermon. The Rev. Mr. Bowers preached a sermon for a collection in aid of the church, which was quite successful. The parsonage was built by the strenuous efforts of the Rev. Levi R. Reese, the pastor, in 1841. The whole cost did not reach four thousand dollars. An error was committed in building. There was quite a hill; and they cut a part of the hill down and made a basement under ground, and ever since the walls have been damp. The rooms have low ceiling. However, the modern style of architecture had not at that time been introduced. The lecture or school-room was commenced by Thomas A. Newman, the then superintendent of the Sabbath school, and finished by his successor, the late John T. Bangs. The school formerly met in the gallery of the church, which, being too large for comfort, the superintendent and teachers determined to build, and they did so. The choir of this church is an attraction. There have never been but four leaders of the choir since the church was organized in 1828. The Rev. William C. Lipscomb was the first. He taught music for the benefit of the church; and the singing under so skillful a leader was quite an attraction. After he moved away from town, he was succeeded by others.

I will now give a list of the different ministers who have had charge of the church, and the respective periods of their ministry here: Rev. William W. Wallace, 1829 to 1830; Rev. Dennis B. Dorsey, 1830 to 1831; Rev. Frederick Styer, 1831 to 1832; Rev. Thomas H. Stockton, 1832 to 1835; Rev. John W. Porter, 1835 to 1836; Rev. Josiah Varden, 1836 to 1837; Rev. Augustus Webster, 1837 to 1839; Rev. Bignal Appleby, 1839 to 1840; Rev. Levi R. Reese, 1840 to 1843; Rev. John G. Wilson, 1843 to 1845; Rev. Joseph Varden, 1845 to 1847; Rev. William Collier, 1847 to 1849; Rev. John Everest, 1849 to 1850; Rev. J.J. Murray, 1850 to 1851; Rev. S.R. Cox, 1851 to 1853; Rev. J.B. Southerland, 1853 to 1855; Rev. Dr. Murray, 1855 to 1857; Rev. David Wilson, 1857 to 1859; Rev. Washington Roby, 1859 to 1861; Rev. Daniel E. Reese, 1861 to 1863; Rev. Daniel Bowers, 1863 to 1865; Rev. D.A. Shermer, 1866 to 1867; Rev. Dr. Bates, 1868 to 1871; Rev. T.D. Valiant, 1871 to 1875; Rev. J.T. Murray, D.D., 1875 to the present time.

GERMAN LUTHERAN CHURCH.

The German Lutheran Church, situated at the corner of High and Fourth Streets, had its origin in this way: Col. Charles Beatty, one of the original founders of the town, had, in 1769, set apart the lot of ground in question, for the sole use and benefit of the Lutheran Church, and caused the same to be so entered and designated on the plat of the town. Soon afterwards, the lot was taken possession of by the German Lutherans, inclosed, and a school-house erected thereon, and was used by the members of the church as a burying ground for upwards of fifty years. During all that time, neither their possession nor title had been questioned, and Colonel Charles Beatty died without making a conveyance of said lot to the trustees of the church, leaving Charles A. Beatty his heir at law. The Court decided "that they could not decree a conveyance of the lot to the trustees, but as they had been in possession of the lot for fifty years, and have used it as a church lot and burying ground, and as the donor, Charles Beatty, and his son and heir at law have declared that the lot belongs to the Lutherans, the Court thinks that the defendants cannot now conscientiously turn the complainants out of possession, and will therefore decree a perpetual injunction."

151

Affirmed by the Supreme Court of United States, 2d Peters, page 566. See, also, 2d Cranch, Circuit Court Reports, page 699.

The subsequent history of the church is detailed in a letter addressed to the chronicler by the Rev. John J. Suman, its former pastor, which we here insert:

"The condition of the Lutheran Church for the past half century, has been rather deplorable. In the memory of the oldest inhabitant (Mr. Hurdle), there has not been any regular preaching of the gospel by ministers of that denomination, until very recently. The lot on which the present building is erected, was for along time unenclosed, and the resting places of the sacred dead were trampled upon by the unhallowed feet of man and beast. These things, it was thought, ought not to be; and a determination was arrived at that they should not longer so exist—For the people had a mind to work.'

"Some time in the year —, a number of persons, mostly among the German population, raised the means to aid in putting up the present building, under the direction of Rev. S. Finckle, D.D., who had long been the pastor of the German Church, located on the corner of 20th and G Streets, in Washington City. The design appears to have, been the combining of a school (German) with the church, and holding the same in the church building. In this they succeeded. But, from various causes, the school was not a very great success—mismanagement, improper qualifications in some of the teachers, and want of proper support, operated to bring the school into disrepute, and prevent its being of any advantage to the church.

"On the 16th of November, 1868, I received a very pressing invitation to preach for the people who desired to worship according to the doctrines and usages of the Lutheran Church.

"On Sunday, January 3d, 1869, I received a formal written call to become pastor of the church, which I accepted in a note to the trustees.

"It is proper here to state, that at this time, there was no regularly organized congregation of the Lutheran denomination in Georgetown. The people (mostly Germans) were held together by an association, seeming to have for its object the

152

support of the school in the church building, as well as to pay off the debt on the latter.

"It was apparent to all, who at that time worshiped in the building, that, under existing circumstances, there was very little prospect of building up a congregation. The school that was held in the building kept it in such a filthy condition that persons would not attend worship there on that account. Unless a change was made in some way the building might as well have been closed, so far as Lutheran interests were concerned. But the question was, how was this change to be effected? For the pastor to inaugurate an effort to make a change would antagonize him with the Germans. This was not to be thought of. Just at this moment, to put it in its mildest form, the misconduct of the teacher of the school induced the trustees of the building to close the same against the teacher; and this formed the entering wedge to accomplishing the desire of the people worshiping there.

"On the 24th day of January, 1869, I was installed, by Rev. George Diehl, D.D., as the first regular pastor of the new church. It was a great day for us few Lutherans.

"On the 27th day of February, 1870, at a meeting of the trustees of the church, James Gosler, George Wetzrich, Henry Wirner, John C. Kiser, and Henry Kiser, and myself as secretary, it was *resolved*, That hereafter the church building be devoted exclusively to church purposes. Truth requires it to be stated that this caused disaffection among the body of Germans. Their hearts were fixed upon the school, and its discontinuance was a great disappointment to them, and caused some very bitter feeling.

"On Sunday, June 5th, 1870, the church, having been repaired, repainted, papered, and renovated, was re-dedicated to the worship of Almighty God: Drs. Butler, Finckle, and Bates participated in the exercises. The Masonic Choir leading the singing for us.

"At the time of my taking charge of the church there was a debt of about one thousand eight hundred dollars resting thereon, and we have been reducing that debt some. At the meeting of the synod of Maryland, at Emmitsburg, they

153

appropriated five hundred dollars towards the payment of this debt, to be raised during the synodical year, which was afterwards raised and paid.

"At this time, arrangements were also made by which Rev. George N. Nixdorff was to visit the Georgetown church, and if he were pleased, he was to become our pastor. Meanwhile, a congregation had been regularly and constitutionally organized—small in number—twelve persons. Rev. Nixdorf visited us, was pleased, and on the first Sunday in April, 1871, he preached his first sermon as pastor of the church.

BAPTIST CHURCH.

The Gay Street Baptist Church was organized June 19, 1866. The following persons composed its constituent members, viz : B.P. Nichols, J.C. Nichols, A.M. Appler, J.G. Hedgman, J.W. Haney, W.B. Brittain, James Nelson, Susannah Nichols, Susan Mattox, Helen M. Appler, and Susan Nelson.

The church was formally recognized July 9, 1866, by a council, of which G.W. Samson, D.D., A.D. Gillette, D.D., J. Berg, C.C. Maddox, and S.R. White were members.

The church worshiped for over two years in a chapel on Market Street, the use of which was courteously granted by the Bridge Street Presbyterian Church. The house of worship at the corner of Gay and Congress Streets was dedicated October 11, 1868. This property was secured to the church in a large measure through the liberality of Mr. James S. Welch, and a legacy from the late John McCutchen of five thousand dollars.

Rev. James Nelson was the first pastor, and served the church until March 1, 1872. He was succeeded by Dr. A.J. Huntington, who resigned July 1, 1874. Rev. G.W. Beale became pastor December 1, 1874, and continues to the present time. The number of members at present is seventy-three.

COLORED CHURCHES.

Mount Zion Methodist Episcopal Church is located on lot No. 78, in Holmead's addition to the town, and is thirty-five by fifty feet. The deed is recorded in liber A.H. No. 33, page 10, from William Morgan to Henry Foxall and others dated June 3d, 1814, when the building was commenced.

Ebenezer Church is located on Beall Street, between Montgomery and Monroe Streets; was erected in 1856; number of members, one hundred and fifty; Sabbath school, one hundred and sixty, with two superintendents and seventeen teachers.

The Colored Baptist Church is located on the corner of Dunbarton and Monroe Streets.

SUTER'S TAVERN IN 1791.

CHAPTER VII.

GEORGETOWN COLLEGE—THE MONASTERY AND ACADEMY OF THE VISITATION—GEORGETOWN COLLEGIATE INSTITUTE—PEABODY LIBRARY AND LINTHICUM INSTITUTE—PUBLIC SCHOOLS.

The historical sketch of Georgetown College is from the pen of Reverend J.S. Sumner, S.J., editor of the *College Journal*. It is such a full and accurate description of the old institution, that to abridge it would be doing injustice to the author as well as to this venerable institution of learning, therefore the chronicler inserts it in full.

"So little is known by the present generation of students of the past history of the college, and so many demands are made from time to time by others for a brief sketch of it, that we think we cannot do better than transfer to our columns a suitable article which appeared in the Washington *Daily Patriot* in June, 1871, and which was prepared, we believe, by a graduate of '63. It is proper, perhaps, to correct an error the writer has fallen into in stating that the north building was erected in 1808. It had remained in a partially finished condition up to that time, but it was really built in 1791, and nearly completed in 1795. From sundry entries in the old account-books (almost the only existing material for reference in the matter of our early history), we judge that students began to lodge in it in December, 1797. On the first of that month there were fifty-nine boarders in the college, and certainly they must have been greatly cramped for room in the attic of the old college, the only place where it seems possible they could have been accommodated.

"Father John Early, who was president when this sketch was written, died May 23d, 1873, and was immediately succeeded by our present superior, Father P.F. Healy, who bad been prefect of studies since 1868 (an office he continues to hold), and vice-president, besides, since 1869.

"Founded before the city of Washington existed, Georgetown College (since the year 1815, when it was raised to the rank of a university, with the power of conferring degrees in any of the faculties), has been one of the most cherished institutions of the District of Columbia, fruitful as is the latter in noted associations

156

and localities. The Alma Mater of hundreds of distinguished and meritorious citizens of the Republic—not one of whom fails to hold in reverence the old walls in which he drew the inspirations of learning and morality—the college in the present, as in the past, has gathered to itself young men not only from all parts of the country, but also from Mexico, South America, and the West Indies. Its best tribute is rendered in the high character of its graduates—men who have carried with them to their distant and nearer homes, after so many successive 'commencements,' the training of high scholarship and the promptings of an honorable ambition. As year by year it has opened its gates in farewell to its departing pupils, it has done so with the consciousness that in preparing them for the arduous duties of practical life, it has no less thoroughly performed its duty than secured the love and veneration of those who are graduating from it.

"It is not necessary to speak of the great ability as instructors and the profound erudition of the gentlemen, members of the Society of Jesus—always the firm champions of education—who conduct, and are connected with the institution. The names of its successive presidents, from the Rev. Robert Plunkett, in the year 1791, to that of its present distinguished and respected head, Rev. John Early, furnish a list of men, eminent for learning and piety, who, as they have from time to time appeared to guide the destinies of the college, have endeared themselves to the community in which they have lived, and to those who have been placed under their charge.

"In recalling some of these former presidents, the mind contemplates many of the most deserving—as they are among the best known of the clergy of the Catholic Church in America—men well-beloved in their days of service in the cause of education, and whose memories—those of the living and of the dead—are faithfully cherished. We should like here to open up the past for a moment, and speak of these men whose names and histories are so intimately connected with much of the greatness and glory of the past years of Georgetown College. We should like to speak of Father Dubourg, who was president in 1796, afterwards Bishop of New Orleans, and later Archbishop of Besançon, in France; of the universally-loved Father William

157

Mathews, for so many years pastor of St. Patrick's Church, in Washington; of Fathers Benedict and Enoch Fenwick, the good brothers, the former afterwards Bishop of Boston; of Fathers James Ryder, Thomas Mulledy, Charles Henry Stonestreet, John Early, and Bernard A. Maguire, men who, each in his way, have done so much to add to the efficiency and reputation of Georgetown College, and the last mentioned of whom still freshly bears the multiplied laurels of long years of presidency of the institution, as he enjoys the widespread reputation of a brilliant orator, an accomplished gentleman, and a churchman of renown.

"A few words regarding the history of Georgetown College will prove interesting. The site of the present institution, on the heights just beyond Georgetown, was selected by the Rev. John Carroll, first Archbishop of Baltimore, shortly after the American Revolution. In the year 1789, the first building was erected. It still stands: the old building that occupies the central position in the south row. Two years after the schools were opened with Rev. Robert Plunkett as first president of Georgetown College. The college now progressed auspiciously, so much so, that in due course of time-namely, in 1808—the long and spacious building on the north side of the grounds was erected. Under Rev. Leonard Neale, (subsequently the second Archbishop of Baltimore, who succeeded Father Dubourg in 1799), the complete college course was arranged, the college having, in 1806, passed under the control of the Society of Jesus, who thus introduced the excellent educational system peculiar to that order.

"Up to the construction of the north building, where now are the 'big boys' dormitories, the library, the parlors, the apartments of the principal officers of the college, the reading room, the 'jug,' etc., it had been customary for the pupils to board with families in Georgetown, but the building of this finely-arranged structure afforded all the accommodation within 'bounds' necessary at the time. It is built after the model of a château in France, and, with its two towers, presents a very handsome and venerable appearance. On May 1, 1815, Congress chartered the 'Georgetown College,' which was then raised to the position of a university. On January 17, 1830, the Philodemic Society was

158

founded by the Rev. James Ryder, at that time vice-president of the college. More space being found necessary about this tune to afford due accommodation to the largely increasing number of pupils, who began to flock to the college even from beyond the limits of the Union, the college buildings were enlarged in 1831, (Rev. Thomas Mulledy, of Virginia, being president), by the erection of the large western wing of the south row, where now are chapel, dining-room, and study-room of the older students. At the same time the western half of the present infirmary was erected, and the grounds of the college, including that beautiful, umbrageous, and extensive promenade known as the 'college walks,' were greatly improved and beautified. These walks are a lasting and perennial adornment to the surroundings of the college.

In 1843, the astronomical observatory of the college was built, under the presidency of Rev. James Ryder, and in 1845—Father Mulledy, being president for the second time—the well-known villa buildings were purchased as a spot for summer recreation for teachers and students. In 1848, the infirmary building was finished. The political agitations of this year in Europe induced many able members of the Society of Jesus to emigrate to this country. This brought an accession of very learned men to the college, such as Fathers Sestini, Secchi, De Vico, and others, who have written and published several books on educational topics since their connection with the college. About this time (Father Ryder being president for the third time), the college gas works and baths were constructed, and, in 1851, that admirably conducted feature of the institution, the medical department of Georgetown College, now in successful operation in this city, was established. Rev. Charles H. Stonestreet succeeded Father Ryder in the presidency in 1851, but having been appointed Provincial of the Society of Jesus, after one year's service he was succeeded by the popular Father Maguire, who, at the early age of thirty-four years, entered upon his first term of president. Under Father Maguire's presidency the college prospered greatly. The number of students increased, and important material additions were made to the college grounds and surroundings. The large new building for the 'small boys,' situated at the eastern end of the south row, was erected in 1854. A fine green-house was built, and extensive gardens were laid out. Father Maguire continued to occupy the president's office until 1858, when he was succeeded by the Rev. John Early, who now so acceptably fills that position.

"The breaking out of the civil war in 1861, seriously hampered the progress of the college. For several weeks, namely, up to July 4th, the peaceful grounds and buildings of the college were used as a barracks for soldiers; the sixty-ninth and seventy-ninth regiments of New York volunteers having been quartered there. In 1862, after the battle of Bull Run, the college was again seized upon by the military authorities, and was converted into a hospital. In 1863 the college was relieved of this burden, and commenced anew its career of prosperity. In 1866, Father Early retired, and was succeeded by Father Maguire, who thus entered upon his second term, to be again succeeded by Father Early, in whose able hands, as in that of his immediate predecessor, the renewed prosperity of old Georgetown College, recovered from the damaging effects of the war, became, as it continues to be, a source of sincere gratification to its legions of friends.

"So far our extract. The article ought to have added that the law department of Georgetown College was organized in 1870, under Father Maguire's administration. In his time, also, the members of the graduating class were assigned rooms. This arrangement, after five years satisfactory experience, may be considered as a permanent one.

"Under the present administration, many desirable changes and improvements have been added. The study of Chemistry, which was formerly confined to a single year, and that the graduating year, now covers two years, beginning with Inorganic in Poetry, and concluding with Organic in Rhetoric. This arrangement leaves more time to the Philosophers for the studies appropriate to their year. A course of English Literature under a special Professor, is also embraced in the years of Poetry and Rhetoric. Provision has been made, besides, for students of English in less advanced classes. Formerly, every student was obliged to conform to the regular curriculum, embracing Greek and Latin, and none were admitted on other conditions.

"Now, those who wish to pursue English branches alone, and do not aspire to graduation, are provided for, and consequently fewer eligible applicants are, turned away. Exercises in Declamation in presence of the assembled classes take place monthly, each speaker being criticized by those of his fellow-students who are called on by the president for their opinion, the president afterwards adding his own. By these means, greater excellence in Declamation is acquired, and is attainable by a larger number than under the old system of theatrical performances, discarded some years since. Class hours have been changed to suit the convenience of day scholars, and greatly to the physical advantage of the boarders, chiefly by giving them a longer recess between the breakfast-hour and the commencement of school duties. With the same view of health and comfort, the old penal confinement of 'The Jug,' alluded to in the above sketch, has been abolished, the dinner-hour has been set back, and many other conveniences have been introduced which it is unnecessary to describe in detail, but which are strongly in contrast with the *quasi* monastic discipline of former years. While physical development and the needs of recreation are further promoted by the two well-appointed gymnasiums, for the larger and the smaller boys respectively, put up by the college, and the two billiard-tables provided for the larger and one for the smaller students, as well as by the Boat Club organization got up by the students themselves. The course of studies is allowed to suffer no detriment, but is promoted as occasion demands. A special impulse has been given of late, in the direction of science, historical enquiry, polemical skill, and mathematical proficiency, by the donation on the part of friends of the college and of the president, of medals in reward for successful efforts in each of these directions. Further developments, towards which preliminary steps have been taken, are in contemplation, but must for the most part await complete realization until the administration is able to erect new buildings, the plans of which are now undergoing final consideration.

161

"The following is the succession of presidents of Georgetown College:

"Rev. Robert Plunket, October 1st, 1791, to June 13th, 1793; immediately succeeded by Rev. Robert Molyneux, to September 30th, 1796; after whom followed Rev. Wm. G. Dubourg, to March 29th, 1799, who subsequently assisted in organizing St. Mary's College, Baltimore. Rev. Leonard Neale then occupied the presidency until September 30th, 1806, having meanwhile, in 1800, been made coadjutor to the Bishop of Baltimore. These appointments were all made by Bishop John Carroll, the founder of the college. In 1806, the Society of Jesus was re-organized and the college committed to its care. Rev. Robert Molyneux, the first Superior of the Jesuits, became president of the college, October 1st, 1806, and died in office, December 9th, 1808. He was succeeded by Rev. William Matthews, a former student of the college, who held office until June 10th, 1810. Rev. Francis Neale had been appointed vice-president of the college, January 1st, 1800; and December 11th, 1810, became president, and remained to September 30th, 1812. Rev. John A. Grassi, S.J., under whom the college developed into a university, succeeded. He was, during the same period, Superior of the Maryland Jesuits. Rev. Benedict J. Fenwick, S.J., a former student, became president on the retirement of Father Grassi, July 31st, 1817. On October 31st, 1818, he was succeeded by Rev. Anthony Kohlman, S.J. (Superior of the Jesuits, 1817 to 1821), until September 15th, 1820. Rev. Enoch Fenwick, S.J., also a former student, filled up the interval until the return of his brother, Benedict, September 15th, 1822, who served until his appointment to the Bishopric of Boston in 1825. Rev. Stephen L. Dubuisson, S.J., followed him, September 9th, 1825, to July 7th, 1826; when Rev. William Feiner, S.J., became president, and gave place March 30th,1829 (a few weeks before his death), to Rev. John Beschter, S.J. Father Beschter held office only until September 13th, of the same year, and was succeeded by Rev. Thomas F. Mulledy, S.J., a former student, until December 23d, 1837, when he became Provincial of Maryland. Father Mulledy's predecessor as provincial, Rev. William McSherry, S.J., another student of

Georgetown College, was his successor as president, and died in office December 18th, 1839. Rev. Joseph A. Lopez, S.J., filled up the interval to April 30th, 1840, and died six months after. Rev. James Ryder, S.J., then held the presidency to January 3d, 1845, and was succeeded by Rev. Samuel F. Mulledy, S.J., who gave place to his brother Thomas, for a second term, from September 6th, 1845, to August 7th, 1848. Father Ryder then returned to the presidency until August 1st,1851. Rev. Charles H. Stonestreet, S.J., an alumnus of the college, was then president until August 15th, 1852, when he was made Provincial of Maryland. Fathers Maguire and Early then alternately held office, each two terms, until 1873, nearly nineteen years. We trust that their successor, Father Healy, an alumnus of Holy Cross, the prosperous daughter of Georgetown, may still preside at Georgetown when her centennial is reached."

The faculty of the college, ever keeping time with the advancement of education, and training the youthful mind to become men in the future, and to do their part in the affairs of life, are not unmindful that a spacious building is necessary to accommodate the increasing number of students coming to the college from all parts of the country. A building is now being erected, which, for magnificent proportions and durability, will be a credit to the college and an ornament to the town. The length of the building is three hundred and seven feet, and occupies the whole front of the college grounds between the north and south wings. The altitude is seventy feet nine and one-half inches; depth is ninety feet at the north end, sixty-three feet and eight inches at the south end, and forty-nine feet in the middle. The building, when completed with the two wings, will form the three sides of a square. The number of windows are two hundred and ninety-two, five feet by ten. The number of doors in the interior, nine. Number of rooms in the whole building, eighty-two. Some of them will be occupied by the library; others will be used by the faculty of the college as parlors and class rooms, and various rooms for the professors in different branches of learning. The number of brick to he used in the construction of the building is estimated at two millions. The quantity of stone called blue gneiss, which is quarried from the banks of the Potomac River, will be five thousand cubic yards used in the construction of the front and sides of the college.

MONASTERY AND ACADEMY OF THE VISITATION.

Our chronicles would be imperfect if we omitted a sketch of a very important institution in our town called the "Monastery," where ladies live in single blessedness. About the year 1792, some sisters belong to the order of "Pon Clares," driven from France by the horrors of the French Revolution, sought refuge in Maryland. The names of the sisters were Maria de La Marche, Abbess of the order of St. Clare, Celeste la Blonde, de La Rochefoncault, and — de St. Luc. They took up their abode in Georgetown. In 1801 they purchased a lot of ground on Fayette Street, in said town, of John Threlkeld. They endeavored to support themselves by opening a school, but they had to struggle constantly with poverty; and on the death of the Abbess, in 1805, Madame de La Rochefoncault, who succeeded her, sold the convent to Bishop Neale, by deed of June 29, 1805, and returned to Europe with her companion. These poor "Clares" had been aided in their labors by Miss Alice Lalor, from Philadelphia (but originally from Ireland), and one or two other pious ladies from the same city. They had, for a time, occupied a small frame house, the site of which is enclosed in the present convent grounds. Bishop Neale, immediately after purchasing the Clarist convent in 1805, installed there these "pious ladies," as they were then called, and by deed of June 9, 1808, confirmed June 9, 1812, transferred the property to Alice Lalor, Maria McDermott, and Mary Neale.

Such was the origin of the Visitation Nuns in the United States. This institution had its trials. In 1824 its financial embarrassments were so great, and the poverty of the community was so extreme, that they came to the resolution of dispersing. But at this juncture relief came. A wealthy Spanish merchant of New York, the late John B. Lasaler, sent two daughters to the convent, paying several years board in advance. This timely aid enabled them to continue their school; and other assistance came afterwards. It was not until 1816 that the institution was regularly established as a Visitation Convent.

Connected with the monastery is a ladies' academy, which ranks among the first educational institutions in the country. The buildings are extensive; fronting three hundred feet on the west side of Fayette Street, also the same distance on Third and Fourth Streets, occupying nearly a square of ground. They have also added to their possessions the tract of land formerly owned by the late John Threlkeld, one of the original founders of the town, where are cultivated all the vegetables and fruits used in the institution; and the grounds are laid out in serpentine walks, around which the ladies promenade for exercise. Thus, from a small beginning, this institution has become one of the wealthiest of our town, without calling upon the Woman's Rights Convention for any assistance or aid whatever.

The chronicler had the pleasure, many years past, to witness at the Monastery the taking of the vail by four young ladies (whose names he will not mention, as it might be a breach of politeness to place the names of ladies in print without their consent). It was on the 4th day of July, 1840, at six o'clock in the morning, when the chapel of the monastery was opened, and from that hour the congregation began to assemble. The small and beautifully ornamented chapel, which the sisters had decorated, with evidence of accomplishment and taste, with its dim light burning before the altar, the solemnity rendered more impressive by the number of silent worshipers who were present, and by the voices of the unseen choir whose chant filled the air, had an effect to prepare the mind for this interesting ceremony. Soon the chapel filled. One of the sisters threw back the curtain which shaded the grating that separated the chapel from the convent, when every eye was turned in that direction. All the nuns were seen to enter in a long procession, and to kneel down the whole length of the aisles, with their heads bent towards the ground in an attitude of humility. Presently, the ladies who were to take the vail were led towards the grating; the chanting ceased, and the organ, touched by a master hand, filled the air with its music. The ladies who were the all absorbing interest of the, ceremony were young, beautiful, and tastefully arrayed in white. The anthem ceased; when the Archbishop, in his canonicals, advanced to the front of the altar, and eloquently addressed the congregation and the novices who were about to enter as members of the Sisters of the Visitation. When the discourse was finished, the Archbishop gave a blessing: after which the novices one by one answered the questions which prepared them to renounce the world; then coming forward for the last time, their baptismal names were renounced and they received their new titles. Thus they passed away from the gaze of their relatives and friends, and the sight of the world, of which their beauty and accomplishments would have rendered them the admiration and the ornament. The whole sisterhood received them; when the peals of the organ again filled the church, and the dark folds of the falling curtain shut them, forever perhaps, from the public sight. They abandoned the cares and vexations of this life, of which they were too young to have felt any of its vicissitudes, to look forward to another world beyond the grave.

GEORGETOWN COLLEGIATE INSTITUTE.

Georgetown Collegiate Institute for Young Ladies, Miss Lucy Stephenson, principal, was first opened for the reception of pupils September 9th, 1872.

This institute has been in successful operation for more than six years. During that time it has been steadily increasing in favor with the public. Since its foundation, fourteen young ladies have graduated, having completed the required course of studies. At the present time there are seventy-three scholars in the institute. In addition to the principal, there are eight teachers assisting her in imparting instruction in the several branches of study taught.

The location of the institute is very desirable, situated at the southwest corner of Congress and Gay Streets.

PEABODY LIBRARY AND LINTHICUM INSTITUTE.

Peabody Library and Linthicum Institute, which was lately established in our town, owe their origin to the liberality of George Peabody and E.M. Linthicum, now deceased.

As the letters and correspondence show the origin of these

institutions, the chronicler avails himself, for the benefit of his readers, of copying from the report of J. Ormond Wilson, Esq., a history of the above institutions, in which can be seen the fertile pen of our fellow-citizen, Josiah Dent, Esq., now one of the Commissioners of the District of Columbia:

"In 1872, when the trustees of the public schools of Georgetown were considering the proposition to erect in a central locality a school building in which they could place their more advanced schools and furnish the city with enlarged and improved school facilities, it was suggested that two philanthropic gentlemen had each given to the city, for educational uses, a considerable fund which had not been applied, and that all of these interests might be united with great mutual advantage. The suggestion was favorably received, and has since been carried out.

"It is deemed proper to give some account of the transactions in the report; and I am indebted to the courtesy of Mr. A. Hyde, one of the trustees of the Peabody Library Association, and of Mr. Josiah Dent, president of the Linthicum Institute, for the following brief histories"

PEABODY LIBRARY.

"This library had its origin in the munificence of Mr. George Peabody, and his intentions are fully set forth in the following letter:

"91 LAFAYETTE STREET, SALEM, 20th April, 1867.
"To W.W. CORCORAN, GEORGE W. RIGGS,
A. HYDE, HENRY D. COOKE, and WILLIAM L. DUNLOP, Esqs.,
of the District of Columbia.

"GENTLEMEN: As most of you are aware, I am, and have been for some time, desirous of making some gift which would be productive of benefit to the citizens of Georgetown, in the District of Columbia, where I commenced business for myself in early youth. I am persuaded that I cannot better do so than by endeavoring to assist them in their own endeavors to cultivate a healthful, moral, and intellectual progress; and I therefore give to you gentlemen the sum of fifteen thousand dollars, to be, by you and your successors, held in trust as a fund for a public library, to be established in the city of Georgetown. This sum I direct to be invested and accumulated until it shall be sufficient, in connection with the amount of accrued interest, and including any donations from other sources, should such be made, to erect a suitable building in the city of Georgetown for a public library, to which the inhabitants of Georgetown shall have free access, under such restrictions and regulations as may, by you and your successors, be deemed necessary and proper. Should you think it best to keep the funds as they are until they shall be sufficient, by accumulation, as before stated, to erect a building which shall not only be suitable for such a library as I have specified, but which shall also contain a lecture-room or hall for lectures for popular instructions, I give you leave to do so. I give you the power to organize, to choose a treasurer, and, if necessary, to obtain an act of incorporation; and I direct that an annual report of the condition of the fund and amount of income be prepared and published by yourselves and your successors. I direct that your board be always composed of five persons, and in case of a vacancy or vacancies occurring in your number, I direct that the same be filled, by vote of the remainder, as soon thereafter as conveniently can be.

"Please to receive inclosed my check on James Tinker, Esq., New York, for fifteen thousand dollars, to be appropriated as directed in this letter.

With great respect, I am your humble servant,

GEORGE PEABODY.

The gentlemen named in the foregoing letter met in the private office of Mr. Corcoran, May 1, 1867, and organized as a board of trustees by electing Mr. W.W. Corcoran, president, and Mr. A. Hyde, secretary. The funds given by Mr. Peabody was ordered to be invested in United States securities, and was so invested at first, but was subsequently changed to ten per cent. mortgages, secured by real estate in Washington City.

"The following reply to Mr. Peabody's letter was made:

"WASHINGTON, May 1st, 1867.
"To GEORGE PEABODY, ESQ., LONDON, ENGLAND.

"DEAR SIR: On the 26th April, Mr. Corcoran had the pleasure to acknowledge the receipt of your esteemed favor of the 20th April, addressed to himself and others therein named.

"In pursuance of the directions contained in this letter, the trustees met at twelve o'clock this day, at Mr. Corcoran's private office, all being present, and they organized by the appointment of Mr. Corcoran as chairman, Mr. Hyde as secretary, and Mr. Riggs as treasurer; and, after a full interchange of views, and to meet your wishes as understood from your letter, it was

"*Ordered*, That the amount to be invested in United States five-twenty Treasury notes, registered in the name of the trustees; the accruing interest to be invested in the same securities until further order of the trustees.

"It was also determined to obtain an act of incorporation, as soon as practicable, under the name of 'The Peabody Library Association of Georgetown,' which, we trust, will meet your approbation; and it will be the pleasure of the trustees, whom you have honored with the custody and direction of this liberal gift to the people of Georgetown, to give full effect to your wishes in this behalf, as already expressed, or that you may hereafter intimate.

"On behalf of the people of Georgetown, we tender you, dear sir, our grateful acknowledgments for this beneficence, and most sincerely wish that you may long be spared to witness the benefits of your enlarged liberality to the people of these and other lands, and to receive and enjoy the admiration and gratitude of those who will be the direct recipients of your bounty, as well as of those who can appreciate the inestimable benefits that will flow to thousands by your most liberal and enlightened munificence.

"We are, dear sir, your obedient servants,

> W.W. CORCORAN,
> GEORGE W. RIGGS,
> A. HYDE,
> HENRY D. COOKE,
> WILLIAM L. DUNLOP.

"The fund was allowed to accumulate, and an annual statement of its condition was made at regular meetings of the board, and published, in conformity with the gift. In November, 1872, the following letter was received from the board of trustees of public schools of Georgetown:

"TO W.W. CORCORAN, ANTHONY HYDE,
HENRY D. COOKE, W.L. DUNLOP, AND GEORGE W. RIGGS,
Trustees of the Peabody Library Fund.
"GENTLEMEN: I am directed by the board of school trustees of the city of Georgetown, to submit for your consideration the following:

"The authorities of the District of Columbia are about to erect a school-house on Second Street, opposite St. John's Church, in Georgetown, of large dimensions, to be of as imposing an exterior as is consistent with a proper economy. The objects sought to be attained by the outlay are the advancement of the cause of education in the town, the elevation of the public school system, and the establishment of better educational facilities for the youth of both sexes, and for the general benefit and prosperity of the community.

"To aid in the accomplishment of their purposes, and at the same time to open up the only way which seems practicable for carrying out, at an early day, the designs of Mr. Peabody for the establishment of a library in Georgetown, the board of trustees of the public schools propose to set apart a room of sufficient dimensions on the ground floor, fronting on Second Street, for the purpose of the Peabody Fund, where a library may be established, free of rent, under the absolute control of your honorable body in every respect, with the privilege of withdrawal whenever such action is desired. It is also designed to provide accommodation for the Linthicum Institute on the same terms, to enable the trustees of that fund to carry out the objects of their trusts. They have already informerly expressed their concurrence in the design, and their desire to accept such a proposition.

"Connected with the building will be a commodious lecture hall, for general lecture purposes; and the managers of the Linthicum Institute contemplate making provision for popular lectures in connection with their other plans.

"It is, in the judgment of the school authorities, safe to predict that the three interests thus combined, while they will remain under separate and independent control, will be, by this combination, of great and lasting benefit to the town, and open an admirable and speedy way for the consummation of the liberal and enlightened intentions of the generous donors of the respective funds referred to.

"As it will have a bearing on the plans of the building, it is desirable to know, at your earliest convenience, whether it will be the pleasure of your honorable body to accept the proposition herein embraced, and the board of school trustees would, therefore, ask early consideration of the same.

"I am, gentlemen, very respectfully,
"Your obedient servant,
W.W. CURTIS, *Secretary.*
"By order of the board of school trustees of Georgetown.

"The proposition contained in the foregoing letter was very carefully considered, and in due time accepted. In the latter part of 1875, a committee, consisting of Messrs. Hyde, and Dunlop, was appointed, with authority to have the rooms properly fitted up and furnished, to purchase the books, and to make all necessary arrangements for opening the library to the public. The committee consulted with Mr. A.B. Spofford, Librarian of Congress, and are greatly indebted for the valuable advice and aid cheerfully given by him. The furniture and appointments are all in the most approved style, and the book shelves will readily hold six thousand volumes. About twelve hundred volumes were purchased, and the library was opened in March, 1875, under rules and regulations governing the Peabody Library Association.

"Mr. Frank Hyde Barbarin was appointed first librarian; but shortly after his appointment was transferred to the banking house of Riggs & Co., and Mr. Frank D. Johns was appointed in his stead. Although so short a time has elapsed since the library was first opened, it is already in successful operation, and a large number of persons are availing themselves of its benefits. The average daily attendance has not been less than twenty, and the number is steadily increasing. The fund now amounts to twenty-five thousand dollars; and the treasurer, after paying all expenses to date, has about two thousand dollars now in hand.

"The following is the present list of officers of the Peabody Library Association: Trustees—W.W. Corcoran, president; George W. Riggs, treasurer; Anthony Hyde, secretary; William L. Dunlop, Henry D. Cooke, Sr. Committee on the Library—A. Hyde, W.L. Dunlop; Committee on Accounts and Expenditures A. Hyde; Frank D. Johns, librarian; G.B. Wibert, janitor.

A. HYDE, *Secretary.*

"By order of the association, July 30, 1876.

LINTHICUM INSTITUTE.

Edward Magruder Linthicum, to whose liberality this institute owes its existence, was born in Montgomery County, Maryland, on the 16th of July, 1797. With no other advantages of education than those furnished by a country school of the times, he embarked, when quite a youth, in mercantile pursuits in Georgetown, District of Columbia, under the auspices of his uncle, Doctor Ninian Magruder, a prominent citizen of the town. At this period Georgetown was a port of considerable commerce.

171

A career of fifty years devoted to active business, and distinguished for integrity, energy, and prudent sagacity, was crowned with abundant success; and the last five years of his life were spent in tranquil retirement. He died at his residence an Georgetown heights, on the 30th of October, 1869, universally respected for his virtues by the community who had been the daily witnesses of his life from youth to old age. That in his last years, free from the cares of business, he was not unmindful of duty and of the highest interests of those among whom his useful and exemplary life had been spent, is attested by the following extract from his last will:

"'Convinced that knowledge and piety constitute the only assurance of happiness and healthful progress to the human race, devoutly recognizing the solemn duties to society which devolve on all its members, and entertaining more especially a sincere desire to contribute in some measure to the permanent welfare of the community among whom my life has been spent, I give to my friends, Doctor Joshua Riley, Josiah Dent, William Laird, Jr., William L. Dunlop, and William A. Gordon, Jr., and to their survivors and successors forever, the sum of fifty thousand dollars in trust, to found, establish, and maintain, in Georgetown, under such conditions and regulations as they may from time to time prescribe and ordain, a free school for the education and instruction of indigent white boys and youths of said Georgetown in useful learning, and in the spirit and practice of Christian virtue; and I advise and direct that said school fund, with all its additions and accretions, except what may be required to provide necessary accommodations for said school, shall, as favorable opportunity may offer, be invested and kept invested in unincumbered real estate, situated in said Georgetown, yielding good rents, and free from all doubt or dispute as to the title thereof on the security of such real estate; and that, in no case of investment on such security, shall the sum invested exceed in amount two-thirds of the estimated cash value of the property by which it is secured. And I further request and enjoin my said trustees that, whenever from any cause a vacancy may exist in their body, the remaining trustees shall, without unnecessary delay, fill the same; so that the number of trustees of said school fund shall never be less than five; and that, in order to perpetuate this trust, the said trustees shall, as soon as may be, cause themselves to be legally incorporated for the purposes hereof; under a suitable name and with all needful powers and immunities. And it is my wish, finally, that my adopted son, Edward Linthicum Dent, should he attain to manhood, shall be elected to fill the first vacancy thereafter existing in said board of trustees.'

"And, by a final provision of his will, Mr. Linthicum contingently dedicated the entire residue of his estate, after payment of a few small legacies, to the same beneficent uses.

"In obedience to the injunction of the testator, the trustees, without delay, applied for an act of incorporation to the Congress of the United States, in the winter of 1870; and a bill for that purpose passed the House of Representatives without objection, but, under adverse influences, failed in the Senate. The trustees then applied to the legislative assembly of the District of Columbia for a similar grant, which was duly accorded to them. Under this charter, the board of trustees of the Linthicum Institute of Georgetown was formerly organized on the 7th of September, 1872, and at once proceeded to arrange for active operations.

"On the 19th of November, 1872, however, the trustees received from the board of trustees of the public schools of Georgetown, through J. Ormond Wilson, Esq., superintendent, the following overtures for the location of the institute in the new school building, the erection of which, on corner of Second and Potomac Streets, was then under consideration:

"To JOSIAH DENT, Doctor JOSHUA RILEY, W.L. DUNLOP,
W. LAIRD, Jr., and WILLIAM A. GORDON, Jr.,
Trustees of the Linthicum Institute.
"GENTLEMEN: I am directed, by the board of school trustees of the city of Georgetown, to submit for your consideration the following:

"You are already aware, through informal conferences with the board, of their design to build a large and imposing school-house on the premises opposite St. John's Church, said premises being situated between High and Market Streets, with a width of about one hundred and twenty-five feet, extending from Second to Third Streets; the house to cost about sixty thousand, and the ground not less than thirteen thousand.

"To increase the usefulness of this enterprise, it is proposed to set apart, free from rent, a room on the ground floor of the main front of said building, for the use and purposes of the Linthicum Institute, and also one for the establishment of the Peabody Library, so arranged as to have each institution under the exclusive control of the respective boards of trustees, with the right to manage their own affairs in their own way, and to withdraw therefrom at pleasure.

"In the department devoted to the purpose of the Linthicum Institute, there will be added a laboratory and other conveniences for scientific lectures and for such school purposes as it is understood the trustees design to establish and maintain.

"It is proposed to combine under one roof the three institutions, each preserving its independency of the other, and each, under separate and distinct control, believing that the usefulness and efficacy of each will thereby be greatly enhanced.

"To aid in carrying out the proposed plan, the board of trustees of the Georgetown schools propose to borrow of the trustees of the Linthicum Institute, the sum of fifty thousand dollars, at the rate of eight per cent. per annum, payable semi-annually; the principal to be refunded at the pleasure of the board, at any time after five years, in sums not less than five thousand dollars; said payments to be secured on the property to be improved, and the money borrowed to be expended thereon; the funds to be placed in the bands of a third party, to be expended as needed for the building, and to bear interest from the date of delivery, or to be taken by the board of school trustees as needed; and the amount so taken to bear interest from the date of delivery. It is understood that the fund belonging to the Linthicurn Institute is in certain bonds (as stated at the informal meeting), and that they are to be received at par by the school authorities.

"It is important that the board of school trustees be informed, at your earliest convenience, of your action in reference to the proposition herein stated.

"I am, gentlemen, very respectfully,
your obedient servant,
W.W. CURTIS, *Secretary.*
"By order of the Board of School Trustees of Georgetown.

"These overtures were favorably received, and it was finally stipulated that, in consideration of a loan by the institute to the public school board of forty thousand dollars secured by lien or mortgage on the school property, suitable accommodations for the use of the institute should be provided in the projected school building.

"This arrangement, of course, was productive of delay in opening the institute, and also of important changes in its plan. It soon became apparent that the greater development and increased accommodations for common school education in Georgetown, which would be secured by the erection of this central and spacious school edifice, would satisfy present wants in respect to day schools for our children. But there is a class of boys and youths of more advanced years, to whose circumstances these schools are not suited whose necessities require them to spend the day in work rather than in school. And to this class the trustees turned their attention as the most needy and worthy beneficiaries of Mr. Linthicum's benevolent provision. They concluded to establish an evening school, to which, after the daily toil is ended, they may resort for such practical instructions as will qualify them for the active duties and business of life. So soon, therefore, as the new edifice was ready for occupancy, a school was organized with three competent teachers, for the instruction of classes from seven to nine o'clock, every evening, except Saturday and Sunday, in the following studies, viz: Penmanship, Book-keeping, Drawing, Arithmetic, Geometry, Chemistry and Physics, the two last being taught experimentally. The school was opened auspiciously on the 1st of October, 1875, in the rooms in the Curtis School Building provided for the use of the institute, under the arrangement referred to above.

PUBLIC SCHOOLS.

The chronicler, availing himself of the admirable report of Samuel Yorke AtLee, Esq., made to the board of trustees in 1876, concerning the public Schools of Georgetown, makes the following extracts in relation to public education, showing how the system commenced and gradually progressed in the town.

LANCASTERIAN SCHOOL.

"Georgetown had been settled sixty years before public

175

attention was turned to the necessity of education, and it is especially worthy of notice that the movement originated amongst the people.

"About a hundred citizens, neither so rich or so poor as to be indifferent to the general welfare, formed themselves into a society for the purpose of imparting to the citizens of Georgetown 'the advantages of education according to the system devised by Joseph Lancaster;' and for defraying the expenses thereof, they agreed to contribute annually about one thousand dollars. They no doubt considered that amount amply sufficient to sustain a school, after complete organization; but they soon discovered that to begin such an undertaking, to purchase a lot, to build a house, and to supply the necessary furniture; would require additional resources.

"To obtain such additional resources, the Lancaster Society, through their trustees, memorialized the corporation. Some response must have been given to that memorial, but we have searched the municipal journal in vain to find it. The memorialists represented a large number of respectable and influential constituents of the corporate authorities, and it is not at all probable that their request was treated with indifference. Legislation, however, seems by general consent, to have been suspended, and meanwhile 'a square of ground was conveyed by the Rev. Leonard Neale to certain persons (the Lancaster Society) for the purpose of carrying on a public system of education.' The Lancaster Society, under these circumstances, and willing to put off as long as possible recourse to the public treasury, may perhaps have withdrawn their memorial and confined their efforts to the erection of a school-house.

"These efforts were successful, and in June, 1811, the mayor, recorder, aldermen, and common councilmen, officially attended the procession of the Lancaster Society for the purpose of laying the corner-stone of the school-house. In five months the building was completed, and a school was begun November 18th, 1811, under Mr. Robert Ould, and contained, before the lapse of many weeks, three hundred and forty boys and girls under tuition. But the trustees disapproved of this indiscriminate crowding of both sexes in one room, and to correct that irregularity, as well as to accommodate the throng daily seeking admission, they renewed their application to the 'Worshipful Corporation.' The trustees congratulated the authorities on the success of a 'plan of education so plain, so unembarrassed, and so ready of execution,' which had been proved by the proficiency of the scholars, and the increasing reputation of the school; expressed their serious objections to an intercourse of the sexes in an assemblage so large and so promiscuous; and as the school-house could not accommodate all the applicants for tuition, they asked the aid of the legal guardians and representatives of the town towards carrying into effect a plan already 'digested,' which would enlarge the accommodations for the boys and extend the facilities of instruction to the girls.

"Either from pride or diffidence, the trustees did not announce this digested plan, but endeavored to propitiate the good will of the city fathers by presenting, as a subject of general regret and sorrowful reflection, that females, the distinguished ornaments of creation, should experience that neglect of education, unhappily too prevalent towards them throughout the world. Following this eloquent appeal a petition was read, signed by ninety-five subscribers to the 'Lancaster School Fund,' all constituents, respectable, influential, and legal voters. This petition frankly represented that an addition to the Lancaster School, for the accommodation of the female scholars, would be a public good, and prayed for an appropriation of money sufficient to build such an addition as would accommodate two hundred female scholars.'

"Neither of these papers bear any date, but the ordinance of May 12th, 1812, is so perfectly responsive to both, that we need not hesitate to assign to them a date prior to the date thereof.

"That ordinance appropriated the sum of one thousand dollars, to be given to the trustees of the Lancaster School, for the express purpose of enabling them to erect an addition to their present school-house to accommodate the females of said school, and prescribed the materials and dimensions of the additional building, which was to be so constructed as to accommodate two hundred and fifty scholars, at the least. A proviso attached to the ordinance betrayed the fear of censorious animadversion. The one thousand dollars was to be paid in annual instalments of two hundred dollars, so that public indignation might be soothed by the long credit, for the last instalment would not be payable until May, 1816.

"But the, result of this legislation relieved the corporation from all fears of censure, and the Lancaster School had, meanwhile, diffused its meliorative influences so widely, that the councils felt authorized to manifest their good will in a more decided manner. Some months before the last instalment of two hundred dollars was due, an ordinance, of October 6,1815, provided that, instead of the trifling annuity theretofore allowed to the Lancaster School, there should thereafter be paid, yearly and every year, to the trustees thereof, the sum of one thousand dollars, for the purpose of assisting the said trustees in defraying the expenses of the school. The conditions annexed to the grant were, that the trustees should receive all destitute children and cause them to be educated; that all children, on completing their education, should be bound out according to the laws in force in the country; that an annual report of the condition of the school be made by the trustees, and that the schools should be subject to occasional visits of four persons out of the councils, for the purpose of inspecting the operation thereof; and to see that order and morality were maintained, as well in as out of the school.

"For nine years the schools were carried on in harmony and to the satisfaction of the community and of the corporate authorities. The annual reports must have been regularly made by the trustees, but, although the utmost freedom of search amongst the archives of Georgetown was allowed to me by their custodian, Mr. Surveyor Forsyth, with the assistance of Mr. J.J. Bogue, an intelligent and polite coadjutor, not one of them could be found. The Lancaster Society seems to have left everything relating to the schools to the discretion of the trustees, and those gentlemen did not, it seems, suppose that the monotonous routine of school-keeping could ever become a subject of inquiry. We are, therefore, left to infer or to conjecture the proceedings of the school trustees from the records of municipal legislation.

"During this period, the corporation was admonished of the

danger of transgressing the line of secular policy in relation to schools. Application for aid in maintaining a free school was made by a religious society. An appropriation of two hundred dollars was granted; and the lot on which the school-house stood was exempted from taxes. But these favors were soon afterwards withheld. The feelings of the American people are deeply and sincerely religious, but their theological opinions are not concordant. Conscience and worship are both equally free, and the increase and prosperity of each church are dependent, exclusively, on private liberality and enterprise.

"For thirty-two years the Lancasterian School had been sustained by private contribution and municipal aid. The list of subscribers to the Lancaster School Fund exhibited the names of few survivors, and those few could not, fairly, be expected to make good the deficiencies in the fund with their individual offerings. They had nobly volunteered to do a good work, and had done it well. They had broken up the fallow ground, ploughed the field, and sowed the seed, and the successive harvests had supplied an entire generation with intellectual and moral nourishment. Their fellow-citizens appreciated their beneficent labors, and, prompted by public opinion, the municipality passed the ordinance of December 31, 1842.

"This ordinance declared that the schools then in operation, and supported by appropriations of the public money, be taken under the exclusive care of the corporate authority, and that guardians thereof be annually appointed, in joint meeting of the two boards, on the first Monday in January;

"That the guardians of the Georgetown school should consist of seven members, two, at least, of whom shall be members of the corporation, and were thereby invested with full powers to keep and manage said schools in such manner as they should deem best;

"And that, soon as the organization of the board of guardians shall have been reported to the mayor, the clerk of the corporation was authorized and directed to transfer and pay the amounts appropriated for education to said guardians.

GEORGETOWN SCHOOL.

"Who constituted the first board of the Georgetown schools is not shown by the legislative record. The regular annual appropriation of one thousand dollars allowed by the ordinance of October 6,1815, seems to have been enough to defray expenses; for, up to November, 1847, only two appropriations, amounting to three hundred and fifty dollars, were required. The guardians kept no journal of their meetings, neither was there found on file any copy of their periodical reports or other document.

"In 1848, however, that omission was supplied; and until the consolidation of 1874, there is a continuous narrative of twenty-six years. The board of guardians for 1848 met on the 5th of January, and were duly organized. The removal of the schools to other rooms was the only remarkable event in their administration until September, when they were served with a copy of a joint resolution, directing the guardians to charge and receive pay for all scholars whose parents or guardians are, in the opinion of a majority of the board, able to pay not exceeding one dollar a month for the general use of the schools. Whereupon, the board *ordered*, That the principals of the school furnish lists of their respective scholars from which the board may ascertain whose parents may be able to pay for the tuition of their children. These directions were not agreeable to the board; for no further mention of nor allusion to the subject appears on the minutes. Inquisitorial duties were imposed on them which no American gentleman could possibly perform; and the councils, by their silence, seemed to attribute the adoption of the joint resolution to inadvertence.

"From 1848 to 1853 was an era of good feeling for the teachers, for their salaries were twice raised; but the unfair discrimination shown against the 'ornaments of creation' in the gradation of salaries recalls the 'sorrowful reflection' suggested by Mr. Robert Beverley. The principal teacher of the male school was allowed five hundred and fifty dollars, while the principal teacher of the female school was allowed only one-half that amount, two hundred and seventy-five dollars, which was, moreover, fifty dollars less than the salary of the assistant teacher of the male school.

"The corporation having been informed, in 1849, by the board, that the interests of the schools required more ample accommodations than those afforded by the hall of the Vigilant Fire Company, passed the ordinance of August 11th, 1849, appropriating twelve hundred dollars for the purchase of the Methodist Episcopal Church on Montgomery Street, and an additional amount, not exceeding eight hundred dollars, for adapting the same to the comfortable accommodation of the schools. The purchase and alterations must have been promptly made. The day, however, when it was first occupied by the schools is not mentioned, but the minutes of November 9, 1850, are dated 'at the new school-house.' In the ordinance purchasing this building, there was a provision that the trustees were to pay interest, annually, on the two thousand dollars to the corporation; but this condition does not appear to have been insisted on, and was formally repealed in 1852.

"In 1851 the councils appropriated, at the request of the board, seventy-five dollars for the purchase of premiums at the annual exhibition, but in 1852 they did not feel able to afford such an expenditure; and, but for the generosity of Mr. W.W. Corcoran, whose father, forty-three years before, made the first appeal to the corporate authorities on behalf of the public schools, the children would have been sorely disappointed. Mr. Corcoran sent one hundred dollars to the board for the purchase of premiums, and annually repeated his donation as long as it was needed.

"In September, 1853, the board ordered that Mr. Craig, the principal teacher of the male school, be allowed five dollars to purchase instruments for pulling teeth. The extraction of teeth was not a punishment, but the toothache was such a common excuse for neglect of lessons and for non-attendance at school, that Mr. Craig came to the conclusion that the removal of the offending member was the best way of maintaining discipline. 'And it was astonishing,' said the trustee who explained this entry, 'it was astonishing to see the business he did! Odontalgia became so contagious or fashionable that Mr. Craig soon filled a quart-cup, more or less, with trophies of his dentistry.'

"The councils having been asked for one thousand dollars, responded by appropriating two thousand five hundred dollars for school expenses in 1855, and the board, having received it, set apart thereof enough to pay incidental expenses, and divided the rest *pro rata* amongst the teachers. In May, 1856, there was some correspondence between the board and the corporation, in the course of which it appeared that the board of trustees had never kept any account-book, and were, therefore, unable to submit to the council a statement of receipts and expenditures. They had depended entirely on the books kept by the clerk of the corporation, but 'they expected to present, if necessary,' at the end of the year, a full and accurate exhibit of the condition of the school fund. In regard to the personnel of the school, they reported one hundred and fifty males enrolled, with an average attendance of one hundred and twelve; and eighty females enrolled, with an average attendance of sixty. The report at the end of the year stated the number of males enrolled at one hundred and fifty-eight, with an average attendance of one hundred and nineteen; and that during the year fifty had been admitted and fifty-two withdrawn. Of the females seventy-one were enrolled, with an average attendance of fifty-six; and that during the year sixty-one had been admitted and fifty-three withdrawn.

"This irregular attendance was to be, no doubt, attributed in part to the crowded benches. The two school rooms had each been partitioned into two, and although the change at first conduced to order and good discipline, the wish of the board to admit as many as possibly could be seated, neutralized these advantages. These inconveniences became so embarrassing, that in March, 1857, the board communicated to the councils their desire to establish an additional school at an estimated expense of nine hundred and thirty-five dollars. But the proximate municipal election and the hope of aid from Congress induced the corporation to postpone legislation on the subject. Meanwhile, the board sought to obtain from the voters at the polls voluntary donations in behalf of the public schools. The attempt failed; but the board soon presented an argument that convinced everybody of the necessity of enlarging the scope of their administration.

"At the meeting in January, 1856, it was determined to canvass the city, so as to ascertain what proportion of the children, between five and eighteen years of age, attended school. In April the canvasser reported -the whole number of such children at two thousand two hundred and seventy-eight; six hundred and seventy-nine of whom were in private schools, and four hundred and sixty-one were in public, free, and parish schools; total, one thousand one hundred and forty; leaving one thousand one hundred and thirty-eight, almost exactly half, of the juvenile population entirely without means of learning. The publication of this census dispersed all objections. In one week afterwards, the board were informed that the remainder of the school fund was made subject to their order, for the purpose of building a new school-house, and a committee was at once instructed to select a site. This was not done, however, until June, 1859, when the purchase of the lot on the corner of High and Market Streets was consummated. The plan of the new building was agreed on in April, 1860, and the contract was awarded in the following May, but it was not occupied before September, 1863, for this was a time of great political distress arid perplexity. The building cost about three thousand dollars; and the expenditure for lot, furniture, salaries, and other indispensable outlay, must have made up a total not less than five thousand dollars.

"The year 1864 lifted up on high the 'ornaments of creation;' for every teacher elected was a 'female.' Even the senior and junior male classes were put under their control. But the board seemed still to be influenced by the traditionary undervaluation of woman's services, and reduced the salary of the teacher of the senior male school to seven hundred and fifty dollars—fifty dollars less than allowed to the male teacher ever since 1856. The scale adopted was, however, an evidence of progress, generally, and was fixed at a more equitable standard than theretofore.

"Music was very cautiously introduced into the schools. On the 7th of October, 1857, it was ordered by the board that 'the children, or such of them as would agree, may be taught music at their own expense.' In the following December, Mr. Magee stated that 'a large number of the scholars had placed themselves under Mr. Hunter, who was teaching them music scientifically, and that their progress was a source of congratulation.' In August, 1860, 'permission was given for the introduction of singing into the schools, provided such arrangements be made without expense to the board.' In April, 1863, Mr. Magee was instructed 'to converse with Mr. Daniel, music teacher, on the subject of giving instruction to the town schools.' In 1864, a music master was included in the academic staff; at a salary of one hundred and fifty dollars.

"From 1865 to 1870, the administration of the board received many tokens of public approbation. The ladies held a fair for the benefit of the schools, in April, 1866; and Mr. Magee handed to the guardians the net proceeds thereof (four hundred dollars), with a recommendation that it be devoted to the establishment of a library for the schools. The board approved the recommendation; but when they took under consideration the room to be provided for the books, the librarian to be appointed and paid to distribute and to take care of them, and the binder's bill for occasional repairs, the project was given up, and, with the consent of the ladies, the money was spent for a piano for use in the higher schools. Major George Hill, Jr., also presented to the six schools as many beautiful silk flags, and Captain Thomas Brown gave nine neatly bound volumes suitable for premiums. All these donors were tendered the thanks of the board.

"New schools were the chief topic at the meetings of the guardians, and the aid of the corporation was again invoked; and a lot, on Prospect Street, about to be sold at that time, was withdrawn from market and transferred to the board. Meanwhile, room was made for thirty scholars more in each of the schools in the High Street building, and the necessary assistant teachers were added to the preceptoral force. In 1868, the corporation appropriated fourteen hundred dollars for the schools, and ordered that city stock be issued to the amount of twenty thousand dollars, the proceeds of which were to be placed to the credit of the school fund. Proposals for a building were at once invited, and of seven, the lowest was for nine thousand seven hundred and thirty-seven dollars, and a contract was accordingly executed.

"In 1868, 1869, and 1870, Congress was memorialized for help, but neither money nor land was available for the District schools, although millions of acres were allotted for maintaining schools in the States and Territories of the Union. In 1869, the teachers' salaries were advanced twenty-five per cent., and the schools were graded as grammar, intermediate, secondary, and primary. About forty children having been reported as awaiting admission on granted permits, two half schools, of thirty scholars each, were organized in the High Street building, and the requisite assistant teachers elected.

"During this period a law had been passed, levying a tax of twenty-five cents on each one hundred dollars of assessed property for the public schools, which yielded about twelve thousand dollars a year. Out of the proceeds the corporation was to be reimbursed for the stock issued in 1868.

"In 1871, the board began their administration full of energy and hope. Four hundred dollars were appropriated for medals and premiums at the June examination. But their proceedings were interrupted by Congress, which, by an act passed February 21, 1871, put the District under a territorial form of government.

"On the 16th of the ensuing June, the following gentlemen were appointed by Henry D. Cooke, Governor of the District, a board of trustees of the public schools of Georgetown, viz: Anthony Hyde, G.W. Beall, C.D. Welsh, W.L. Dunlop, W.W. Curtis, C.S. Ramsburg, and F.W. Moffat. The first regular meeting of the board was held October 3, and organized by the election of Anthony Hyde, president, and W.W. Curtis, secretary.

"At the meeting, January 5,1872, the salaries were thus graded: teachers of the male and female grammar schools each, one thousand dollars; teachers of intermediate, eight hundred dollars; of secondaries, seven hundred dollars: of primaries, six hundred and fifty dollars; music teacher, two hundred dollars. Thus were the 'ornaments of creation,' at last, ranked according to the uses they performed; for which just act the names of these gentlemen ought ever to be held in grateful remembrance.

"Under the new form of government, all public expenditures

185

had to be estimated and submitted to the legislature through the comptroller. In response to a communication from that officer calling attention to this law, the board reported, as necessary for the current expenses of the year, the sum of fifteen thousand dollars.

"But a project was under consideration in the board which involved the expenditure of a much larger amount, and which, if successfully consummated, would secure the permanent prosperity of the public schools of Georgetown. Some desirable lots were for sale, suitable for a commodious and elegant school building worthy of the city and of the cause; but the ground and the house would cost not less than seventy-five thousand dollars. The ways and means of raising this amount were the subject of frequent consultations. To these consultations Governor Cooke and superintendent Wilson were invited, and contributed essentially to a favorable conclusion. The District government could not give any aid, as the expenditures by the board of public works had emptied the public treasury; and so utterly were the Territorial finances deranged, that the salaries of the teachers in the public schools of Washington, Georgetown, and the county had not, for some months, been paid. In this strait, Mr. W.W. Corcoran volunteered the loan of a sum sufficient to pay the salaries for two months. The offer was gratefully accepted, and Mr. Corcoran advanced twenty-five thousand five hundred and ninety dollars, without interest.

"The consultations, meanwhile, were continued, and resulted, finally, in a proposed coalescence of interest between the 'Peabody Library Fund,' the 'Linthicum Institute,' and the public schools of Georgetown. George Peabody had donated fifteen thousand dollars to certain trustees, for founding a public library in Georgetown, and Edward Linthicum had bequeathed fifty thousand dollars for establishing schools for free instruction to the children of that city. The negotiations preliminary to this union were not encouraging, but an arrangement satisfactory to all parties was finally agreed to, and the monument of that satisfactory arrangement is the Curtis school-house. In that spacious and elegant building, named in honor of Mr. W.W. Curtis, president of the existing board, are ample

186

accommodations for the Peabody Library, which now consists of about fifteen hundred volumes, with space for five thousand more. There are also, for the use of the Linthicum Institute, rooms for scholastic exercises and for public teachers. The rest of the edifice is occupied by eight public schools. Mr. Adolph Cluss was the architect.

"In 1873 a new primary School, the sixth, was established, and the board estimated the expenditures for the year ending June 30, 1875, at eighteen thousand dollars; but their proceedings were again interrupted by a remodification of the local government. By act of June 20, 1874, the Territory was transmuted into a province, and the administration thereof was invested in a triumvirate commission. The Commissioners consolidated the school boards of Washington, Georgetown, and of the county into one board of nineteen trustees, eleven of whom were to be residents of Washington, three of Georgetown, and five of the county. This board has jurisdiction over all the public schools of the District, without discrimination of color. Every change of official management, howsoever advantageous, is disagreeable to persons accustomed to the old routine; and this change was, no doubt, inconvenient to some. But experience has reconciled all. Instead of many different organizations for a similar purpose, the entire District contributes all its resources, and concentrates all its energies to a single end, and all harmoniously co-operate in measures productive of more general good.

"The following statement exhibits the condition of the schools in Georgetown"

Number of scholars	1,439
Number of teachers: male, 1; female, 21	22
Salaries of teachers	$ 17,200.00
Expenditures, including payment of previous debts	89,107.15
Receipts	33,037.30
Value of school property	137,350.00
Average cost, each scholar	22.80

"The history of the schools in Georgetown embraces sixty-six years, during which period we have seen, despite all vicissitudes, annual improvement. The trustees never neglected their duties.

Out of nearly four hundred meetings, there were not twenty nonquorums. No one seemed to consider his appointment as a sinecure, but discharged his high duties with fidelity and industry. The places of many of these faithful servants have been vacated by death or other casualty, but as examples of official punctuality and energy we recall the names of Brown, Shoemaker, Jewell, Tenney, Bangs, Osborn, Magee, Addison, Hyde, Ould, Adler, Marbury, Beall, King, Magruder, Dunlop, Ramsburg, Curtis, and Moffat.

"The guardians never 'despised the day of small things.' They were just as solicitous for the welfare of the humble Lancasterian School as they could have been for that of a renowned university. They took a heart interest in the scholars, and, in their treatment of them, seemed to bear in mind that they were soon to become their fellow-citizens. Allusions to their gratuitous tuition were never obtrusively made, and nowhere on their minutes or on any document can be found the word 'pauper.' 'Charity scholars' was used in an ordinance of 1812, but the epithet was never repeated. It was *ordained*, indeed by the corporation, that the scholars, after completing their education, were to be 'bound out,' according to the laws of the country, and that parents able to pay for their children's tuition should be required to do so; but neither provision was ever insisted on. Indeed, the 'free' schools of Georgetown were, from the beginning, animated with a patriotic and independent spirit.

"The Corporation of Georgetown was always friendly to the schools, and assured their success by its enlightened policy. It was, indeed, cautious at times, as it behooved delegated authority to be, but the solicited aid was never refused.

"Georgetown has now seventeen public schools, containing about fifteen hundred scholars; but a large proportion of her juvenile population is unprovided with schools, and it is impossible for that city to supply them. The necessity of education and the inadequacy of her resources to impart it have been repeatedly made known to Congress, but no relief has been granted. Lands worth more than a hundred millions of dollars have been given to the States for universities and schools; and even to the Territories more than thirty million acres have been granted for like uses, but not a section nor a rood to the District of Columbia!"

CHAPTER VIII.

OAK HILL CEMETERY, AND GENEROSITY OF W.W. CORCORAN—HOLYROOD CEMETERY—PRESBYTERIAN BURYING-GROUND—METHODIST BURYING-GROUND.

Oak Hill Cemetery, located on the heights of town and bordering on Rock Creek was, previous to it occupancy as a cemetery, known to our old residents as *Parrott's Woods*; and the hills, covered with lofty oaks, extended their shady bowers in every direction. It was the play ground of the school-boy, and the resort of the weary citizen from the cares and turmoils of city life. Many of our citizens who, when boys, have romped and played under the wide spreading oaks, gathering acorns in playful mirth, or hunted over the ground with dog and gun, little thought that it would be their final resting place under that Divine injunction–"dust thou art, and unto dust thou shalt return." This grove was dedicated by common consent to the celebration of the 4th of July, where the Sunday school children of our town were wont to assemble and celebrate the birthday of American liberty in prose and song; but their voice of music is no longer heard, and wafted by the western breeze to the shores of the Atlantic; neither do we hear the bursts of eloquence which flowed from the lips of the impassioned orator when mind infused itself into mind, but in their stead, silence reigns supreme. Some of the towering oaks have been leveled with the ground, and the willow and the cypress will supply their place, and the outspreading branches and sombre foliage of the funeral yew will be planted there.

This cemetery owes its origin to Col. William W. Corcoran, a native and former resident of Georgetown, who conceived the idea of laying out a burial place for the public good; and, consequently, he purchased fifteen acres of land of Lewis Washington, of Jefferson County, Virginia; and when the charter of the Oak Hill Cemetery Company was passed by Congress on the 3d day of March, 1849, he generously conveyed this land to the company for the purpose of a cemetery. More land has since been added, until the number of acres have increased to thirty-six; and the whole is divided into lots of such sizes as to

190

GRAVE OF JOHN HOWARD PAYNE AT OAK HILL CEMETERY.

191

suit the means of every family. The number of lots sold up to the present time exceeds twelve thousand, and the number of interments four thousand.

The generous donor who originated the cemetery, has continued his beneficent donations from time to time, in laying out and embellishing the grounds at his own expense. There has always appeared to be a silent effort made to bury in oblivion what ever was done by Col. Corcoran towards the cemetery, until a committee was appointed by the lot-holders, February, 1869. When they became aware of the fact, that the records of the company afforded no account of the origin of the cemetery, at the time of its institution, now twenty-eight years ago, it was known to all that the originator of the cemetery was Col. Corcoran, and that to his taste and munificence, the company are indebted for this beautiful burial place. The general knowledge and recognition of the fact was probably the reason why it was not made a matter of special record on the journal of the company; but this omission, has, no doubt, been remedied, and the history of the origin of the cemetery has been engrossed on the books of the company.

From the record of the investigation by the committee appointed to examine into the affairs of the cemetery company, it has been ascertained that the following donations have been made by Col. Corcoran:

Expenditures in purchase of land June 7th, 1848 .	$ 3,000.00
Expenditures for dwelling house and chapel, from 1850 to 1853	9,400.10
Expenditures for iron railing, from 1852 to 1853	3,582.54
Expenditures for improving grounds	24,176.28
Ditto for various other purposes	79,841.08
Making a total of	$120,000.00

The committee expressed their surprise that no record whatever is to be found of these original donations, either on the journal or account-books, and would beg to recommend that suitable entries be made of all these matters before anything else is done. If this has not been done, the chronicler will record them in his book, to be read as long as his book will last.

If we take a stroll through the cemetery, we find that

neatness and order reigns supreme. The lots are laid out with mathematical skill, the most of them containing three hundred square feet of ground; others, again, have a larger number of square feet, and are suitable for the erection of a vault or mausoleum. We see here the granite monument erected to E.M. Stanton, the great War Secretary of President Lincoln, who died on 24 December, 1869; also the monument to General Jesse Lee Reno, who fell at the battle of South Mountain, on the 14 September, 1862; also a spacious tomb to Samuel Hooper, a Representative from Massachusetts, who died February 14,1875; and a monument to Bodisco, the Russian Minister, who died January 28th,1854; also to Charles B. Fisk, the chief engineer of the Chesapeake & Ohio Canal, who completed it to Cumberland. A lofty monument is erected to Fowler, who died at sea in 1850. Intestate and unmarried, his heirs in the District of Columbia inherited his fortune, and erected this monument to his memory. There are two mausoleums in the cemetery; one erected by Col. Corcoran; the other is the Van Ness mausoleum, transferred from H Street, Washington City, and said to be a copy of the temple of Vesta. This tomb is constructed of stone, and is an open dome with pillars, and a deep vault beneath; and is said to have cost thirty-four thousand dollars. Just in the rear of the chapel is a monument erected to the memory of Major George Peter, who died June 22d, 1861. He commanded the Artillery Company from Georgetown at the battle of Bladensburg, on 24 August, 1814. John Kurtz was 1st lieutenant, the late Judge Morsell was 2d lieutenant, James A. Magruder was 8d lieutenant. Major Peter, after the war, represented his district in Congress for several years.

HOLYROOD CEMETERY.

This cemetery is situated at the junction of High, Fayette, and Madison Streets, and embraces several acres of ground. It is situated on a high elevation, from which a full view of Washington and Georgetown, and all parts of the District, can be obtained. It is a lovely place for a city of the dead; and when laid out into lots and graveled walks, with a plantation of trees, will compare with any cemetery in the District in beauty and location.

193

To improve a cemetery requires considerable labor and money, which might be raised by the ladies of the congregation doing as the ladies of the Presbyterian congregation did when their cemetery was in a state of dilapidation going to the lot-holders and collecting five dollars from one, and ten from another; and those who were not able to pay, to give a few days' labor in the cemetery. In this way Holyrood would soon improve in appearance, and become a resort for strangers as well as the citizens of the town. Certainly, those who are lot-holders ought to take a pride in beautifying the grounds. One could plant flowers, another trees, others could gravel the walks.

PRESBYTERIAN BURYING-GROUND.

This cemetery lies between Fourth and Fifth and Market and Frederick Streets, in Georgetown, in square number — on the new map, and is probably the oldest burying-ground in the town.

The following communication was published in our town paper some forty years past:

"MR. EDITOR: Once in a year, for many years past, have I made a pilgrimage to the grave-yard (belonging, I believe, to the congregation of the Presbyterian Church, in the northwestern part of Georgetown,) to drop a silent tear upon the tombs of departed children and friends; but language cannot describe my feelings on visiting the mansions of the dead a few days since. It would have been difficult to believe that the grounds belonged to a Christian community had I not known that they did. The broken fences, open gates, and grazing cattle upon the very grass that flourished over the bosoms of departed worth; the marks of sacrilegious destruction upon the monumental pile by idle, rude, and vulgar hands, sickened my very soul, and almost determined me not to be buried in a place appropriated for the dead, or even to allow a turf to mark the spot where my remains may rest. A NON-RESIDENT."

When the above communication made its appearance, a number of ladies of the Presbyterian congregation called a meeting of the lot-holders, and determined to have the grounds placed in a suitable condition; for that purpose they made collections among the lot-holders, and had a new fence erected, the briers and bushes cut down, the lots sodded, and the walks graveled; so that it has from that day to the present a genteel appearance, to attract the eye of a stranger or non-resident. This was the principal burying ground until the laying out of Oak Hill Cemetery in 1850.

In looking over the tombstones, the chronicler discovers that Robert Peter, the first mayor of Georgetown, died November 15, 1806, aged eighty years; John Barnes, who was collector of the port of Georgetown for twenty years, and founder of the poor-house, died February 11, 1826, aged ninety-six years; James Gillespie, Member of Congress from North Carolina, died January 11, 1805; Mary Bohrer, wife of John P. Bohrer, died August 8, 1844, in the ninety-seventh year of her age; Elizabeth Thompson died March 9, 1847, aged eighty-seven years; William Waters, a soldier of the Revolution, died August 19, 1859, in the ninety-third year of his age; Col. George Beall, born in Georgetown, February 26, 1729, died October 15, 1807, in the seventy-ninth year of his age. The town must have been a village at the time of Col. Beall's birth.

METHODIST BURYING-GROUND.

This burying-ground lies upon the banks of Rock Creek and the road leading to Lyons' Mill. This ground was conveyed by Thomas Beall to Ebenezer Eliason and others, by deed dated October 13, 1808, recorded March 6, 1809, in liber V, page 295. It was divided into lots, and many of them have been sold to various citizens of the town and used for the burial of the dead. There is a disposition to sell this ground and apply the proceeds to other purposes, but this cannot be done. The best way is to turn it over to Mount Zion Church, on condition that they keep up the fence and put the grounds in order.

CHAPTER IX.

"The committee to whom was referred the duty of collecting the books, records, and relics of Potomac Lodge, No. 5, and of making a report on the same, respectfully submit the following report, in which they have briefly sketched the history of the lodge, and of Masonry in Georgetown, as connected with the books, records, and relies collected by them.

"In order of date, the first relic that we find belonging to the lodge is an old bible, published in Edinburgh in 1754, with this inscription on the fly leaf: 'A present from Mr. Colin Campbell to St. Andrew's Lodge, the 30th January, 1773, Bladensburg.' This bible has been in the possession of our lodge from its first organization, under its present name, in 1806. It may have belonged to a Lodge once in existence at Bladensburg, which was at that time a place of more importance than at present, but, according to our oldest living member, as received by him through tradition, it belonged to the first lodge of Masons that ever was in Georgetown, and was presented to it by a resident of Bladensburg.

"We know that lodges of Masons were formed in this country when colonies of Great Britain, under charters granted both from the Grand Lodge of England and the Grand Lodge of Scotland, and, their work being somewhat different, they held no Masonic intercourse with each other until after the revolutionary war, when they came together and formed Grand Lodges. It is probable, from the name, that this was one of the lodges of Scotch Masons, and we know that the first lodges here, and this lodge when reorganized in 1806, were mostly composed of Scotch men.

"Our oldest member, Bro. James King, who was initiated in 1810, says that at the time, and for some years afterwards, this was the only bible used in the lodge.

"Of this ancient lodge we know nothing except by tradition; but we find that at a meeting of the Grand Lodge of the State of

Maryland, on the 21st of April, 1789, a petition was presented from a number of respectable brethren from Georgetown on Potomac River, praying for a warrant from the Grand Lodge to authorize them to convene as a regular lodge, which petition was granted; and Brothers Fierer and Grier being present, were, agreeably to the request of the petitioners, installed as Master and Senior Warden, and, at the same time, received their warrant, authorizing them to hold their lodge at Georgetown, on the river Potomac, in Maryland, distinguished by the No. 9.

"Of this lodge we possess no record or relic but the gavel used by Gen. George Washington, then President of the United States, at the laying of the corner-stone of the Capitol, September 18th,1793, and by him then, according to tradition, handed to the Master of the lodge. The following account of the ceremony of laying the corner-stone of the Capitol was published in a newspaper in Georgetown, on September 21st, 1793; and as it is very rare and interesting, and shows the connection of this lodge with the Masonic ceremonies, we give it in full:

"GEORGETOWN, *September 21, 1793.*

"On Wednesday one of the grandest Masonic processions took place for the, purpose of laying the cornerstone of the Capitol of the United States, which, perhaps, ever was exhibited on the like important occasion. About ten o'clock, Lodge No. 9 was visited by that congregation so graceful to the craft, Lodge No. 22, of Virginia, with all their officers and regalia; and directly afterwards appeared, on the southern banks of the great river Potowmack, one of the finest companies of Volunteer Artillery that hath been lately seen, parading to receive the President of the United States, who shortly came in sight with his suite, to whom the Artillery paid their military honors; and his Excellency and suite crossed the Potowmack, and was received in Maryland by the officers and brethren of No. 22, Virginia, and No. 9, Maryland, whom the President headed, and preceded by a band of music; the rear brought up by the Alexandria Volunteer Artillery, with grand solemnity of march, proceeded to the President's square, in the city of Washington, where they were met and saluted by No. 15, of the city of Washington, in all their elegant badges and clothing, headed by Brother Joseph Clark, Rt. W.G.M., P.T., and conducted to a large lodge prepared for the purpose of their reception. After a short space of time, by the vigilance of Brother Clotworthy Stephenson, Grand Marshal P.T., the brotherhood and other bodies were disposed in a second order of procession, which took place amidst a brilliant crowd of spectators of both sexes, according to the following arrangement, viz:

"'The surveying department of the city of Washington; Mayor and Corporation of Georgetown; Virginia Artillery; commissioners of the city of Washington, and their attendants; stone-cutters; mechanics. (Here follow all the various officers of Freemasonry, amongst whom appears Grand Master P.T., George Washington; Worshipful Master of No. 22, Virginia.)

"'The procession marched two abreast in the greatest solemn dignity, with music playing, drums beating, colors flying, and spectators rejoicing, from the President's square to the Capitol, in the city of Washington, where the Grand Marshal ordered a halt, and directed each file in the procession to incline two steps, one to the right and one to the left, and faced each other, which formed an hollow oblong square, through which the Grand Sword Bearer led the van, followed by the Grand Master P.T. on the left, the President of the United States in the center, and the Worshipful Master of No. 22, Virginia, on the right; all the other orders that composed the procession advanced in the reverse of their order of march from the President's square to the southeast corner of the Capitol, and the artillery filed off to a destined ground to display their maneuvers and discharge their cannon; the President of the United States, the Grand Master P.T., and Worshipful Master of No. 22, taking their stand to the east of a huge stone, and all the craft forming a circle westward, stood a short time in awful order.

"'The artillery discharged a volley.

"'The Grand Marshal delivered the commissioners a large silver plate with an inscription thereon, which the commissioners ordered to be read, and was as follows:

"'This southeast corner-stone of the Capitol of the United States of America, in the city of Washington, was laid on the

18th day of September, 1793, in the thirteenth year of American Independence, in the first year of the second term of the Presidency of George Washington (whose virtues in the civil administration of his country have been so conspicuous and beneficial, as his military valor and prudence have been useful in establishing her liberties), and in the year of Masonry 1793, by the President of the United States, in concert with the Grand Lodge of Maryland, several lodges under its jurisdiction, and Lodge No. 22, from Alexandria, Virginia.

THOMAS JOHNSON,
DAVID STUART   } Commissioners.
DANIEL CARROLL,
JOSEPH CLARK, R.W.G.M.P.T.
JAMES HOBAN,   } Architects.
STEPHEN HALLATE,
COLLIN WILLIAMSON, *M. Mason.*

"'The artillery discharged a volley.

"'The plate was then delivered to the President, who, attended by the Grand Master P.T. and three Most Worshipful Masters, descended to the cavazion trench and deposed the plate, and laid it on the corner-stone of the Capitol of the United States of America, on which was deposited corn, wine, and oil, when the whole congregation joined in reverential prayer, which was succeeded by Masonic chaunting honors and a volley from the artillery.

"'The President of the United States and his attendant brethren ascended from the cavazion to the east of the corner-stone, and there the Grand Master P.T., elevated on a triple rostrum, delivered an oration fitting the occasion, which was received with brotherly love and commendation. At intervals, during the delivery of the oration, several volleys were discharged by the artillery. The ceremony ended in prayer, Masonic chaunting honors, and a fifteen volley from the artillery.

"'The whole company retired to an extensive booth, where an ox of five hundred pounds weight was barbecued, of which the company generally partook, with every abundance of other recreation. The festival concluded with fifteen successive volleys from the artillery, whose military discipline and maneuvers merit every commendation.

"'Before dark the whole company departed, with joyful hopes of the production of the labor.'

"Two members of this lodge (No. 9), Gen. James Thompson and John Mountz, for over fifty years clerk of the corporation of this town, died only ten years ago, in 1855. Both visited our lodge in 1854, and testified that the gavel in our possession, to the best of their knowledge and belief, was the same used by General Washington at the laying of the corner-stone of the Capitol.

"In 1854, Bro. John Mountz, in response to a communication from this lodge, addressed us the following letter:

"'I was secretary of Lodge No. 9, now Potomac Lodge, No. 5, in the year 1793, and am now in the eighty-third year of my age and have never had occasion to regret my connection with our ancient and honorable order. I was present and near our late brother, George Washington, first President of the United States, when he laid the first corner-stone of the Capitol of the United States, on the 18th of September, 1793, which he did Masonically with a marble gavel, which, I believe, is the one now in possession of your lodge.

"'I am, brethren, sincerely, your brother,
JOHN MOUNTZ.

"'To JAMES GOSZLER, W.M., WALTER H.S. TAYLOR, S.W., JOHN S. MOORE, J.W., of the brethren of Lodge No. 5, Georgetown, D.C.

"GEORGETOWN, D.C., *June 18, 1854.*'

"According to Bro. James King, this gavel was the one used by the Master of the lodge at the time he was initiated, in 1810, and for some years afterwards, up to 1818. A committee, of which he was chairman, made a report September 28th, 1846, concerning the Washington gavel, from which we will give an extract:

"'This gavel was manufactured for M.W. Bro. General George Washington, for the express purpose of laying the corner-stone of the Capitol of the United States, in Washington City, in the year 1793, and used by him on that occasion, and then deposited in Lodge No. 9, of Mary land.'

"According to tradition, General Washington, after the

ceremony was performed, presented the gavel to Lodge No. 9, by placing it in the hands of the Master, who, at that time, was Valentine Reintzel, afterwards elected the first Master of Potomac Lodge, No. 43, of Maryland, when it was reorganized in 1806, which office he held until 1810; and in 1811, when the Grand Lodge of the District of Columbia was formed, be was chosen as the first Grand Master.

"It is singular that we can nowhere find this lodge formed in 1789, recorded by any other name than that of Lodge No. 9. Although it seems in 1793 to have been in a very flourishing condition, yet from some cause it soon afterwards ceased to exist as then organized.

"Bro. John Mountz, Secretary of Lodge No. 9, in 1793, has said that it received great accessions of members, and fell to pieces by its own weight, and as all its members have passed away, this is all that we can probably know of the cause of its suspension.

"On 22d October, 1795, a petition was again received by the Grand Lodge of Maryland, from a number of brethren in Georgetown, praying for a warrant, and recommended by Federal Lodge, No. 15, city of Washington, which petition was granted, and the secretary ordered to make out a warrant for the lodge, under the title of Columbia Lodge, No. 19.

"The charter for Federal Lodge, No. 15 (the first lodge formed in Washington), had been granted by the Grand Lodge of Maryland, September 12th, 1793, just six days before the corner-stone of the Capitol was laid.

"Of Columbia Lodge, No. 19, we have one book of records, commencing with its by-laws, and then the proceedings of the lodge from 7th November, 1795—James Thompson, Master, and John Reintzel, Secretary; to 12th December, 1796, Charles Minor, Master, and James Thompson, Secretary.

"James Thompson, first Master and then Secretary of this lodge, died in 1855, and visited our lodge in 1854, when, with Bro. John Mountz, he testified to his belief in the authenticity of the Washington gavel.

"The accounts of this lodge are kept in pounds, shillings and pence, Maryland currency. Members were fined *3s. 9d.* (half-a-dollar) for non-attendance, and on every stated meeting night, refreshments were furnished to the brethren. The 13th article of their bylaws provides for the appointment of a committee of three, to furnish refreshments, under the direction of the lodge, on all stated meeting nights, which were on the second Monday of each month, and at every stated meeting the account for refreshments furnished at the preceding one, would be read, passed and ordered to be paid. Of this lodge it is probable we possess but a small part of the records. On 12th December, 1796, the last meeting of which we have any account, they elected their officers for the ensuing year, accepted an invitation from Federal Lodge, No. 15, to ,join them in procession on the next St. John's day, and passed a bill to pay for refreshments furnished at the last stated meeting, amounting to *£1.3s.9½d.*, all tending to show that the lodge was then in a vigorous and healthy state, but at some time between that date and 1806, they, too, suspended operations.

"As all the members of Lodge No. 19, have also passed away, we do not know the reasons why, or the time when the lodge ceased, and we have been unable to trace any tradition on the subject.

"In November, 1806, we find from our next book of records, that a number of Masonic brethren, having the good of Masonry at heart, as well as for their own convenience as that of others, think it proper that there should be a lodge held in Georgetown, and for that purpose had a meeting, when it was unanimously agreed that each of the subscribers should pay into the hands of their trusty brother, Thomas Pryse, the sum of five dollars for the benefit of the same. The names of ten brethren are recorded as agreeing to this, and Thomas Pryse was authorized to attend the meeting of the Grand Lodge of Maryland, to be held at Easton on the 12th of November, 1806, with a petition signed by these ten, praying for a warrant to establish a lodge. On the 18th November, 1806, a meeting of the brethren was held, when Bro. Pryse informed them that he had attended the meeting of the Grand Lodge, and obtained a charter. They then appointed committees to select and get in order such things as would be necessary for the lodge. One of these committees consisted of

202

Valentine Reintzel, William Knowles, and Thomas Beatty; and their duty was to collect and receipt for the jewels, &c., in possession of John Laird and Adam King. At their third meeting, 22d November, 1806, this committee reported that they had obtained all the jewels, &c., in the possession of John Laird and Adam King.

"At their fourth meeting, on 19th December, 1806, the lodge was organized, with Thomas Pryse as Master, under the name of Potomac Lodge, No. 43, and on the same night went into an election for officers, when Valentine Reintzel was chosen Master, and Daniel Kurtz, Secretary, and from that period to this time the lodge has uninterruptedly kept up its organization without any suspension, first as Potomac Lodge No. 43, of Maryland, and when the Grand Lodge of the District of Columbia was formed in 1811, as Potomac Lodge, No. 5, of that jurisdiction.

"The intimate connection between the three lodges that thus succeeded one another in this town, under charters from the Grand Lodge of Maryland, is shown by the fact, that two of the four brethren on the committee to obtain the jewels, &c., viz: Valentine Reintzel, and Thomas Beatty were, according to the published proceedings of that Grand Lodge, delegates to it from Lodge No. 9, at the semi-annual communication held at Easton, Maryland, on 19th April, 1791, and the name of Valentine Reintzel appears as delegate from, and Master of, Lodge No. 9, at the communication of 11th April, 1793. The names of others of the brethren who assisted, in 1806, in organizing Potomac Lodge, No. 43, appear both as members of Lodge 19, and Lodge No. 9. Each lodge seems to have been partly composed of the same brethren as members, and they followed so close in succession as to have inherited the one from the other, without dispute, all property, jewels, and records of the preceding lodge, just the same as if there had only been a reorganization, which in fact it was, although from some cause the charter had lapsed each time, and they obtained a new one with another name and number for the lodge.

"We can observe that our late Bro. John Mountz takes this view of it, when in his letter to the lodge, he says: 'I was Secretary of Lodge No. 9, now Potomac Lodge No. 5, in the year

1793.' About the same time, also, Bro. James Thompson, in response to some inquiries from this lodge, addressed to us the following letter:

"'WASHINGTON CITY, MAY 23, 1854.

"'BRETHREN: In responding to your inquiries I offer the following remarks: I am now in the eighty-sixth year of my age, and have belonged to our ancient and honorable order upwards of sixty years. *I was Master of your lodge, then Columbia Lodge, No. 19*, in the year 1795, and Secretary in the year 1796. Appointed delegate to represent the lodge at the Grand Communication held in the city of Baltimore in July, 1796. Elected Secretary for the year 1797.

"'I was one of eight oarsmen, and pulled the stroke oar of the barge that conveyed Bro. George Washington across the Potomac, at Georgetown, on one of his visits to the East, and stood near, and saw him when he laid the corner-stone of the Capitol in 1793.

"'I am, brethren, most sincerely yours,

J. THOMPSON.

"'TO THE WORSHIPFUL MASTER, WARDENS AND BRETHREN,
of Potomac Lodge, No. 5, Georgetown.'

"Here were two living witnesses of the circumstances, both active members of No. 9, and No. 19, and frequent visitors to our lodge during their life, who concur in the same view, and evidently consider No. 9, No. 19, and No. 43, of Maryland, or No. 5, of the District of Columbia, as identically one and the same lodge, even if, when reorganized, they had taken a different name and number.

"During the suspension of the lodge, the Washington gavel had been in the possession of Valentine Reintzel, Master of Lodge No. 9, in 1793, and when it was reorganized as Potomac Lodge, No. 43, it was by him brought forward as the property of the lodge, and as we mentioned before, ordinarily used as the Master's gavel up to 1818.

"Following the reorganization as described as Potomac Lodge, No. 43, we have its records from 19th December, 1806, to June 20th, 1808, when Valentine Reintzel was still the Master, and Daniel Kurtz, Secretary. The same book also contains the first by-laws of the lodge, which are longer, and have many more rules than are now customary, and commence with the following curious preamble:

"'We, the Master, officers and members of Potomac Lodge, No. 43, of the most ancient and honorable fraternity of Free and Accepted Masons, duly constituted by charter from the Grand Lodge of Maryland, bearing date the 12th day of November, A.D., 1806, and now in opened lodge assembled at our lodge room in Georgetown, this — day of January, 1807, *Annoque Lucis*, 5807, in order to pay homage and adoration to the Grand Architect, whose divine wisdom having resolved to form the world, and reduced a wild chaos to a fair, regular and permanent system; and who not only traced out the whole plan of the Universe, but gave life and being, form and figure, to every part of what before had been a rude undigested and immovable heap of matter, who said, 'Let there be light, and there was light,' and the dull, heavy and terrean parts of matter which over-clouded the expansion, obeyed the Almighty fiat, and began to range into form and order, and for the purpose of disseminating brotherly love, relief and charity; and to maintain the principles of benevolence and religion inculcated by our order—have made, established, and confirmed the following articles, as a constitutional code, for the government of ourselves and our successors.'

"Our next book of records seems at its commencement, to have had several leaves torn out, and now begins with the proceedings of a meeting held December 17th,1809, when the same brethren as before were still respectively Master and Secretary, but at an election held that evening, A.L. Joncherez was elected Secretary, instead of Daniel Kurtz, and from this date we have continuous records to the 19th August, 1811, when it is recorded in the secretary's writing— 'This journal ends at this last regular meeting.' Daniel Kurtz then Master, and William Calder, Secretary; but, afterwards, in the back of the same book, we have records of meetings August 31st,1812; February 15th, March 15 and 18, April 5th, May 17th, June 21st and 24th, August 25th, September 20th, and December 20th, 1813. It is probable the regular records for that time are lost, and these were only notes taken by the secretary on the nights of meeting, as many of them are written with a lead pencil, and few are signed.

"Until 1810, the lodge met in the third story of the dwelling-house of Valentine Reintzel, then Master. This was a three-story brick house, situated on the west side of Jefferson Street, between the canal and Water Street, and was standing until about eight years ago, when it was destroyed by fire. But, at that time, having much increased in numbers, they were desirous of securing to themselves a more suitable place for their meetings.

"They first presented a petition to the corporation proposing to join them in erecting at the market space a building which might serve as a town house and a Masonic Hall, but finally leased a lot on Jefferson Street; and on October 18th, 1810, it is recorded that *this lodge in ample Masonic form* laid the corner-stone of a building to be constructed for a Masonic Hall on the lot thus leased.

"The proceedings on that occasion are spread in full on our records, and we give a concise abridgment of them. The brethren formed in procession at their lodge-room, and went from there to the lower bridge, where they met their brethren from Washington; they then proceeded along the water side to the market space, thence to Bridge Street, where they were joined by the mayor, members of the corporation, and magistrates of the place; then along Bridge to Jefferson Street, and down Jefferson Street to the place where the ceremony of laying the corner-stone was performed; thence to the Presbyterian Church, where an appropriate discourse was delivered by Rev. Bro. Elliott, after which they went back to Jefferson Street, where the craft were called from labor to refreshment, and they partook of a collation prepared for the occasion.

"The building erected at this time was finished by the following summer, and is still standing on the west side of Jefferson Street, and just north of the canal. In 1840, it was sold by the lodge and stockholders to Mr. Philip Gormley.

"Our now venerable brother, James King, was initiated on December 17th, 1810. He is still a member of our lodge, and is

206

probably the oldest living Mason in the District of Columbia.

"The Grand Lodge of the District of Columbia was formed by delegates from five lodges, on January 8th, 1811, when Valentine Reintzel, for years the Master of Lodge, No. 43, and in 1793, Master of Lodge, No. 9, was chosen as the first Grand Master; and our lodge henceforth was designated as Potomac Lodge, No. 5, of the District of Columbia, instead of No. 43, of Maryland.

"We regret to say that we were unable to find any of the records of the lodge from December 20th,1813, to January 24th, 1825. There is no doubt the lodge was in existence, and its records regularly kept, and in, at least, as prosperous a state as they had previously been. In 1818, the bible now used in the lodge was presented to it by Bro. George Richards, then Master. Previous to that time, the old bible referred to at the commencement of this report had been used. In 1818, a Chapter of Royal Arch Masons were formed in Georgetown, and through accessions, chiefly from members of Potomac Lodge, No. 5, soon attained a flourishing condition. In 1823, our lodge returned to the Grand Lodge the names of twenty-four brethren as members, with Daniel Kurtz as Master, and William Calder, Secretary; and in 1824, the names of thirty members, and William Hayman, Master, and Edward Deeble, Secretary. During the intervening period, as near as we have been able to ascertain, Daniel Kurtz was Master in 1813, 1814, 1815, and 1816; John Wiley in 1817; George Richards in 1818, and James King in 1819, 1820, 1821, and 1822.

"Our next book of records commences with the proceedings of a meeting held January 24th, 1825, when John Myers was Master, and Edward Deeble, Secretary, and ends with the meeting on April 11th, 1836, when John Myers was again Master, and Thomas Holtzman, Secretary.

"It was during part of this period, from 1827 to 1836, that the anti-masonic excitement raged so fiercely, happily, not with so much intensity in this locality as in others, where Masonic lodges were forced to yield to the popular frenzy and suspend their operations, some of them for several years. The effect of this excitement on our lodge for a while, seems actually to have caused an increase in the number of its members. Probably, because persecution had its usual effect in binding the objects of it more closely together, and the attention of individuals amongst our citizens, who otherwise would not have thought of it, was called to the consideration of Masonry. They wished to examine for themselves what this thing was, then so vilified; and many of them sought and gained admission to our lodge, and became, afterwards, worthy and acceptable members. The only notice taken of it in our records is, that on May 10th, 1830, Bro. Lorenzo Dow delivered an address in the lodge to its members and a large number of visiting brethren, giving them an interesting account of the present excitement and its tendency, and adding some wholesome advice. This was the celebrated and eccentric itinerant preacher, Lorenzo Dow, who was neither afraid nor ashamed to avow himself a Mason during the time popular feeling ran highest, and was most bitter against them. In 1834, he died in Georgetown, at the house of one of our members, P.M., George W. Haller; and our records show that on February 4th, 1834, the brethren of Potomac Lodge, No. 5, formed in procession to pay the last tribute of respect to their deceased brother, Lorenzo Dow, and went to the house of Bro. Haller, and there received the body, and then, with the remains of the deceased, the procession moved to Holmead's burying-ground,[1] where they were deposited with their kindred earth, and the usual Masonic ceremonies performed by the Master and brethren.

"Our next book of records commences with the proceedings of a meeting held April 25th,1836, John Myers, Master, and Thomas Holtzman, Secretary, and ends with the record of the meeting of October 27th, 1845, Edgar Patterson, Master, and James Goszler, Secretary.

"During 1836 and 1837, through the inattention and falling off of its members, the lodge was at a very low ebb, and was only kept up by the exertions of some few of the more zealous of the brethren. In 1837 but five meetings were held during the entire year. Perhaps this was owing to the reaction from the anti-

---

1. Before the destruction of Holmead's, Dow's remains were removed to Oak Hill Cemetery.

masonic excitement which was then passing away. But on February 19th, 1838, a meeting was held, John Myers, Master, and Samuel Cropley acting as Secretary, when they reorganized the lodge by passing the following resolution:

"'*Resolved*, That the members present are of the opinion that this lodge ought to be recognized, and that those members who have from time to time assembled here for the purpose be now considered as the only members, viz: John Myers, Jeremiah Orme, Henry W. Tilley, Samuel Cunningham, William Jewell, Samuel Cropley, Daniel Kurtz, William Hayman, Samuel Clark, Hiram Howard, Sebre Howard, Daniel Ragan, Jonathan Y. Young, and Robert Boyd; and that it be so represented to the Grand Lodge, and that the residue be dropped from the roll for non-regular attendance, and so reported. That all dues charged on the lodge books be abandoned as uncollectible, and that regular dues be collected from the acknowledged members from and after the regular meeting in this month from which the reorganization is to be dated.'

"Of the fourteen brethren who thus in 1838 reorganized the lodge, but three, we believe, are now living; and but two, Henry W. Tilley and Samuel Cropley, are now members of it. In December, 1840, James King, who had for some years been absent from Georgetown, was, by a resolution of the lodge, admitted a member on the same terms as the original fourteen who thus reorganized the lodge, and on the same evening was elected the Master.

"In 1840 the lodge and stockholders sold the house on Jefferson Street, erected in 1810 for a Masonic Hall, but for some time afterwards rented, and still held their meetings in, the upper story; but in 1842 they bought a house on Washington Street, opposite to the Union Hotel, the third story of which they fitted up as a lodge room, and thenceforth met in it.

"During the years 1843,1844, and 1845, from some cause of dissatisfaction with the Grand Lodge of the District of Columbia, this lodge made persistent efforts to withdraw from its jurisdiction. At one time a committee was appointed to communicate with the Grand Lodge of Maryland on the subject. Committees of conference were also appointed to meet committees from the Grand Lodge of the District of Columbia in reference to it, and on May 5th, 1845, a resolution was offered and passed, proposing to surrender the charter, and appointing a committee to ascertain and report the state of the funds of the lodge, and also to confer with the proper officers of the Grand Lodges of Virginia and Maryland, to ascertain what course should be pursued to obtain a charter from either of said Grand Lodges.

"In 1811 our lodge appears to have drawn rather reluctantly from the jurisdiction of the Grand Lodge of Maryland, to assist in forming the Grand Lodge of the District of Columbia, and from the notices on our record, a feeling of discontent with the Grand Lodge to which they were attached seems frequently to have existed. As one illustration, we will cite that on November 25th, 1830, Brothers Kurtz, Haller, and Myers were appointed a committee, 'Respectfully to memorialize the Grand Lodges of the District of Columbia and State of Maryland upon the re-ceding of this lodge back to the jurisdiction of the Grand Lodge of Maryland.' After 1845 our lodge appears to have become better contented with their condition, for from that tune we find no record of any more propositions of the kind.

"The next book of records contains the proceedings of the lodge from November 24th, 1845, when Edgar Patterson was Master, and James Goszler, Secretary, to December 20th, 1854, when James Goszler was Master, and George Thompson, Secretary.

"In 1852 the lodge sold the building on Washington Street, which they had occupied since 1842, and rented part of the third story of Forrest Hall, which they fitted up and furnished as a Masonic lodge room, in which to hold their meetings.

"For some years past the Masonic fraternity in the United States had been gradually recovering from the depressing influences of the anti-masonic excitement. Other secret societies had appeared in the meantime, which, by their popularity and vast increase, seemed for awhile to over-shadow our beloved institution; but Masonry, the oldest secret society now existing, by its sterling good qualities, gradually won its way to command again, as it deserved, the respect of our countrymen generally. Soon after their removal to Forrest Hall, our lodge felt the benefit of the general revival of an interest in Masonry; and from this cause, together with the zeal and attention of its officers and members, and probably, also, the change of the place of meeting to a more central location in the town, speedily had a considerable addition to its membership of worthy brethren and a rapid increase of its prosperity.

"Our next book of records commences with the proceedings of a meeting held December 27th,1854, when James Goszler was Master, and M. Adler, Secretary, and ends with the record of the proceedings of the meeting of October 10th, 1859, when the same brethren were still respectively Master and Secretary.

"We have now arrived at times in the history of our lodge, which, doubtless, are familiar to most of our brethren, for it was during this period that, perhaps, a majority of our present members were initiated. Our lodge was no longer feebly keeping its existence by the untiring exertions of a few zealous brethren, but with the revival of an interest in Masonry, numbers were seeking admission into its sacred retreats, and our gates were besieged with the applicants for entrance. In spite of the predictions of the anti-masons in 1836, that Masonry would soon pass away with other relics of barbarism, and be classed among the things that were, and that posterity would wonder that their ancestors could take pleasure in its solemn and unmeaning mummery, and be deluded by such a dangerous and wicked institution, Masonry had now become more popular than ever before in its history in this country, and more firmly rooted amongst our people.

"With its increase of numbers and prosperity, the lodge soon became desirous of having a more spacious and convenient lodge room, in a building erected especially for Masonic purposes. After several propositions, they finally, in 1858, purchased for three thousand dollars the property on which our Masonic Hall now stands, then occupied by some old brick houses. The purchase money was advanced on the security of the property by one of our brethren. The lodge subscribed for five hundred dollars in stock, and the remainder was taken entirely amongst our members, with one exception, and that one a brother Mason; and the property is now owned, with that exception, exclusively by the lodge and its individual members. On the 19th of August, 1858, after a procession of the brethren, the corner-stone of the building was laid in ample Masonic form, after which an address was delivered by the Grand Master, George C. Whiting, at the close of which he highly praised our members for their spirit shown in the attempt, by the members of a single lodge, to erect in the heart of the city such a building, to be devoted exclusively to Masonic purposes. The building was finished by the following May, 1859, when the lodge took possession of it, and first met in the lofty, spacious, and convenient room we now occupy. It cost about eleven thousand dollars, considerably more than was estimated, which, added to three thousand dollars paid for the property, makes the entire cost about fourteen thousand dollars. What debts were incurred in its erection have mostly been paid, and we have every reason to believe that in two or three years they will all be liquidated, and the property will be owned, free from any incumbrance, by the lodge and stockholders.

"Our next book of records, containing the proceedings from October 10th, 1859, to the present time, is the one now in use by the secretary; and as we have not had it in our possession, not deeming that it was our duty according to the resolution under which we are acting to obtain it, we do not notice any of the events that have happened since that time. They are familiarly known to most of our brethren.

"We have dwelt more upon the history of our lodge in past times than in those with which we are contemporaneous, and have endeavored to redeem from forgetfulness and record those things, the memory of which is rapidly passing away with the actors in them. Our records are now well kept and carefully preserved; and at some future time, if desired, some of the brethren can take up the history of the lodge where we have left off.

"Up to 1813, and, perhaps, even later, the regular business of the lodge, even to the election of officers, was transacted in the E.A. degree, and, unless for the purpose of conferring one of the other degrees, was always opened in that degree. After

1825, the lodge was generally opened in the M.M. degree, but up to 1841, would occasionally be opened, and all the regular business, such as reading the proceedings of last meeting, receiving petitions for initiation, referring them to committees, &c., be carried on either in the E.A. or F.C. degrees; and when they expected to work in either of those degrees they generally opened in them.

"In 1795 and 1796, the Past Master's degree was conferred by the lodge on nearly all their members, and up to 1843 or 1844, that degree was conferred by the lodge on any officer elect, and occasionally on any brother who wished to receive it.

"According to our records, our lodge seems to have had and exercised the power to do many things to which it is not now considered competent, unless by direction and consent of the Grand Lodge. For instance, with an applicant for initiation or for any degree, our lodge exercised the power within itself to declare it a case of emergency, and to initiate a candidate or confer the degrees at any time they saw fit; also to make arrangements for, and have a Masonic procession at, any time or on any occasions the officers and members judged best. Also, without permission from, or consultation with, the Grand Lodge, to lay, Masonically, the corner-stones of public buildings. We may mention, among others, that in 1811 this lodge laid the corner-stone of the Lancaster School-house; in 1829, of the Methodist Protestant Church, and in 1831, of the Georgetown Poor-house, all in this town. On May 25th,1829, it is recorded on our minutes that an application was made to this lodge to lay the corner-stone of the first lock on the Chesapeake & Ohio Canal, whereupon it was resolved: 'That in case the Grand Lodge refuse (they being first invited) this lodge will undertake to perform that ceremony.' It was finally done by the Grand Lodge, who at first, on account of the anti masonic excitement so prevalent at that time, hesitated to undertake it; but it is evident that our lodge then had no doubt of their power and ability, with or without the Grand Lodge or their permission, to do the same.

"We only chronicle the facts, and from these it appears certain that the subordinate lodge now has less, and the Grand Lodge claims and exercises much more power than in former times.

"We herewith present in all seven books of records, four ledgers, one used in 1810 and 1811, one from 1824 to 1836, one from March, 1845, to March, 1856, and one used from March, 1856, to January 1st,1862; also, two stock books, one from 1825 to 1828, concerning the stock in the old Masonic Hall, on Jefferson Street, and one from 1843 to 1853, concerning the stock in the building on Washington Street.

"We append a list of books in our possession belonging to the lodge, but have been unable to obtain many which, according to the records, have from time to time been purchased by or given to it; for instance, of the *Freemason's Monthly Magazine* we have only been able to find fifty-two numbers, although the lodge subscribed to it from 1843 to 1862, and had several volumes bound, which we also were unable to find.

"Respectfully submitted,

JOSEPH LIBBEY, JR.,
CHARLES M. MATTHEWS,
Committee.

"GEORGETOWN, D.C., *November 6, 1865.*"

SKETCH OF THE CHESAPEAKE & OHIO CANAL.

The State of Maryland, by the numerous acts of its legislature passed in 1826, 1827, 1830, 1831, 1835, 1836, 1843, and 1845, made large appropriations for the completion of the canal, and assumed entire control over the same, by the election of a president and directors, who would push on the work to its fixed destination. After many years of financial adversity, and difficulties of every kind to contend with, and frequent change of its president and directors, James M. Coale was finally elected president. Mr. Coale was a gentleman of great financial skill, and possessed of industry and indomitable perseverance in any undertaking, especially in the then deplorable condition of the canal company. He was elected president of the canal company in August, 1843. The company was prostrated and paralyzed, and its prospects were gloomy in the extreme. It was destitute of means and devoid of credit. It was overwhelmed with difficulties. In addition to its enormous liabilities to the State of

214

Maryland, which were secured by mortgage liens on the canal and its revenues, the debts and obligations of the company due to individuals by the treasurer's report of October 1st, 1843, amounted to one million one hundred and seventy-four thousand five hundred and sixty-six dollars. Some of these creditors, to whom large amounts were due for work, had been reduced from affluence to poverty by the failure of the company to meet its engagements. President Coale, when he entered upon the duties of his office, infused new life and vitality into the company.

In the year 1842 the Legislature of Maryland, with a view of reducing the liabilities of the State and severing its connection with internal improvement companies, passed a law authorizing the treasurer of the State to sell all of Maryland's interest in the public works. He was authorized to sell the whole of the interest of Maryland in the Chesapeake & Ohio Canal Company (at that time amounting to eight millions of dollars) for five millions, payable in bonds or certificates of debts of the State, bearing an interest not less than five per cent. After advertising the sale of the State's interest in numerous newspapers, he did not receive a single bid.

When president Coale took charge of the canal, with a view to its final completion, it was only navigable to dam No. 6, one hundred and thirty-four miles from Georgetown, to which point it had been finished in 1839, leaving fifty miles in an unfinished condition to complete it to Cumberland, the cost of which was then estimated by the chief engineer at one million five hundred and forty-five thousand dollars. The United States and the citizens of the District of Columbia and all the private stockholders had long previously discontinued their assistance, and the State of Maryland, which had from the beginning sustained the company under all disasters, was no longer able to render assistance. It had nothing to depend upon to sustain it but the receipts from tolls and water rents, and these were insufficient to discharge current expenses.

The chronicler, availing himself of the numerous reports made by the president to the stockholders, will quote from them numerous extracts which will give a general outline of the completion of the canal to Cumberland.

"In former years, and before its treasury had become exhausted, the deficiencies for these purposes bad been supplied from the appropriations of the State and the general funds of the company. Although the practice of receiving scrip, in payment of tolls, had been abandoned, a debt had been accumulated, and was in arrear for current expenses incurred during the three preceding years, to the amount of sixty-nine thousand two hundred and fifty-six dollars and sixty-five cents, which was, principally, due to the agents and laborers, then on the finished portion of the canal, for services that were indispensable to its operations. It was difficult to obtain even the necessary supplies of provisions for the hands, and far more difficult, under the circumstances, to retain them in service. In consequence of heavy breaches in the canal, produced by the extraordinary freshets of April and September, 1843, which were repaired principally by the aid of accommodations from the banks, the deficit at the close of that year was unusually large and embarrassing. The whole revenues of the year only amounted to forty-seven thousand six hundred and thirty-five dollars and fifty-one cents, and the current expenses to eighty-three thousand seven hundred and ninety-two dollars and eighty cents, showing an excess of expenses over income to the amount of thirty-six thousand one hundred and fifty seven dollars and twenty-nine cents. Such was the melancholy condition of the Chesapeake & Ohio Canal Company in the year 1843. It could scarcely have been considered a very politic step for any set of gentlemen to connect themselves with the company at that period, for the purpose of endeavoring to retrieve it from its fall, and complete the canal to Cumberland; for the way of the world, generally, is to give credit to official labor, not according to the difficulties it has to overcome, but according to the measure of success with which it is crowned, and the chances of success were clearly against them.

"In January, 1844, the company succeeded, after much controversy, in rescuing from assumed forfeiture £15,500 of the sterling bonds, which, in 1839, had been hypothecated in England, and which had been regarded as irrecoverably lost, together with a small amount of coupons overdue, by means of which it was enabled to discharge, to a considerable extent, the debts for current expenses, and, also, which was imperatively called for, put the canal in somewhat better order than it had previously been. But the relief thus afforded was, necessarily, but temporary in its character, and some permanent increase in the income became a subject of indispensable necessity, to maintain the navigation, and keep in motion the operations of the company. With a view to secure this as far as practicable, until the canal should be finished to its available terminus when expedients would no longer be necessary, an arrangement was concluded with the Baltimore & Ohio Railroad Company, in September, 1843, by which that company agreed to fix the charge for the transportation of coal at two cents per ton per mile from Cumberland to dam No. 6, there to be transferred to the canal; and at that rate to transport it for any person or persons so long, as in their judgment, it should not interfere with their general trade nor require a material augmentation of their machinery. By reason of this arrangement, four thousand eight hundred and seventy-one tons of coal were transported on the canal during the year 1844, nearly the whole of which was transferred from the railroad at dam No. 6 ; and even with the aid of this amount, which was merely a beginning of the trade, the tolls of the year, for the first time, exceeded fifty thousand dollars of available funds. In the years 1841 and 1842, the tolls were nominally above that sum, but scrip was then received in payment, which was bought at about fifty cents on the dollar; and the principal articles of trade on the canal were then put at the highest rate of tolls authorized by the charter, so that the increased charge might, in sonic respect, compensate for the depreciated value of the funds in which it was paid.

"The arrangement with the Baltimore & Ohio Railroad Company, if it had been continued and carried out in good faith on their part, would, both in its immediate effects and future results, have been of much benefit to this company in the then existing state of its affairs. It was, however, for very unsound and unsatisfactory reasons, as given, abandoned by the railroad company in May, 1845, soon after the passage of the act providing for the completion of the canal to Cumberland, which, probably, had more effect in producing the abandonment than the grounds upon which it was placed. But the arrangement was merely intended by this company as the expedient of the day. The paramount and controlling importance of the early completion of the canal to Cumberland was always kept steadily in view. From the belief that the previous failures to obtain the necessary legislation from Maryland to enable the company to accomplish this great object, had resulted from a want of proper information in regard to the state of its affairs and the expediency of completing the canal, the president and directors in November, 1843, presented a special report to the stockholders, designed for publication, and to be submitted to the general assembly at the ensuing session, in which those objects were fully and clearly explained. The idea which had been started several years previously, and which was at that time revived with increased zeal and ardor, that the facilities of connection with the railroad at dam No. 6, superseded the necessity of extending the canal beyond that point, was likewise combated and refuted; and the policy and indispensable necessity of completing the work to Cumberland, merely viewing it as a financial measure to Maryland, made manifest. The plan suggested, in consideration of the prostrate credit of the State, and which was alleged to be practicable if unencumbered with injurious restrictions, was the waver by the legislature of the State liens on the revenues of the canal, so as to empower the company to issue its bonds, with preferred liens on its revenues, to an amount not exceeding two millions of dollars. In principle and amount, it was similar to the measure which had been proposed and rejected by the legislature at the December sessions of 1841 and 1842.

"After showing that bids had been made to finish the canal for a less sum, in current money, than the engineer's estimate, which was one million five hundred and forty-five thousand dollars, the report proceeded:

'In order, however, to give full strength to the credit of the company, so as to enable it to procure the required sum, upon fair and advantageous terms, it will be indispensably necessary to waive the State liens to a much larger amount, so that a broad and tangible basis may be presented for the bonds to rest upon. By this same means, the company will have to provide for the payment of the accruing interest on the sum that may be required for the construction of the work, until the net revenues of the canal become adequate to the purpose, which, cannot justly be calculated on until a year after it reaches Cumberland, unless, indeed (which was one of the objects of the connection), the coal trade shall be so much built up, under the operation of the arrangement with the railroad company, as to give it a sufficient tonnage immediately upon its being completed to that point. But this expectation ought not to govern the action of the legislature in this behalf. The better fortified the bonds are, the greater will be their value; and as no more will be issued than will be necessary to finish the work and pay the interest on the cost thereof, in aid of the net tolls of the canal until they become sufficient for the purpose, together with a small outlay for repairs and improvements on the finished portion of the line, it will be to the interest of the State to leave a broad margin to the credit of the company. With this view, and to provide against all contingencies, we would recommend a waiver of the State liens to such amount as may be found necessary for those purposes, not exceeding the sum of two millions of dollars. This we would consider an ample and available provision for all the demands in the premises.'

"But, notwithstanding the obvious policy of the State, the Legislature of Maryland at the December session, 1843, were not yet prepared to adopt the measure suggested. The report of the company had been published too late to have any decided effect at that time. The elections had all previously taken place, and the members had been chosen under the influence of long cherished prejudices against the company in consequence of the misfortunes or improvident measures of a former period of its history, and in ignorance of the real issue they were called upon to decide. No act was accordingly passed at that session.

"At the December session, 1844, the application was renewed with unabated ardor and an array of additional arguments. The officers of the company stood almost alone in the vindication of the measure. The friends, who, on former occasions, had gathered together to aid and support the company in its times of difficulty, were no longer seen. There were no gatherings in primary meetings and no State convention to encourage and sustain it in its struggles for relief. Instead of friends to help, it was, indeed, surrounded by enemies to oppose. The city of Baltimore, oblivious of its past support and of its earnest advocacy in former years of the completion of the work to Cumberland, now took decided grounds in opposition to it. The columns of the press of the city teemed with essays and communications adverse to the measure which had been proposed. The railroad company also, after all their previous protestations of enduring amity, with more diplomatic skill, sought to crush the effort by statements intended to show that a connection between the railroad and the canal at dam No. 6 rendered a further prosecution of the latter work wholly unnecessary. They likewise, and doubtless with a similar object, asserted that 'many years would elapse before the demand for coal would require more than one hundred thousand tons in any one year, whatever facilities of transportation may be afforded.' If the same powerful opposition had been arrayed against the completion of the canal at the December session, 1834, or even at that of 1835, the work at either of those periods would, most probably, have been stopped; for, even with the active and combined exertions of the immediate friends of both of the great internal improvement companies, backed by the whole influence of the city of Baltimore, the appropriations on those occasions were obtained with great difficulty, and, as regards the latter, only after a prolonged struggle. But the subject in 1844 presented a very different aspect. It was now no longer a question of internal improvement merely, but also a question of finance—not whether the vast treasury of wealth which was locked up in the bosom of the mountains of Alleghany County should be opened and its contents added to the general aggregate of the State's resources by some facility of internal improvement, but whether the millions which the State had invested in the Chesapeake & Ohio Canal Company should be given up as irretrievably lost, or an effort be made to save and render them productive. Maryland had already expended seven millions of dollars in the prosecution of the canal, and had never anticipated a return from it until after the work should be finished. Neither more money nor the State's credit was now solicited. All that was asked of her was, that as she was herself in pecuniary difficulty, arising mainly from her support to this company, and as her investments in it must remain valueless and unproductive until the canal should be completed to Cumberland, she would waive her unprofitable liens on the revenues to such an extent only as would enable the company to finish the work upon a preferred pledge of its future resources. Although, as we have remarked, the opposition was influential, there was not wanting upon the floor of the house of delegates at the December session, 1844, Marylanders who fully appreciated the deep importance of the completion of the canal, and whose strong judgments and fervid eloquence were earnestly enlisted in favor of the plan that had been recommended. After a long and arduous struggle, the act waiving the liens of the State (1844, ch. 281,) under which the canal has now been completed, was passed. But it was only finally passed on the 10th of March, the last day of the session by the limitation of the constitution, and received merely a majority of one vote in each house of the general assembly; and it was not passed even thus and then, until the bill originally proposed, which fairly embodied the application of the company, had been rejected in the house of delegates, and ultimately so materially modified that some of its most prominent advocates pronounced it valueless, and were disposed to abandon its support.

"The act authorized the board of president and directors to borrow or raise on the bonds of the company, to be executed in a prescribed manner, and secured by a pledge of the revenues and tolls that may hereafter accrue on the canal and its works between Georgetown and Cumberland, such sum or sums of money as would be required to pay for the completion of the canal to Cumberland, under a contract or contracts thereafter to be made by the board and approved by the Maryland State agents, and the necessary expenses appertaining thereto; and also to pay the interest on the bonds issued under the act, in aid of the net revenues, until they became sufficient for the purpose after the debts in arrear for repairs and officers salaries are discharged; with a proviso that the whole amount of the bonds issued should not exceed one million seven hundred thousand dollars. The bonds were directed to be countersigned and approved by the Maryland State agents, or a majority of them; and the company was forbidden to sell or hypothecate them at less than their par value; but it was authorized to make contracts payable in them at par, and to pay thus for the whole or any part of the work, instead of raising money for the purpose, if the president and directors should deem it most expedient. The rights and liens of the State upon the revenues of the company were postponed and waived in favor of the bonds, so as to make them and the interest to accrue thereon preferred liens on the revenues, as above mentioned, with an express reservation, however, that the president and directors shall, at all times, have the authority to use and apply such portion of the revenues and tolls as, in their opinion, may be necessary to put and keep the canal in good condition and repair, provide the requisite supply of water, and pay the current expenses of the company.

"The interest on the bonds, at the rate of six per cent. per annum, was to be made payable on the first of January arid July in each year, and the principal in not less than thirty-five years; the State, however, retaining the right to redeem them, upon payment of the principal and interest due thereon, at any time that, in the opinion of the legislature, the interest of the State might require it, but in no event was it to be held responsible for such payment.

"So soon as the revenues should be more than sufficient to pay the interest on the bonds and the interest on the certificates of debt issued to the creditors of the Potomac Company, under the 12th section of the charter, which is not to exceed five thousand dollars per year, the company was required to pay to the treasurer of the State, out of the surplus net revenues, such sum, not exceeding an average of twenty-five thousand dollars a year, dating from the first of January next after the completion of the canal to Cumberland, as may be necessary to constitute an adequate sinking fund; and the treasurer was directed to receive such annual payments, under the responsibilities of his office, and to invest and accumulate the same, until a sufficient amount should be thus obtained to pay the principal of the bonds that may be issued, which he was directed to pay at maturity. Until the bonds were paid the said fund was to be considered as held for that purpose by the State of Maryland as agent for the company.

"The president and directors were authorized to execute any deed, mortgage, or other instrument of writing that should be deemed necessary or expedient to give the fullest effect to the provisions of the act; and the company was required to execute to the State of Maryland and deliver to the treasurer a further mortgage on the canal, its lands, tolls, and revenues, subject to the liens and pledges made, created, or authorized by this act, as additional security for the payment of the two million loan made by the State under the act of December session, 1834, ch. 241, and the interest in arrear and to accrue thereon.

"This act was, however, not to take effect until its provisions were approved, assented, and agreed to by the stockholders of the company in general meeting assembled; and it was expressly provided that no bond should be issued under it until after one or more of the incorporated companies of Alleghany County, or other corporations or individuals, should, by an instrument or instruments of writing in due form, with ample security, to be approved by the agents representing the interest of the State in the company, or a majority of them, and the governor, guaranty to the company an aggregate transportation, on the entire length of the canal between Georgetown and Cumberland, of not less than an average of one hundred and ninety-five thousand tons of tonnage per year for five years, dating from the end of six months after the canal shall have been completed to Cumberland. Such is the synopsis of the leading provisions of this important measures.

"At the same session of the general assembly, the company, upon application, also obtained the passage of an act, amendatory of the charter, in regard to the adoption of by-laws, and the protection of the canal from injury, with some necessary provisions to prevent frauds upon the revenues, which was

223

ratified and confirmed by Congress, after many efforts for the purpose, in September, 1850.

"In the charter of the Chesapeake & Ohio Canal Company, prior to the year 1844, there was no express power given to the company to borrow money for the construction or completion of the canal, and its right to do so had been much doubted. Even the force and validity of the mortgages which it bad executed to the State of Maryland to secure the payment of the two millions loan had been called in question. Besides this, the time limited by the charter for the completion of the canal to Cumberland had expired in 1840, and since that period; the corporation had existed merely by the sufferance of the sovereignties which had created it. No steps had previously been taken to procure amendments in either of these vital points. In the confident belief that the measure which had been suggested by the company at that time for the completion of the work in some shape, must, sooner or later, prevail; and that it would prove ineffectual unless the omissions and defects in the charter, to which we have referred, were first remedied and supplied, the board of president and directors, at the session of 1843, transmitted a memorial to the Legislature of Virginia, asking for the passage of an act providing for the amendments indicated, and also enlarging the powers of the company in regard to the right of extending the canal by a slack-water improvement to the mouth of Savage River, whenever it should hereafter deem it expedient to do so. A draft of a bill embracing the provisions desired, and containing a reservation as to the liens of Maryland, accompanied it. The Legislature of Virginia promptly acted upon the subject and passed the bill in the form in which it was presented, with some slight and unimportant additions, on the 20th of January, 1844. The act provides for an enlargement, and extension of the time for the completion of the canal to Cumberland, to the 1st of January, 1855; and an express authority is conferred on the president and directors, or a majority of them assembled, to borrow money, from time to time, to carry into effect the objects authorized by the charter of the company, to issue bonds or other evidences of such loans, and to pledge the property and revenues of the company for the payment of the same, and the interest to accrue thereon, in such form, and to such extent, as they may deem expedient, with a proviso, saving the, prior rights or liens of the State of Maryland, under the mortgages which had been executed by the company to this State, except in so far as they should be waived, deferred, or postponed by the Legislature of Maryland. The amendment, in regard to the slack-water improvement beyond Cumberland was to the effect already mentioned. The assent of the Legislature of Maryland was given to this act on the 8th of February, 1844, and it was confirmed by Congress, and approved by the President of the United States, on the 17th of February, 1845.

"At a general meeting of the stockholders of the company, assembled at the office of the company in Frederick, on the 29th of April, 1845, the president and directors submitted authenticated copies of these several acts of Virginia, Congress, and the State of Maryland, amendatory of the charter, and they were duly accepted, and thus became a part of the charter of the company. At the same meeting, and on the same day, the president and directors also submitted to the stockholders the act of the general assembly of Maryland, entitled, 'An act to provide for the completion of the Chesapeake & Ohio Canal to Cumberland,' which we have already explained; and they passed a resolution accepting and agreeing to its provisions, and authorizing the acceptance to be communicated to the treasurer of Maryland in the manner prescribed, and the mortgage to the State to be executed as required. The acceptance was immediately communicated to the treasurer of Maryland, and the act thereupon went into effect. The mortgage, which was executed to the State, and delivered to the treasurer, pursuant to the provisions of the seventh section of the act, bears date the 8th of January, 1846.

"The important amendments to the charter, which have been described, were finally ratified by Congress about one month before the passage of the act, waiving the liens for the completion of the canal. They were appreciated by the professional gentlemen who occupied seats in the Legislature of Maryland, in their consideration of the merits of the measure, as may be inferred from the provision made for the new mortgage to the State. Without them, as we have heretofore intimated, the act of the 10th of March, 1845, would have been wholly unavailable. Even fortified and sustained by them, serious doubts were generally entertained whether the conditions of the act could be fulfilled and complied with, or, if complied with, whether, with the limited amount and kind of means contemplated and authorized by its provisions, the company could secure the completion of the canal to Cumberland. These doubts, unfortunately, tended to increase the intrinsic difficulties of the act.

"In the year 1841, the chief engineer made a detailed estimate of the work done and to be done on the fifty miles above dam No 6, and on the 1st of December, 1842, after the operations on the line had ceased, he estimated the amount then required to complete the canal to Cumberland at one million five hundred and forty-five thousand dollars.

"In consequence of a change made in the character of certain portions of the masonry, and for other causes, requiring a variation in the previous estimates, the chief engineer made a revised estimate in August, 1845, and, with an allowance of fifteen per cent. for land damages, superintendence, and other contingencies, estimated the cost of completing the canal at one million four hundred and four thousand four hundred and seventy-one dollars. The work previously executed between dam No. 6 and Cumberland, amounted, as then ascertained, to two million eight hundred and ninety-two thousand dollars.

"The first requirement of the act of December session, 1844, ch. 281, to give effect to its operative provisions, was the execution of the guaranty of tonnage, and its approval in the mode prescribed. Until this should be accomplished no bond could be issued under it. A condition of similar character had rendered abortive the act of March session, 1841, authorizing a loan of two millions of dollars of State securities to the company, as has been shown. The same result was generally predicted for this, and the impression produced an unfavorable effect, and caused a listlessness on the part of the incorporated companies of Alleghany County, whose assistance had been most confidently relied on. But, by persevering exertions, and the active and efficient co-operation of the friends of the canal in the District of Columbia and the western counties of Maryland, the full amount of guaranty required by the act was obtained. Three of the incorporated companies ultimately joined in the measure to a limited amount. The instruments of guaranty were prepared in such a form as to divide the responsibility, and enlist the largest number of guarantors. Twenty-eight instruments of this description were executed and delivered to the company. They were laid before the governor and the Maryland State agents, and received their approval on the 29th of July, 1845.

"By the fulfilment of this embarrassing condition, the president and directors of the company were placed in a situation to avail of the benefits of the law, and, after a long and toilsome struggle against difficulties, which at times seemed almost insurmountable, they finally succeeded in completing the canal under it.

"Without dwelling on the details of the various negotiations and proceedings which took place, or averting to the critical position of affairs on several occasions, we will trace, briefly, the progress of events to the final accomplishment of the purposes of the law, and, after a reference to a few antecedent transactions, which it is proper to notice, hasten to a conclusion.

"It has been seen that the act of 1844 did not place any money at the disposal of the company for the completion of the canal, furnish it with State bonds, as on previous occasions, nor even waive the liens to the extent recommended, and clothe it with available power to raise money on its own bonds to be issued under the act; but, in effect, merely authorized the board of president and directors to issue the company's bonds, upon a pledge of its disencumbered revenues, to an amount not exceeding one million seven hundred thousand dollars, for the purpose of completing the canal to Cumberland, then estimated to cost one million five hundred and forty-five thousand dollars in money, and of paying certain expenses necessarily growing out of a fulfilment of this provision, which, at a moderate calculation, could not have been computed at less than one hundred and fifty thousand dollars, and which have actually somewhat exceeded that sum; and to render this limited amount of the bonds of the company sufficient for the objects indicated in the act, the liens of the State, then having priority, were waived and postponed in their favor. Little more than one year previously, these liens, together with the whole interest of the State in the company, amounting in all to upwards of eight millions of dollars, had been advertised for sale in the money markets of Europe and America, upon an offer to receive therefor the sum of five millions of dollars in Maryland State bonds, which then commanded less than fifty cents on the dollar, without attracting a bid or eliciting a single inquiry upon the subject; and their waiver, by the State, could only give value to the liens that were to be preferred to them, in proportion as it gave assurance of the completion of the canal.

"In the general depreciation of American securities at that period, with Maryland herself in discredit, and in view of the comparatively small means allowed for the accomplishment of the ends proposed, a sale of the bonds at par was utterly unattainable, and a resort to a contract, payable in the bonds, and covering all the subjects necessary to be provided for, became the only practicable course for the company to pursue, and it was accordingly adopted. After duly advertising for proposals, the board of president and directors, with the approval of the Maryland State agents, concluded an agreement to that effect on the 25th of September, 1845. The contract was full of details, and guarded with the utmost care in all its provisions. For the consideration of one million six hundred and twenty-five thousand dollars of the bonds to be issued under and pursuant to the act of 1844, ch. 281, the contractors, four in number, bound themselves to commence the work within thirty days, and within the period of two years finish the canal to Cumberland, according to the plans and specifications of the 1st of December, 1842, estimate as modified and explained by certain memoranda attached thereto, to pay to a trustee, for the use of the company, in twenty-one monthly instalments, an aggregate sum of one hundred thousand dollars in money, to enable the board of president and directors to liquidate land claims, engineering and other incidental expenses, and to pay the interest on the bonds to be issued under the act until, and including the half year's interest that would fall due, after the work had been finished. The bonds were to be paid at their par value only as the work progressed and the respective provisions of the contract were complied with. The payments for construction were to be based upon the chief engineer's estimates of work actually executed, which were to be made out monthly, the company reserving the right to retain a certain percentage as security; and by way of super added obligation to the execution of the instrument, the parties executed their bonds, with approved security, to the company, to commence the work within thirty days, and to prosecute it at an expenditure of at least one hundred and fifty thousand dollars. The contractors also bound themselves to cash, at *par*, the remaining seventy-five thousand dollars of bonds authorized to be issued by the act, if required to do so by the company. To the board of president and directors was reserved full power to declare the contract abandoned upon a non-compliance on the part of the contractors with any of its material provisions. And with a view of guarding all the bonds issuable under the act from depreciation, and of insuring the accomplishment of the undertaking, a provision was incorporated that no bonds should be paid to the contractors for the execution of the work until they had given bond with ample security for the fulfilment of the entire contract, or concluded an arrangement for the negotiation of such amount of the company's bonds to which they might become entitled, as would afford to the Maryland State agents and the board of president and directors a reasonable guaranty of their ability to comply with their engagements.

"The above is a concise outline of the principal provisions of the original contract. It was not at the time deemed probable that the security for the large amount that would be required could be given, and the avowed reliance of the contractors was on an arrangement for the disposal of the bonds. They did not, however, we believe, suppose that this could be effected until after the State of Maryland had provided for the resumption of the payment of interest on the State debt, because they had ascertained, and, indeed, the company had previously been distinctly informed, by its London correspondents, that capitalists regarded 'the interests of the company and the State so interwoven,' that whilst the State's securities were dishonored the company's bonds could not be negotiated. The contractors thought that their own private means and resources would enable them to prosecute the work until after the close of the ensuing session of the legislature, and it was confidently believed, on all sides, that at that session provision would be made for the public liabilities, and that they could then make a satisfactory negotiation. Soon after the date of the contract, therefore, they commenced the work between dam No. 6 and Cumberland, and prosecuted it until June, 1846, when, the legislature having met and adjourned without passing an act to restore the credit of the State, and their private means being exhausted, they were compelled to suspend operations.

"The last report made by the chief engineer, previous to the suspension, showed that the work done under the contract according to the revised estimate of August, 1845, which he took as his guide, amounted to the sum of fifty-five thousand three hundred and eighty-four dollars. The contractors, however, had received from the company no part of this sum, as they bad not yet placed themselves in a situation to be entitled to payments. Although applications were made for an advance of bonds, none had yet been issued.

"The company having made known its willingness to allow the contractors a reasonable time to mature their financial arrangements, they continued actively engaged in the effort to make a negotiation, and secured the services of several distinguished gentlemen and financiers to aid them. One of the contractors went to England for the purpose of giving his personal attention to the subject, and with the assistance of conditional promises, obtained from the capitalists on this side of the Atlantic, succeeded in arranging for a negotiation there, predicated mainly upon the resumption of payment by Maryland, but with reservation of a right to the parties to decline if a change should take place in the money market. As in the case of the loan for the benefit of the Illinois and Michigan Canal, two experienced gentlemen bad previously been appointed by the

English capitalists, to inquire into the probable productiveness of the canal when finished, and other matters submitted to them; and they had fully examined the whole subject and made an elaborate and favorable report. At December session, 1846, this state of things was known to the legislature, and the friends of the canal were among the most zealous and indefatigable advocates for the restoration of State faith, both on account of the good name of the State, and the known bearing of the measure upon the procurement of means for the completion of the canal. On the 8th of March, 1847, the Legislature of Maryland passed a law for funding the arrears and punctually paying the interest accruing on the State debt after the 1st of October, 1847. On the application of the contractors, the Legislature of Virginia, on the 8th of March, 1847, passed an act, accommodated to the terms of the contract, in regard to a negotiation, and authorizing a guaranty of the bonds to the amount of three hundred thousand dollars, which gave additional efficacy to the provisions of the act of 1844; and in the succeeding month, the District cities and certain citizens of Alexandria, subscribed, on similar terms, for one hundred thousand dollars of the bonds at their par value, for the purpose of aiding the work. But the guaranty and subscriptions were all conditional, and their availability depended upon the contractors obtaining from other sources an amount of money, which, when super added to their aggregate, would constitute a fund sufficient for the completion of the canal. It was supposed that this amount had already been secured by the conditional arrangement that had been made in England, in as much of the difficulties which then existed had been removed, and the application in that quarter was accordingly renewed. The prospect of success was for a time flattering, but contrary to all expectations, the London parties, through their agent in Boston, abruptly withdrew from the negotiation just as it was about to be concluded, upon the ground that, though Maryland had resumed payment, a change had taken place in the money market. This was the reason given, but it was not considered as the influencing cause of the course that was pursued. The Boston agent had desired distinct and specific information in regard to the questions, Whether the canal could be finished with the aggregate sum of money which would be realized by the contractors from the proposed arrangement, viz: one million one hundred thousand dollars, which they considered sufficient for their purposes; and, secondly, whether it could be completed with the whole amount of bonds authorized to be issued by the company, under the act of 1844. These inquiries were propounded on the 14th of April, 1847, to one of the gentlemen who, at the instance of the London capitalists, had made the investigations in regard to the canal in 1846, and who was an engineer of approved experience. His reply bears date the 17th of the same month. To the first question, his answer was distinctly in the negative; in reference to the second, he stated that, if all the bonds at the command of the company could be disposed of without serious loss, and certain legitimate modifications, which he indicated were made in the character of the work, the means provided would be sufficient, but, in his opinion, not otherwise. It was doubtless these replies, to receive which the Boston agent had deferred his final answer for several days, that produced the failure of the negotiation; for the withdrawal of the proposition of the London capitalists was, thereupon, decisive and absolute.

"The prospects of the company were at this period discouraging. After sounding all the depths of the money markets on both Sides of the Atlantic, and offering the bonds at a great discount, the contractors, though aided and strengthened by the Virginia guaranty and the par subscriptions of Alexandria and the District cities, had been unable to effect an arrangement for the funds required by them to comply with their engagements, and the disinclination of capitalists to purchase the bonds, had arisen, not from an apprehension in regard to the productiveness of the canal when finished, but from a belief in the inadequacy of the amount of bonds authorized and the amount of money that could be realized therefrom for the accomplishment of its completion. And whilst the aspect was thus gloomy without, the state of affairs was scarcely more favorable within. During the years 1846 and 1847, this region of country was visited with a series of freshets, which in magnitude and rapidity of succession were without example. Considerable damage was done by them to the canal, particularly on the lower division, and scarcely was sufficient time afforded to mend the breaches occasioned by one, before they were renewed by another inundation of the Potomac. In the straightened condition of the finances of the company, when it could barely struggle along, in ordinary years, with its annual receipts, this increase of expenses was exceedingly embarrassing. With the aid of temporary loans obtained from the banks, however, the damage was repaired.

"In regard to the contract for the completion of the canal, the president and directors of the company yielded to circumstances, and, planting themselves firmly upon the position originally assumed—that they would issue no bonds until a satisfactory negotiation had been consummated—acquiesced in a further delay of the operations. The early completion of the canal, important as it was undoubtedly considered, was not the subject of most solicitude, either with them or the friends of the company generally. Under the act of 1844, as we have seen, it was not a question of time, but a question of practicability; not whether the canal could be finished by a given day, but whether it could be finished with the means provided for the purpose. By the omission of the contractors to prosecute the work continuously, their contract was liable to forfeiture at the pleasure of the president and directors of the company; but such a measure, even under the existing unfavorable appearances, could have produced no benefit, but on the contrary would have tended to make things worse. If the contract had been annulled, the Virginia guaranty and the par subscriptions of Alexandria and the District cities, which the contractors had secured and brought to their assistance, would have gone down with it, and the company would have been thrown back upon the sheer provisions of the then discredited act of 1844 for the means to complete the canal to Cumberland. Under these circumstances, therefore, the president and directors forbore to exercise their power of annulment, and the prudence of their course was justified by the result. Although the last effort of the contractors to raise the requisite means to comply with their contract seemed decisive of

233

failure, it was only the prelude to a final arrangement.

"So soon as the London capitalists abandoned the negotiation, the attention of the contractors and their agents was turned exclusively to this country. Two of the gentlemen whose assistance they had engaged, issued a pamphlet bearing date the 10th of July, 1847, in which they explained the provisions of the act of 1844, and the contract made under it for the completion of the canal; referred to the guaranty act of Virginia, and the subscriptions of Washington, Georgetown, and Alexandria, and to an agreement made with the sub-contractors, by which they consented to receive two hundred thousand dollars of the bonds at par in payment for their work; and exhibited a statement, showing the sum of money which, in their judgment, would be sufficient to accomplish the undertaking. This sum was one million one hundred and seventy-two thousand one hundred and sixteen dollars, and it was arrived at by a calculation based upon subcontracts which, it was stated, had been previously entered into by the contractors for about two-thirds of the work remaining to be executed between dam No. 6 and Cumberland. To the exposition thus made the attention of capitalists was invited, and on the 13th of October, 1847, the contractors, through the medium of three distinguished gentlemen of the North, two of whom were the authors of the above-mentioned pamphlet, succeeded in finally concluding a satisfactory negotiation. According to its terms, which assumed that six hundred thousand dollars of the bonds had been disposed of at par in the manner above indicated, the contractors agreed to sell to certain parties residing principally in Boston, New York, and Washington City, at the rate of sixty cents on the dollar, eight hundred and thirty-three thousand three hundred and thirty-three dollars of bonds they were to receive from the company at par, upon a compliance with the respective provisions of their contract, leaving still of the consideration therein mentioned a margin of one hundred and ninety-one thousand six hundred and sixty-seven dollars of the bonds undisposed of, which were regarded as a reserved fund to supply deficiencies if they should occur. They also at the same time constituted and appointed the three gentlemen, alluded to, their agents and attorneys in the execution of their contract for the completion of the canal, and authorized them to receive the bonds from the company, from time to time, as they should become payable under its provisions, and sell or distribute them in conformity with the arrangement.

"The Maryland State agents and board of president and directors, in view of the entire arrangement made by the contractors, including the guaranty and par subscription, and of the guards and conservative provisions of the contract for the work, considered the clause in reference to a negotiation as now sufficiently complied with, and accordingly consented to issue and pay out the bonds as the work proceeded.

"We will here remark that a mortgage, pursuant to the 6th section of the act of 1844, to give full effect to its provisions, was subsequently executed by the company, and bears date the 6th of June, 1848.

"Some time after the execution of the contract for the completion of the canal, two of the original contractors withdrew from the co-partnership, and Thomas G. Harris, of Washington County, Maryland, became associated with the remaining two, who were James Hunter, of Virginia (whose indomitable perseverance and indefatigable exertions merited better fortune than ultimately befel him in his connection with the work), and William B. Thompson, of the District of Columbia. The three became associated in a firm under the name of Hunter, Harris & Co. The contract was accordingly so modified in November, 1847, and the time for completion having been extended, and other satisfactory alterations made in its provisions, under some of which certain specific parts of the work were dispensed with, and changes in the plan of construction made in a few others, with a view to a saving of cost, which was then found absolutely necessary, the operations were resumed and, under the pressure of constant embarrassments, with appeals to the company, frequent and urgent, for relief, which was, from time to time, extended to them, as often, and as far, as it could be allowed without hazarding the completion of the canal, were steadily prosecuted under the immediate management of Messrs. Hunter & Harris, until the 11th of March, 1850, when they were suspended in consequence of the pecuniary difficulties of the contractors, arising from the large sacrifices they had sustained in their sales of the bonds. They had, indeed, for some time previously, avowedly abandoned the hope of profit, but were stimulated to perseverance in the prosecution of their arduous undertaking, by an honest ambition to complete the canal and comply with their engagements. The suspension, however, only lasted for a few days. Messrs. Hunter, Harris & Co., made an assignment of their interest in the contract to two of their agents and attorneys for the benefit of their creditors. The work was again put in motion, under the assignment, and its prosecution continued until the middle of July, 1850, when the agents and assignees finally stopped operations and abandoned it, from an inability, under the very disagreeable and difficult circumstances in which they were placed to complete the canal, with the remaining means that were applicable to the purpose.

"Upon the certificate of the chief engineer in regard to the facts of the case, the board of president and directors, on the 17th of July, formally declared the contract abandoned, and on the following day entered into a new contract with Michael Byrne, of Frederick County, for the final completion of the canal. The aggregate of the work remained to be done at this period was inconsiderable, but it consisted of unfinished parts, at numerous places along the line between dam No. 6 and Cumberland, and was, consequently, tedious and troublesome in its execution. Mr. Byrne commenced promptly and prosecuted it with diligence. He had so far progressed by the 10th of October, 1850, that, on that day, the canal was opened for the purposes of navigation throughout the entire line to Cumberland, and the through trade then commenced. He, however, still continued to press forward the work, which, being now of an external character only, did not interfere with the passage of boats, and on the 17th of February, 1851, the final payment was made to him under and pursuant to the provisions of his contract. From that period may be dated the completion of *the Chesapeake & Ohio Canal to Cumberland.* The terms of the contract with Mr. Byrne, and the payments of all the bonds issued under the Maryland act of 1844, ch. 281, together with the parties to whom and the purposes for which the bonds were issued and paid, have been stated and explained in the preliminary report which precedes this narrative, and need not be here repeated.

"The Chesapeake & Ohio Canal, between Georgetown and Cumberland, lies on the north or Maryland side of the river, with the advantages of a southern exposure, and pursues the immediate valley of the Potomac throughout its whole length, except at a point called the Pawpaw Bend, about twenty-seven miles below Cumberland, where it passes through the mountain by a tunnel three thousand one hundred and eighteen feet in length, and lined and arched with brick laid in cement, by which about six miles in distance have been saved. From the Rock Creek basin in Georgetown, where it first reaches tide-water, to the basin at Cumberland, is one hundred and eighty-four and four-tenths miles, and the total rise from the level of mid-tide at Georgetown to the Cumberland basin, is six hundred and nine and seven-tenths feet. This ascent is overcome by seventy-four lift-locks, and a tide-lock that connects Rock Creek basin with the Potomac River. From a point about a mile west of Rock Creek basin, the Alexandria Canal, seven miles in length, diverges from the Chesapeake & Ohio Canal and crosses the Potomac River by an aqueduct eleven hundred feet long, and connects with tide-water at Alexandria. The Chesapeake & Ohio Canal is constructed for a depth of six feet throughout. From Georgetown to Harper's Ferry, sixty miles, it is sixty feet wide at the surface, and forty-two feet at the bottom. From Harper's Ferry to dam No. 5, forty-seven miles, the width at the surface is fifty feet, and at the bottom thirty-two feet; and from dam No. 5 to Cumberland, seventy-seven and one-half miles, the surface width is fifty-four feet, and the bottom thirty feet. The average lift of the locks a little exceeds eight feet. They are one hundred feet long and fifteen feet wide in the clear, and are capable of passing boats carrying one hundred and twenty tons of two thousand two hundred and forty pounds.

"The present supply of water for the canal is drawn entirely from the Potomac. For this purpose. dams are constructed across the river at seven different points.

"From a statement made out by the clerk from the books of

the company, with an additional allowance for a few small unsettled claims, it appears that the cost of the Chesapeake & Ohio Canal, from the mouth of Tiber Creek in the city of Washington to the town of Cumberland, a distance of one hundred and eighty-five and seven-tenths miles, for construction, engineer expenses, lands and other contingencies properly applicable to construction, amounts, in the aggregate, to the sum of eleven million seventy-one thousand one hundred and seventy-six dollars and twenty-one cents, or fifty-nine thousand six hundred and eighteen dollars and sixty-one cents per mile."

On the 10th of October, 1850, the Chesapeake & Ohio Canal was completed from Georgetown to Cumberland. The following boats loaded with coal started for the District of Columbia: *Southampton, Elizabeth, Ohio,* and *Delaware,* belonging to the Merchants' Line of McKaig & Agnew, and the *Freeman Rawdon* belonging to the Cumberland Line. The levels not being full of water in the new portion of the canal, the boats had great difficulty in passing down, frequently running aground; and it was not till the 17th day of October (when the chronicler was standing on the aqueduct), that he saw the first boat from Cumberland, the *Freeman Rawdon.* In going around the bend of the canal, at the Columbian Foundry, a gun was fired announcing her arrival as the first boat from the coal regions. She was soon afterwards followed by other boats; and thus the canal trade was opened to Georgetown, and has continued ever since, except when interrupted by breaches in the bank of the canal occasioned by heavy freshets in the river.

The quantity of coal shipped from Cumberland to Georgetown since the completion of the canal to 31st of December, 1876, was ten millions two hundred and fifteen thousand two hundred and six tons. The capital stock of the company was eight million two hundred and twenty-six thousand five hundred and ninety-three dollars and sixty-seven cents; the loan by the State of Maryland was two million dollars, on which interest is to be added to 31st of December, 1876, making in the aggregate the sum of four million four hundred and ninety-five thousand dollars. Other expenses of the company, such as guaranteed dividends, payable out of the net profits of the canal, nine million fifty-six thousand two hundred and fifty dollars; tolls collected, water rents, and other revenues, seven million eight hundred and fifty-five thousand eight hundred and fifty-two dollars. The number of boats cleared to Georgetown from 1870 to 31st of December, 1876, was forty-eight thousand nine hundred and forty-nine, bringing five million four hundred and sixty-three thousand four hundred and fourteen tons of coal; the number of boats loaded at Cumberland from 1872 to 31st of December, 1876, was as follows; at the Potomac wharf, ten thousand eight hundred and fifty-three; at the Basin wharf, fourteen thousand four hundred and four; at Consolidation wharf; ten thousand three hundred and thirty-two. The use of steamers on the canal for the transportation of freight will supersede the towing of boats by horses and mules. There are now sixteen steamers running from Cumberland to Georgetown; and during the year 1876 the following number of trips were made by them: the *Arcturus*, twenty-nine round trips; the *New Era*, twenty-seven round trips; the *L. Patten*, twenty-four round trips; the *A. Lovel*, eighteen round trips; the *Star, No. 1*, fifteen round trips; the *Star, No. 2*, fifteen round trips; the *W.T. Weld*, fifteen round trips; the other steamers made from two to thirteen trips each.

Receipts from all sources, including
    stock and loans $35,746,301.07
The whole expenditures of the canal
from its beginning to 31st of Decem-
ber, 1876, have been . . . . <u>35,659,055.06</u>
    Net balance on hand $87,246 01

THE OUTLET LOCK.

To give greater facility to the passage of boats from the canal to the river, a company was formed, in 1875, to build and erect a railway or inclined plane, about a mile above Georgetown, that would pass loaded boats from the canal to the river without the trouble of passing through a series of locks. This invention was projected by our fellow-townsman, H.H. Dodge, Esq., president of the Potomac Lock and Dock Company, and was designed and worked up in its details by

W.R. Hutton, chief engineer of the Chesapeake & Ohio Canal. The caisson or tank, turbine waterwheel, and all the machinery was built at the Vulcan Iron Works of H.A. Ramsey & Co., of Baltimore.

A railway was constructed in a diagonal line to the river, some six hundred feet long, consisting of several tracks. On the middle track is the caisson, one hundred and twelve feet long, seventeen feet wide, and eight feet deep, closed at each end by gates. On each side of the caisson are several cars, filled with stone and rocks, to balance the caisson when descending the inclined plane with a loaded boat. The mode of operation is as follows: The caisson is first run up to the canal gate, or fore-bay, when the front gate of the caisson is opened, and, being filled with water, the loaded boat is floated into the caisson, which displaces a bulk of water equal to its weight. As soon as the boat is in, the gate of the caisson is closed, when, by the operation of the turbine wheel and the cables fastened to the caissons, the boat gradually descends to the river, while the counter weights ascend. As soon as the caisson has reached the river, the gate is opened, and the boat passes into the Potomac. An empty boat can then pass in, and, displacing but little water, is light, and easily drawn up the inclined plane to the canal, the counter weights; which before ascended, now descending as the empty boat approaches the top of the railway.

On the 30th day of May, 1877, a serious accident happened at the outlet lock by some derangement of the machinery, while a loaded boat was being passed down the railway, by which accident Michael Reynolds, Sylvester Carroll, and John W. Mead were killed.

The Potomac Lock and Dock Company had used every precaution to have the machinery made of the best iron, to prevent accidents and insure success in the working of the lock; but all human foresight is not sufficient to guard against unexpected occurrences, as was shown in this case. And it appears that the loss of life is an incident in all public undertakings, as in the building of the Capitol, State Department, and other public buildings, railroads, and canals, where human life has been lost. As regards the accident above described, no blame can be attached to the owners of the outlet lock.

The great advantage derived from the construction of this work is the short space of time required to pass a boat through the lock and then to the wharves of Georgetown. To pass a boat from the same point down the level of the canal, and then through a series of locks to the basin or the river, would require two and one-half hours, even admitting that the prism of flotation is perfect in every lock before a boat is floated into it; but by the new lock, and the assistance of a steam tug, a loaded boat is floated to the wharf at any part of the town in less than a half hour.

ACT OF CONGRESS PROVIDING A FORM OF GOVERNMENT FOR THE DISTRICT OF COLUMBIA.

"*Be it enacted by the Senate and House of Representatives of the United States of America in Congress assembled,* That all the territory which was ceded by the State of Maryland to the Congress of the United States for the permanent seat of the Government of the United States shall continue to be designated as the District of Columbia. Said District, and the property and persons that may be therein, shall be subject to the following provisions for the government of the same, and also to any existing laws applicable thereto not hereby repealed or inconsistent with the provisions of this act. The District of Columbia shall remain and continue a municipal corporation, as provided in section 2 of the Revised Statutes relating to said District, and the Commissioners herein provided for shall be deemed and taken as officers of such corporation; and all laws now in force relating to the District of Columbia, not inconsistent with the provisions of this act, shall remain in full force and effect.

"SEC. 2. That within twenty days after the approval of this act, the President of the United States, by and with the advice and consent of the Senate, is hereby authorized to appoint two persons, who, with an officer of the Corps of Engineers of the United States Army, whose lineal rank shall be above that of captain, shall be Commissioners of the District of Columbia, and who, from and after July 1st, 1878, shall exercise all the powers

241

and authority now vested in the Commissioners of said District, except as are hereinafter limited or provided, and shall be subject to all restrictions and limitations and duties which are now imposed upon said Commissioners. The Commissioner who shall be an officer detailed, from time to time, from the Corps of Engineers by the President for this duty, shall not be required to perform any other, nor shall he receive any other compensation than his regular pay and allowance as an officer of the Army. The two persons appointed from civil life shall, at the time of their appointment, be citizens of the United States, and shall have been actual residents of the District of Columbia for three years next before their appointment, and have, during that period, claimed residence nowhere else; and one of said three Commissioners shall be chosen president of the Board of Commissioners at their first meeting, and annually and whenever a vacancy shall occur thereafter; and said Commissioners shall, each of them, before entering upon the discharge of his duties, take an oath or affirmation to support the Constitution of the United States, and to faithfully discharge the duties imposed upon him by law; and said Commissioners appointed from civil life shall each receive for his services a compensation at the rate of five thousand dollars per annum, and shall, before entering upon the duties of the office, each give bond in the sum of fifty thousand dollars, with surety as is required by existing law. The official term of said Commissioners appointed from civil life shall be three years, and until their successors are appointed and qualified; but the first appointment shall be one Commissioner for one year and one for two years, and at the expiration of their respective terms their successors shall be appointed for three years. Neither of said Commissioners, nor any officer whatsoever of the District of Columbia, shall be accepted as surety upon any bond required to be given to the District of Columbia; nor shall any contractor be accepted as surety for any officer or other contractor in said District.

"SEC. 3. That as soon as the Commissioners appointed and detailed as aforesaid shall have taken and subscribed the oath or affirmation hereinbefore required, all the powers, rights, duties, and privileges lawfully exercised by, and all property, estate, and effects now vested by law in the Commissioners appointed under the provisions of the act of Congress approved June 20th, 1874, shall be transferred to and vested in and imposed upon said Commissioners; and the functions of the Commissioners so appointed under the act of June 20th, 1874, shall cease and determine. And the Commissioners of the District of Columbia shall have power, subject to the limitations and provisions herein contained, to apply the taxes or other revenues of said District to the payment of the current expenses thereof, to the support of the public schools, the fire department, and the police, and for that purpose shall take possession and supervision of all the offices, books, papers, records, moneys, credits, securities, assets, and accounts belonging or appertaining to the business or interests of the government of the District of Columbia, and exercise the duties, powers, and authority aforesaid; but said Commissioners, in the exercise of such duties, powers, and authority, shall make no contract, nor incur any obligation other than such contracts and obligations as are hereinafter provided for, and shall be approved by Congress. The Commissioners shall have power to locate the places where hacks shall stand, and change them as often as the public interests require. Any person violating any orders lawfully made in pursuance of this power shall be subject to a fine of not less than ten nor more than one hundred dollars, to be recovered before any justice of the peace in an action in the name of the Commissioners. All taxes heretofore lawfully assessed and due, or to become due, shall be collected pursuant to law, except as herein otherwise provided; but said Commissioners shall have no power to anticipate taxes by a sale or hypothecation of any such taxes or evidences thereof, but they may borrow, for the first fiscal year after this act takes effect, in anticipation of collection of revenue, not to exceed two hundred thousand dollars, at a rate of interest not exceeding five per centum per annum, which shall be repaid out of the revenues of that year. And said Commissioners are hereby authorized to abolish any office, to consolidate two or more offices, reduce the number of employees, remove from office, and make appointments to any office under them authorized by law; said Commissioners shall have power to erect light, and maintain lamp posts, with lamps, outside of the city limits, when, in their judgment, it shall be deemed proper or necessary: *Provided*, That nothing in this act contained shall be construed to abate in any wise or interfere with any suit pending in favor of or against the District of Columbia or the Commissioners thereof, or affect any right, penalty, forfeiture, or cause of action existing in favor of said District or Commissioners, or any citizen of the District of Columbia, or any other person, but the same may be commenced, proceeded for, or prosecuted to final judgment, and the corporation shall be bound thereby as if the suit had been originally commenced for or against said corporation. The said Commissioners shall submit to the Secretary of the Treasury, for the fiscal year ending June 30th,1879, and annually thereafter, for his examination and approval, a statement showing in detail the work proposed to be undertaken by them during the fiscal year next ensuing, and the estimated cost thereof; also the cost of constructing, repairing, and maintaining all bridges authorized by law across the Potomac River within the District of Columbia, and also all other streams in said District; the cost of maintaining all public institutions of charity, reformatories, and prisons belonging to or controlled wholly or in part by the District of Columbia, and which are now by law supported wholly or in part by the United States or District of Columbia; and also the expenses of the Washington Aqueduct and its appurtenances; and also an itemized statement and estimate of the amount necessary to defray the expenses of the government of the District of Columbia for the next fiscal year: *Provided*, That nothing herein contained shall be construed as transferring from the United States authorities any of the public works within the District of Columbia now in the control or supervision of said authorities. The Secretary of the Treasury shall carefully consider all estimates submitted to him as above provided, and shall approve, disapprove, or suggest such changes in the same, or any item thereof, as he may think the public interest demands; and after he shall have considered and passed upon such estimates submitted to him, be shall cause to be made a statement of the amount approved by him, and the fund or purpose to which each item belongs, which statement shall be certified by him, and delivered, together with the estimates as originally submitted, to the Commissioners of the District of Columbia, who shall transmit the same to Congress. To the extent to which Congress shall approve of said estimates, Congress shall appropriate the amount of fifty per centum thereof; and the remaining fifty per centum of such approved estimates shall be levied and assessed upon the taxable property and privileges in said District other than the property of the United States and of the District of Columbia; and all proceedings in the assessing, equalizing, and levying of said taxes, the collection thereof, the listing return and penalty for taxes in arrears, the advertising for sale and the sale of property for delinquent taxes, the redemption thereof, the proceedings to enforce the lien upon unredeemed property, and every other act and thing now required to be done in the premises, shall be done and performed at the times and in the manner now provided by law, except in so far as is otherwise provided by this act: *Provided,* That the rate of taxation in any one year shall not exceed one dollar and fifty cents on every one hundred dollars of real estate not exempted by law, according to the cash valuation thereof: *And provided further,* Upon real property held and used exclusively for agricultural purposes, without the limits of the cities of Washington and Georgetown, and to be so designated by the assessors in their annual returns, the rate for any one year shall not exceed one dollar on every one hundred dollars. The collector of taxes, upon the receipt of the duplicate of assessment, shall give notice for one week, in one newspaper published in the city of Washington, that he is ready to receive taxes; and any person who shall, within thirty days after such notice given, pay the taxes assessed against him, shall be allowed by the collector a reduction of five per centum on the amount of his tax; all penalties imposed by the act approved March 3d, 1877, chapter 117, upon delinquents for default in the payment of taxes levied under said act, at the times specified therein, shall, upon payment of the said taxes assessed against such delinquents within three months from the passage of this act, with interest at the rate of six per cent. thereon, be remitted.

"SEC. 4. That the said Commissioners may, by general

245

regulations consistent with the act of Congress of March 3d, 1877, entitled 'An act for the support of the government of the District of Columbia for the fiscal year ending June 30th, 1878, and for other purposes,' or with other existing laws, prescribe the time or times for the payment of all taxes and the duties of assessors and collectors in relation thereto. All taxes collected shall be paid into the Treasury of the United States, and the same, as well as the appropriations to be made by Congress as aforesaid, shall be disbursed for the expenses of said District, on itemized vouchers, which shall have been audited and approved by the auditor of the District of Columbia, certified by said Commissioners, or a majority of them; and the accounts of the said Commissioners and the tax collectors, and all other officers required to account, shall be settled and adjusted by the accounting officers of the Treasury Department of the United States.

Hereafter, the Secretary of the Treasury shall pay the interest on the three-sixty-five bonds of the District of Columbia, issued in pursuance of the act of Congress approved June 20th, 1874, when the same shall become due and payable; and all amounts so paid shall be credited as a part of the appropriation for the year by the United States toward the expenses of the District of Columbia, as hereinbefore provided:

"SEC. 5. That, hereafter, when any repairs of streets, avenues, alleys, or sewers within the District of Columbia are to be made, or when new pavements are to be substituted in place of those worn out, new ones laid, or new streets opened, sewers built, or any works, the total cost of which shall exceed the sum of one thousand dollars, notice shall be given in one newspaper in Washington, and if the total cost shall exceed five thousand dollars, then in one newspaper in each of the cities of New York, Philadelphia, and Baltimore also for one week, for proposals, with full specifications as to materials for the whole or any portion of the works proposed to be done; and the lowest responsible proposal for the kind and character of pavement or other work which the Commissioners shall determine upon shall in all cases be accepted: *Provided, however,* That the Commissioners shall have the right, in their discretion, to reject

246

all such proposals: *Provided,* That the work capable of being executed under a single contract shall not be subdivided so as to reduce the sum of money to be paid therefor to less than one thousand dollars. All contracts for the construction, improvement, alteration, or repairs of the streets, avenues, highways, alleys, gutters, sewers, and all work of like nature shall be made and entered into only by and with the official unanimous consent of the Commissioners of the District, and all contracts shall be copies in a book kept for that purpose, and be signed by the said Commissioners, and no contract involving an expenditure of more than one hundred dollars shall be valid until recorded and signed as aforesaid. No pavement shall be accepted nor any pavement laid except that of the best material of its kind known for that purpose, laid in the most substantial manner; and good and sufficient bonds to the United States, in a penal sum not less than the amount of the contract, with sureties to be approved by the Commissioners of the District of Columbia, shall be required from all contractors, guaranteeing that the terms of their contracts shall be strictly and faithfully performed to the satisfaction of and acceptance by said Commissioners; and that the contractors shall keep new pavements or other new works in repair for a term of five years from the date of the completion of their contracts; and ten per centum of the cost of all new works shall be retained as an additional security and a guarantee fund to keep the same in repair for said term, which said per centum shall be invested in registered bonds of the United States or of the District of Columbia, and the interest thereon paid to said contractors. The cost of laying down said pavement, sewers, and other works, or of repairing the same, shall be paid for in the following proportions and manner, to wit: When any street or avenue through which a street railway runs shall be paved, such railway company shall bear all the expense for that portion of the work lying between the exterior rails of the tracks of such roads, and for a distance of two feet from and exterior to such track or tracks on each side thereof, and of keeping the same in repair; but the said railway companies, having conformed to the grades established by the Commissioners, may use such cobblestone or

Belgian blocks for paving their tracks, or the space between their tracks, as the Commissioners may direct; the United States shall pay one-half of the cost of all work done under the provisions of this section, except that done by the railway companies, which payment shall be credited as part of the fifty per centum which the United States contributes toward the expenses of the District of Columbia for that year; and all payments shall be made by the Secretary of the Treasury on the warrant or order of the Commissioners of the District of Columbia or a majority thereof, in such amounts and at such times as they may deem safe and proper in view of the progress of the work: That if any street railway company shall neglect or refuse to perform the work required by this act, said pavement shall be laid between the tracks and exterior thereto of such railway by the District of Columbia; and if such company shall fail or refuse to pay the sum due from them in respect of the work done by or under the orders of the proper officials of said District in such case of the neglect or refusal of such railway company to perform the work required as aforesaid, the Commissioners of the District of Columbia shall issue certificates of indebtedness against the property, real or personal, of such railway company, which certificates shall bear interest at the rate of ten per centum per annum until paid, and which, until they are paid, shall remain and be a lien upon the property or against which they are issued together with the franchise of said company; and if the said certificates are not paid within one year, the said Commissioners of the District of Columbia may proceed to sell the property against which they are issued, or so much thereof as may be necessary to pay the amount due; such sale to be first duly advertised daily for one week in some newspaper published in the city of Washington, and to be at public auction to the highest bidder. When street railways cross any street or avenue, the pavement between the tracks of such railway shall conform to the pavement used upon such street or avenue, and the companies owning these intersecting railroads shall pay for such pavements in the same manner and proportion as required of other railway companies under the provisions of this section. It shall be the duty of the Commissioners of the District of

Columbia to see that all water and gas mains, service pipes, and sewer connections are laid upon any street or avenue proposed to be paved or otherwise improved before any such pavement or other permanent works are put down; and the Washington Gas Light Company, under the direction of said Commissioners, shall, at its own expense, take up, lay, and replace all gas mains on any street or avenue to be paved, at such time and place as said Commissioners shall direct. The President of the United States may detail from the Engineer Corps of the Army not more than two officers, of rank subordinate to that of the engineer officer belonging to the Board of Commissioners of said District to act as assistants to said Engineer Commissioner, in the discharge of the special duties imposed upon him by the provisions of this act.

"SEC. 6. That from and after the 1st day of July, 1878, the board of metropolitan police and the board of school trustees shall be abolished, and all the powers and duties now exercised, by them shall be transferred to the said Commissioners of the District of Columbia, who shall have authority to employ such officers and agents and to adopt such provisions as may be necessary to carry into execution the powers and duties devolved upon them by this act. And the Commissioners of the District of Columbia shall, from time to time, appoint nineteen persons, actual residents of said District of Columbia, to constitute the trustees of public schools of said District, who shall serve without compensation and for such terms as said Commissioners shall fix. Said trustees shall have the powers and perform the duties in relation to the care and management of the public schools which are now authorized by law.

"SEC. 7. That the offices of sinking fund commissioners are hereby abolished; and all duties and powers possessed by said commissioners are transferred to, and shall be exercised by, the Treasurer of the United States, who shall perform the same in accordance with the provisions of existing laws.

"SEC. 8. That in lieu of the board of health now authorized by law, the Commissioners of the District of Columbia shall appoint a physician as health officer, whose duty it shall be, under the direction of the said Commissioners, to execute and enforce all laws and regulations relating to the public health and vital statistics, and to perform all such duties as may be assigned to him by said Commissioners; and the board of health now existing shall, from the date of the appointment of said health officer, be abolished.

"SEC. 9. That there may be appointed by the Commissioners of the District of Columbia, on the recommendation of the health officer, a reasonable number of sanitary inspectors for said District, not exceeding six, to hold such appointment at any one time, of whom two may be physicians, and one shall be a person spilled in the matters of drainage and ventilation; and said Commissioners may remove any of the subordinates, and from time to time may prescribe the duties of each; and said inspectors shall be respectively required to make, at least once in two weeks, a report to said health officer, in writing, of their inspections, which shall be preserved on file; and said health officer shall report in writing annually to said Commissioners of the District of Columbia, and so much oftener as they shall require.

"SEC. 10. That the Commissioners may appoint, on the like recommendation of the health officer, a reasonable number of clerks, but no greater number shall be appointed; and no more persons shall be employed under said health officer, than the public interests demand and the appropriation shall justify.

"SEC. 11. That the salary of the health officer shall be three thousand dollars per annum; and the salary of the sanitary inspectors shall not exceed the sum of one thousand two hundred dollars per annum each; and the salaries of the clerks and other assistants of the health officer shall not exceed in the aggregate the amount of seven thousand dollars, to be apportioned as the Commissioners of the District of Columbia may deem best.

"SEC. 12. That it shall be the duty of the said Commissioners to report to Congress at the next session succeeding their appointment a draft of such additional laws or amendments to existing laws as in their opinion are necessary for the harmonious working of the system hereby adopted, and for the effectual and proper government of the District of

Columbia; and said Commissioners shall annually report their official doings in detail to Congress on or before the first Monday of December.

"SEC. 13. That there shall be no increase of the present amount of the total indebtedness of the District of Columbia; and any officer or person who shall knowingly increase, or aid or abet in increasing, such total indebtedness, except to the amount of the two hundred thousand dollars, as authorized by this act, shall be deemed guilty of a high misdemeanor, and, on conviction thereof, shall be punished by imprisonment not exceeding ten years, and by fine not exceeding ten thousand dollars.

"SEC. 14. That the term 'school houses' in the act of June 17th, 1870, chapter 30, was intended to embrace all collegiate establishments actually used for educational purposes, and not for private gain; and that all taxes heretofore imposed upon such establishments, in the District of Columbia, since the date of said act are hereby remitted, and where the same or any part thereof has been paid, the sum so paid shall be refunded. But if any portion of any said building, house, or grounds in terms excepted is used to secure a rent or income, or for any business purpose, such portion of the same, or a sum equal in value to such portion, shall be taxed.

"SEC. 15. That all laws inconsistent with the provisions of this act be, and the same are hereby, repealed.

"Approved, June 11, 1878."

THE END.

INDEX

253

254

255

258

261

262

265

269

271

273

277

279

280

281

282

283

285

286

289

290

T

293

Other Heritage Books by Wesley E. Pippenger:

Alexandria (Arlington) County, Virginia Death Records, 1853–1896

Alexandria City and Arlington County, Virginia Records Index: Vol. 1

Alexandria City and Arlington County, Virginia Records Index: Vol. 2

Alexandria County, Virginia Marriage Records, 1853–1895

Alexandria Virginia Marriage Index, January 10, 1893 to August 31, 1905

Alexandria, Virginia Marriages, 1870–1892

Alexandria, Virginia Town Lots, 1749–1801
Together with the Proceedings of the Board of Trustees, 1749–1780

Alexandria, Virginia Wills, Administrations and Guardianships, 1786–1800

Alexandria, Virginia 1808 Census (Wards 1, 2, 3, and 4)

Alexandria, Virginia Death Records, 1863–1896

Alexandria, Virginia Hustings Court Orders, Volume 1, 1780–1787

*Connections and Separations: Divorce, Name Change and Other
Genealogical Tidbits from the Acts of the Virginia General Assembly*

Daily National Intelligencer *Index to Deaths, 1855–1870*

Daily National Intelligencer, *Washington, District of Columbia
Marriages and Deaths Notices (January 1, 1851 to December 30, 1854)*

*Dead People on the Move: Reconstruction of the Georgetown Presbyterian
Burying Ground, Holmead's (Western) Burying Ground, and
Other Removals in the District of Columbia*

Death Notices from Richmond, Virginia Newspapers, 1841–1853

District of Columbia Ancestors, A Guide to Records of the District of Columbia

District of Columbia Death Records: August 1, 1874–July 31, 1879

District of Columbia Foreign Deaths, 1888–1923

District of Columbia Guardianship Index, 1802–1928

*District of Columbia Interments (Index to Deaths)
January 1, 1855 to July 31, 1874*

District of Columbia Marriage Licenses, Register 1: 1811–1858

District of Columbia Marriage Licenses, Register 2: 1858–1870

*District of Columbia Marriage Records Index
June 28, 1877 to October 19, 1885: Marriage Record Books 11 to 20*
Wesley E. Pippenger and Dorothy S. Provine

*District of Columbia Marriage Records Index
October 20, 1885 to January 20, 1892: Marriage Record Books 21 to 30*

District of Columbia Marriage Records Index
January 20, 1892 to August 30, 1896: Marriage Record Books 31 to 40

District of Columbia Marriage Records Index
August 31, 1896 to December 17, 1900: Marriage Record Books 41 to 65

District of Columbia Probate Records, 1801–1852

District of Columbia: Original Land Owners, 1791–1800

Early Church Records of Alexandria City and Fairfax County, Virginia

Georgetown, District of Columbia 1850 Federal Population Census
(Schedule I) and 1853 Directory of Residents of Georgetown

Georgetown, District of Columbia Marriage and Death Notices, 1801–1838

Husbands and Wives Associated with Early Alexandria, Virginia
(and the Surrounding Area), 3rd Edition, Revised

Index to District of Columbia Estates, 1801–1929

Index to District of Columbia Land Records, 1792–1817

Index to Virginia Estates, 1800–1865
Volumes 4, 5 and 6

John Alexander, a Northern Neck Proprietor, His Family, Friends and Kin

Legislative Petitions of Alexandria, 1778–1861

Pippenger and Pittenger Families

Proceedings of the Orphan's Court, Washington County,
District of Columbia, 1801–1808

The Georgetown Courier *Marriage and Death Notices:*
Georgetown, District of Columbia, November 18, 1865 to May 6, 1876

The Georgetown Directory for the Year 1830: to Which is Appended, a Short
Description of the Churches, Public Institutions, and the Original
Charter of Georgetown, and Extracts of the Laws Pertaining
to the Chesapeake and Ohio Canal Company

The Virginia Gazette and Alexandria Advertiser:
Volume 1, September 3, 1789 to November 11, 1790

The Virginia Journal and Alexandria Advertiser:
Volume I (February 5, 1784 to January 27, 1785)

Volume II (February 3, 1785 to January 26, 1786)

Volume III (March 2, 1786 to January 25, 1787)

Volume IV (February 8, 1787 to May 21, 1789)

The Washington and Georgetown Directory of 1853

Tombstone Inscriptions of Alexandria, Volumes 1–4

CPSIA information can be obtained
at www.ICGtesting.com
Printed in the USA
LVOW13s1741220218
567560LV00013B/1441/P

9 781585 496716